SEX DRIVES

SEX DRIVES

Fantasies of Fascism in Literary Modernism

Laura Frost

CORNELL UNIVERSITY PRESS

ITHACA & LONDON

First published 2002 by Cornell University Press
First printing, Cornell Paperbacks, 2002

Printed in the United States of America

Library of Congress Cataloging-in-Publication Data

Frost, Laura Catherine, 1967–
    Sex drives : fantasies of fascism in literary modernism/Laura
Catherine Frost.
        p. cm.
    Includes bibliographical references and index.
    ISBN 0-8014-3894-2 (cloth : alk. paper)—ISBN 0-8014-8764-1 (pbk. : alk.
paper)
        1. Fascism in literature.   2. Sex in literature.   3. Literature,
Modern—20th century—History and criticism.   I. Title.
    PN56.F35 F76 2002
    809'.93358—dc21   2001003179

Portions of chapter 6 appeared as " 'Every woman adores a Fascist': Feminist Visions of Fascism from *Three Guineas* to *Fear of Flying*" in *Women's Studies* 29
(spring 2000). Copyright by OPA (Overseas Publishers Association) N.V. with
permission from Gordon and Breach Publishers and Taylor & Francis Ltd. Poems from *The Collected Poems of Sylvia Plath*, edited by Ted Hughes, copyright (c)
1960, 1965, 1971, 1981 by the Estate of Sylvia Plath, are reprinted by permission of
HarperCollins Publishers, Inc., and Faber and Faber. Excerpts from Virginia
Woolf's *Three Guineas* have been reproduced with the kind permission of Harcourt, Inc., and The Society of Authors (London) as the Literary Representative
of the Estate of Virginia Woolf. Excerpts from Jean Genet's *Funeral Rites*, copyright 1988, are reprinted by permission of Grove/Atlantic, Inc.

Cornell University Press strives to use environmentally responsible suppliers and
materials to the fullest extent possible in the publishing of its books. Such materials include vegetable-based, low-VOC inks and acid-free papers that are recycled,
totally chlorine-free, or partly composed of nonwood fibers. Books that bear the
logo of the FSC (Forest Stewardship Council) use paper taken from forests that
have been inspected and certified as meeting the highest standards for environ-
mental and social responsibility. For further information, visit our website at
www.cornellpress.cornell.edu.

Cloth printing   10 9 8 7 6 5 4 3 2 1
Paperback printing   10 9 8 7 6 5 4 3 2 1

Contents

Illustrations

Acknowledgments

I am grateful for the generous institutional and financial support I received while working on this project. Through the Columbia University Department of English and Comparative Literature, I received several President's Fellowships and grants from the Mellon Foundation and the Whiting Foundation. While an assistant professor in the English department at Yale University, grants from the Whitney Humanities Center, the Fund for Lesbian and Gay Studies, and the Frederick W. Hilles Publication Fund of Yale University enabled the final research for the book and revisions of it.

When I was first formulating this project, I fortuitously began working with D. A. Miller, whose intellectual audacity and exciting influence changed the way I think about scholarship. I am especially grateful for his guidance, in the early stages, in helping me articulate a critical approach that was less policing and more provocative. David Damrosch's encouragement and humor rendered alienating rites of passage more enjoyable and made it possible for me to take risks with my work. I am grateful to Nancy K. Miller for her inspiring feminist scholarship and professional generosity. Franco Moretti's suggestion that I look at Vercors's *Silence of the Sea* and his illuminating reading of a draft of the resulting chapter proved very useful. Andreas Huyssen, Sylvère Lotringer, and George Stade all read an early version of the manuscript, and I thank them for their detailed responses. David Kastan and Michael Seidel helpfully supported my work at Columbia. Conversations with Ursula Heise were formative in defining this project, as was a conversation with Robert O. Paxton about Vichy. Carol Siegel has been an energizing friend and mentor whose e-mail calls-to-arms kept me going.

I am most appreciative to Catherine Rice at Cornell University Press for supporting this project, seeing potential in its early form, and guiding me through crucial revisions. My anonymous readers provided me with enormously useful reports. I thank Karen Hwa for her care with the manuscript and my expert copyeditor, Jane Marie Todd, who polished my prose and asked perceptive questions. My thanks to Sandy Welsh and Ruth Yeazell for their kindness and encouragement while I was revising the book and to Michael Trask for reading my proposal. Conversations with Nigel Alderman, Douglas Brooks, Sarah Cole, Elizabeth Dillon, Anke Finger, Amy Hungerford, Alex Lee, Pericles Lewis, Celia Marshik, Becka McKay, and Michael Thurston also helped me to refine my thoughts about the project. I also want to thank the Interlibrary Loan Office at Columbia for tracking down numerous propaganda texts for me, Erica Sayers in the English office at Yale, Adam Boxer at Ubu Gallery, and Amy Woods at the Kinsey Institute.

Teri Reynolds, Victoria Rosner, and Miranda Sherwin listened to my ideas at every stage and have read innumerable drafts. I thank them for their critical acumen, loyalty, and affection. They and Anna Brickhouse, Camille Cauti, and Nancy Castro have been superb friends over a number of years. My deepest thanks to Victoria for her sharp readings and giddy humor in the last stages of this project. Finally, throughout the years I spent writing this book and long before, I have been buoyed by my parents' unflagging support. Their intellectual curiosity and enthusiasm for creative work have always been exemplary to me.

No person has contributed as much to this book as Tim Griffin, with whom I have imagined and reimagined these ideas. His thoughts on art, philosophy, and language have been a constantly productive and pleasurable challenge to my own. His wit and patience have sustained me. This book is for him, with love.

SEX DRIVES

Introduction
"Fascinating Fascism"

Bodies bound in snug uniforms, trussed with straps and boots: in November 2000, a *New York Times* article proclaimed "fascist chic" "the Latest Look." Designers, architects, stylists, and historians of design confessed their enthusiasm for uniforms, bondage-inspired clothes, gladiatorial bodies, and the turgid, monumental shapes of neoclassical buildings. The language of the discussion—seductive power, alluring restraint, fetishism, sex appeal—repeated a common refrain that "fascist chic" is a distinctly libidinal phenomenon, despite the repression and violence of fascism itself.[1] In the decade before the *Times* heralded the return of "fascinating fascism" in popular culture, there was an odd proliferation of literature that emphasized fascism's perverse erotics. A number of literary accounts of Nazism written in this period—Steve Erickson's *Tours of the Black Clock* (1989), Kris Rusch's *Hitler's Angel* (1997), Ronald Hayman's *Hitler and Geli* (1997), and Ron Hansen's *Hitler's Niece* (1999)—dwelled on the sadomasochistic predilections of Adolf Hitler.[2] In the same period, several novels imagined fascist characters in sexualized, perverse scenarios, including Emily Prager's *Eve's Tattoo* (1992), Sherri Szeman's *The Kommandant's Mistress* (1993), and Bernhard Schlink's international best-seller (and Oprah's Book Club selection), *The Reader.*[3] Scholars, too, wrote about fascism in terms of sexual deviance. Roger Eatwell began his 1996 study, *Fascism: A History*, with the observation that "for most people, the word *fascism* conjures up visions of nihilistic violence, war, and Götterdämmerung. Fascism has a sexual side too—but it is a world of German uniforms and discipline, of bondage and sadomasochism, rather than love" (xix).

This millennial moment inevitably evokes Susan Sontag's 1974 essay "Fascinating Fascism," which asked why "much of the imagery of far-out sex" in contemporary culture is paradoxically "placed under the sign of Nazism." Sontag was responding to fascist imagery in popular culture and pornography thirty

1

years after the war, in the United States as well as Europe. Youth culture such as punk adopted swastikas and bondage-wear, and a flurry of films in the 1960s and 1970s, including Kenneth Anger's *Scorpio Rising* (1963), Luchino Visconti's *The Damned* (1969), and Liliana Cavani's *The Night Porter* (1974), explored an imagined erotics of fascism.[4] A year after Sontag's essay appeared, Michel Fou-

Liliana Cavani, *The Night Porter* (1974). Courtesy of the Museum of Modern Art / Film Still Archive

cault commented that "every shoddy erotic fantasy is now attributed to Nazism. . . . Aren't we witnessing the beginnings of a re-eroticization of power, taken to a pathetic, ridiculous extreme by the porn-shops with Nazi insignia that you can find in the United States[?]"[5]

If "fascinating fascism" remains as mysterious today as it was in the 1970s, it is in part because it is not strictly a phenomenon of the late twentieth century. Representations of sexualized fascism were not born in U.S. sex shops in the 1970s or in design studios of the 1990s. They began much earlier in an artistic form not usually associated with contemporary popular culture: literary modernism. Fiction of the early to mid-twentieth century, written by some of the most significant nonfascist British and French authors, abounds in images of women pining for tyrants, men craving the hand of a master, and soldiers whose uniforms serve as arousing aphrodisiacs. These startlingly explicit representations of fascism anticipate the tropes that turn up forty years later in works such as *The Night Porter*.

This book traces the literary genealogy of eroticized images of fascism and explores why brutal European dictatorships became so widely associated with eroticism and sexual deviance that "fascinating fascism" came to constitute a major theme in twentieth-century fiction. These fictions, I argue, are complex explorations of how political and national identities are constructed around and shored up by particular sexual identities. They are as revealing of the democratic imagination as they are of fascism.

This is not a history of fascism but rather an examination of literary texts that imagine fascism as a libidinal phenomenon. My interest in these texts is in how the literary imagination responds to and is shaped by cultural history. While this occasionally leads me to discuss nonliterary material, including visual propaganda, I am most interested in identifying discursive patterns and isolating recurring tropes of eroticized fascism across a range of literary texts. I will not, then, offer a broad theory of fascist ideology or reiterate psychosocial explanations of fascist dynamics. Instead, I will take the erotic pulse of these authors in order to understand why fascism, with its history of brutality and hatred, became improbably associated with exotic eroticism and sexual deviance. Rather than begin with the common premise that fascism is an especially libidinal politics or that sexuality is a key to understanding fascism, I will examine how that premise came to be widely shared, if not openly recognized.

While many historians have documented repressive fascist policies on gender and sexuality, cultural critics have paid equal attention to the erotic relation of fascist leaders to the masses, the libidinal dynamics of fascist militarism, and the sexual practices of individual fascists. A number of literary and cultural critics have examined sexualized representations of fascism, including Alice Yaeger Kaplan (*Reproductions of Banality*), Klaus Theweleit (*Male Fantasies*), Cinzia Sartini Blum (*The Other Modernism*), Barbara Spackman (*Fascist Virilities*), Jeffrey Herf (*Reactionary Modernism*), Andrew Hewitt (*Fascist Modernism* and *Political Inversions*), and Erin G. Carlston (*Thinking Fascism*). Kaplan's and Theweleit's work in particular explores the libidinal underpinnings of fascism in ways that have been very influential on this book. However, my material and methodology are quite different from these critics'. The above-mentioned studies primarily describe fascism in the places of its actualization (Vichy France, Germany, Italy, and so on), and they focus almost exclusively on writers who were active participants in fascist movements or, at least, who voiced their approval of them. These studies locate in the writings of the so-called fascist modernists—including Ezra Pound, Wyndham Lewis, Louis-Ferdinand Céline, Ernst Jünger, F. T. Marinetti, Gabriele D'Annunzio, Pierre Drieu la Rochelle, and Robert Brasillach—articulations of fascist ideology: anti-Marxism, anticapitalism, xenophobic nationalism, antidemocracy, racism, a belief in natural social hierarchy, a combination of nostalgia for a romanticized preindustrial past and an infatuation with a technologized future. The fascist modernists also give voice to fascism's rhetoric of eroticized antagonism, glorified violence, and masculine virility, as well as its fear and oppression of women and homosexuals. For example, Marinetti's sexualized paeans to power in *Let's Murder the Moonshine* ("See the furious coitus of war, gigantic vulva stirred by the friction of courage, [the] shapeless vulva that spreads to offer itself to the terrific spasm of final victory" [61–62]) reiterate the violently sexualized discourse of Mussolini, Hitler, and other fascist propagandists.

Studies of fascist modernism usefully demonstrate how these writers reflect the oppressive ideology of fascism. Yet these studies do not explain the large number of writers who do not subscribe to fascist politics but nevertheless produce fictions of eroticized fascism, including Aldous Huxley, Christopher Isherwood, D. H. Lawrence, George Bernard Shaw, George Orwell, Jean Genet, Jean-Paul Sartre, Isaac Babel, Alfred Döberlin, Klaus Mann, Virginia Woolf, Georges Bataille, Marguerite Duras, and many others. These authors quite strikingly adopt many of the same tropes as the "fascist modernists," but they do so alongside a rejection of fascist politics. In interwar Britain, for example, Lawrence spins tales of virile authoritarian leaders to whom his characters are drawn but whose exercise of power and political violence they also fear. Christopher Isherwood compares the sadomasochistic sex trade in decadent Weimar Germany to the violent Nazi presence that builds like a dark storm cloud throughout his *Berlin Stories* and

Down There on a Visit.[6] Aldous Huxley's panoramic novel of British culture between the wars, *Point Counter Point* (1928), depicts a protofascist leader, a handsome and brutal "tinpot Mussolini" whose presence induces in one woman, over and against her politics, a corporeal enthrallment. Glandular representations of fascism also proliferate in France, where, during the Occupation, fascism hit closer to home. In Genet's 1949 novel *Funeral Rites*, Nazi soldiers, collaborators, and Hitler himself are depicted in erotic scenes. In another novel published the same year, *Troubled Sleep* (*La mort dans l'âme*), Jean-Paul Sartre, well known for his antifascist politics, imagines a male character who is aroused by the beautiful bodies of the Nazi soldiers marching into Paris. Marguerite Duras's memoir *The War* shows a female Resistance fighter's attraction to a Nazi collaborator with "a body made for pleasure" (150). I take these representations of nonfascist eroticized fascism as my focus, reading them not as idiosyncratic eruptions of bad taste or political bad faith but rather as a consistent literary theme that expresses a major reevaluation of sexuality and politics in the period. Drawing on a wide range of texts, from propaganda to psychological theory, but focusing on fiction, I will trace how sexualized fascism emerges as a trope in works that span the entire century, both during and after the historical imposition of fascist dictatorships.

This material presents a problem of ideological disjunction rather than continuity. Since these fictions are based on a fundamental asymmetry between political and sexual representation, the critical models offered in studies of fascist modernism, which presuppose an ideological consistency, are not adequate for my purposes. For example, in *Reproductions of Banality*, Alice Yaeger Kaplan poses a rhetorical question that is central to studies of fascist modernism: "What ideology could make it clearer than fascism does that people have a sexual, as well as material, interest in their political life?" (23). The implied answer to Kaplan's question is that no ideology could make this clearer, and that fascism demonstrates sexual interests more than, say, democracy or socialism. My response to Kaplan's question is to ask another: Why is fascism privileged as a particularly sexual ideology? One possibility is that the fascists themselves spoke in sexualized imagery—for example, Hitler's declaration that "Germany is my bride." However, most of the authors I will examine are not as influenced by such primary accounts of fascism as they are by the account of fascism presented in the Allied nations, mediated through the nationalist discourses of propaganda and war reportage, for example, in which fascism is described as culturally debased and sexually deviant. It seems to me that the best way to pursue the question of fascism's relationship to sexuality is not to take that relationship for granted but rather to look at how the assumption that fascism can reveal the nature of sexual interests and investments was produced. I begin, then, with an examination of the cultural factors that influence an author's understanding of the fascist enemy and subsequent construction of fascism in fantasy. My primary questions are: Where do images of eroticized fascism come from (that is, where and why are they produced); what do they mean in relation to their particular historical context; and what purposes do they serve for a particular author? These questions do not necessarily preempt psychoanalysis, and I will use psychoanalytic concepts such as fetishism and intersubjectivity when useful. Psychoanalysis is not, however, my primary methodology (although all of these texts could be examined in terms of psychoanalytic paradigms to produce fairly predictable interpretations). Part of the reason for this is, as I will explain in chapter 1, that psychoanalytic discourse itself participates in the eroticization of fascism and hence is part of the phenomenon rather than an impartial explanatory tool. More importantly, my goal here is not to propose a broad theoretical model of fascist desire or an abstract model for reading the unconscious but rather to examine the specific discourses that influence an author's understanding of the fascist enemy and to offer a taxonomy of literary tropes of eroticized fascism.

I will argue that eroticized fascism cannot be adequately explained as a generalized expression of sexual domination or fascist mesmerism but is rather a response to specific discussions about the enemy that can be traced back to World War I. I contend that fictions of eroticized fascism are part of an antifascist culture that persistently sexualizes fascism, and that these fictions point to a democratic insistence that fascism be construed as sexually deviant. I will build on George L. Mosse's argument in *Nationalism and Sexuality* that a culturally shared ideal of "respectability" is central in the construction of modern European national identity and that the designation of certain sexual behaviors as "deviant" or "abnormal" is pivotal in the solidification of respectability. Mosse points out that Nazi ideology made "sexual deviants" central targets of oppression, and that the Nazis extended characteristics associated with deviance (effeminacy and homosexuality, for example) to other targets, such as Jews and gypsies.

Standards of sexual normality and deviation were just as central to the construction of respectability and national identity in modern Britain, France, and the United States as they were in Germany. In these countries in the early to mid-twentieth century, democracy was so integral to their national identity that specific nationalisms were often eclipsed in antifascist discourse by an international ideology of democracy. In the Allied nations, a selected form of sexuality—heterosexuality founded on equality, respect, and nonviolence—was validated as a reflection of democratic national ideals, while particular sexualities that did not fall into line with this norm were designated "fascist." Sadomasochistic eroticism, for example, was not supposed to be a part of democratic or socialist politics, where the peaceful, nonviolent treatment of everyone was ostensibly the credo. Fascism, therefore, with its institutions of oppression and domination, became the sadomasochistic politics par excellence. Male homosexuality was also, in these discourses of respectable, democratic national sexuality, frequently associated with fascism. The range of gender and sexual object choices represented by the authors discussed in this book makes it clear that there is no demographic particularly likely to eroticize fascism. Authors who explore sexual practices popularly associated with fascism, as well as those authors who do not view fascism as sexually aberrant, have a different stake in the dominant construction of fascism, and their fictions reflect this.[7]

Since this is a pannational project that spans several historical periods, I will briefly clarify my organization and selection of material. First, I have not attempted to construct a seamless chronological continuum or a single national focus. Rather, I have selected a number of historical moments— Britain and France during World War I and the interwar period, France during the Occupation and immediately after Liberation, the United States ten and forty years after the war—marked by significant fictions that together establish the tropes of eroticized fascism. Each text is obviously defined by national and historical circumstances, as well as by each author's interests. I will account for differences in representation: for example, why a text written early in the years of the Occupation, such as Vercors's *Silence of the Sea*, imagines a more realistic Nazism than a surrealist text imagining the aesthetic properties of fascism in 1936; and I will show how differences in the proximity to fascism—Duras's versus Plath's experience and understanding of Nazism, for example—culminate in a different way of imagining fascism in fiction. I am also interested in showing the many continuities among these texts in order to highlight the striking similarities between authors of different nationalities and periods and to establish a genealogy of eroticized fascism. I have focused on authors from the Allied nations—Britain, France, and the United States—whose governments had a coordinated propaganda effort and a common vision of the enemy.[8] (There are, however, many German and Italian antifascist fictions of eroticized fascism—for example, Thomas Mann's "Mario and the Magician" and Leonida Répaci's *The Desert of Sex*[9]—and they typically follow the same patterns I outline here. The parallels will be suggested in my treatment of Hans Bellmer, a German artist, in chapter 3.)

I have limited my discussion to historically precise examples of fascism in an effort to forestall the all too common conflation of fascism with any form of oppression, in which fascism becomes, as Foucault puts it in *Power/Knowledge*, a "floating signifier" (139). I address only explicit representations of fascism. The exception is chapter 1, which demonstrates how the prefascist depiction of authoritarian Germany influenced the later understanding of fascism. My illustration of this in chapter 2, on Lawrence, accordingly examines authoritarian or protofascist movements. There is a fair amount of controversy among historians and political scientists about which political movements are properly described as fascist and which are more accurately described as right-wing or authoritarian (those "forces of the new right" that Stanley G. Payne maintains are "distinct from both leftist revolution and fascist radicalism" [*Fascism: Comparison and Definition*, 15]).[10] Definitions depend on which ideological features the theorist chooses to emphasize. Although scholars of fascism often refer to a "fascist minimum" that establishes the distinct ideological features of fascism, there are many versions of what constitutes that minimum. Roger Griffin, for example, names two totalitarian movements as fascist—Hitler's National Socialism and Mussolini's Italian Fascism—as distinguished from "para-fascist" or authoritarian right-wing movements such as those in Spain, Britain, France, Portugal and Japan (*Fascism*, 9). Although Juan Linz ("Some Notes Towards a Comparative Study of Fascism in Sociological Historical Perspective" in Walter Laqueur's *Fascism: A Reader's Guide*, 385–99), Zeev Sternhell (*Neither Right Nor Left: Fascist Ideology in France*), Stanley Payne (*A History of Fascism*), and other scholars have made different distinctions, rehearsing the finer points of those debates is not central to my project here. My goal is not to offer a new reading of fascism but rather to examine the specific ways that those political movements defined as fascist in a particular fiction are represented: that is, what fascism means to these writers, and how they imagine it.

Although I will retain "fascism" as a general term throughout the following chapters when the authors themselves do so, the specific form of eroticized fascism discussed here is almost invariably Nazism. Certainly, the cult of the leader was strong in most fascist movements of the period. Mussolini vigorously promoted himself as a virile leader, posing for publicity photographs in macho pursuits such as skiing bare-chested, climbing mountains, and charming flocks of women. Once Hitler came to power, however, National Socialism was the fascist movement most often portrayed in an erotic light in British, French, and U.S. literature. Although sexualized images of Mussolini and Franco appear occasionally, the most elaborately realized eroticized fictions of fascism are usually based on Nazism. As I will explain in chapter 1, German fascism had a strong set of national associations for British, French, and U.S. readers, which developed out of the treatment of German authoritarianism in World War I propaganda. Neither Italy, which was a British/French ally in World War I, nor Spain had such a stark national typology in place before World War II. Moreover, Germany's acts of invasion had a great deal to do with the way it was perceived in World War I and following. Nazism was, then, for British, U.S., and French writers of this period a kind of "Ur-Fascism" and surfaces as such throughout the literature.

In uncovering the genealogy of fictions of eroticized fascism, I aim to assess literary modernism and one of its unrecognized legacies and to address a recurring sexual fantasy in fiction that has not received much critical attention. In some respects, eroticized fictions of fascism appear to be modernist business as usual—the shock of the new—but in other ways they necessitate a revision of our understanding of modernist literary concerns. These renderings of fascism are part of the modernist assault on bourgeois values and on the faith in rationality and humanism, and they reflect a common fascination with violence and social transgression among writers and artists who lived through World War I.[11] Eroticized fantasies of fascism are solipsistic and private—classic characteristics of modernism—but they are also intensely engaged with history and politics. Fictions of eroticized fascism appear both to conform to and to challenge the (now mostly discredited) claim that modernism evades or represses history. One might suppose that a great deal of history must be suppressed to imagine fascism as erotic. These authors often aestheticize fascism, but they also establish a clear historical frame that emphasizes the violence of fascism. Literary treatments of eroticized fascism, then, act on contradictory impulses in modernism, making historical fascism the ground of the text and treating fascism as malleable in fantasy.

If images of eroticized fascism are continually produced, why is it that they have not yet been treated as an important feature of twentieth-century culture? The reason, it seems to me, lies in the critical desire to rehabilitate or reclaim culturally transgressive sexualities and fantasies and to recuperate them for liberal politics. But fictions of eroticized fascism demonstrate that fantasy is not necessarily coherent, politically useful, or instrumental, and it is the very fantasies that express desires inhospitable to progressive politics and reformist discourse that are the most difficult to address. Erotic investments and identifications of a nature that are, as Leo Bersani puts it in *Homos*, "not always gratifying to acknowledge" (64), have proven intransigent to analysis. Fictions of eroticized fascism contradict the expectation that politics and fantasy are necessarily consistent. Instead, they suggest that fantasy and politics are often not in alignment, and that the politically forbidden and repudiated is just as likely, if not more so, to be the substance of erotic fantasy as the permitted, the moral, and the chosen good.

While it is fairly easy to recognize that fantasy and political commitment can be asymmetrical when the politically undesirable object of fantasy is not too threatening, when the "bad object" is fascism, the political referent is too strong, too loaded, and the fantasy is intolerable. In his essay "The Aryan Boy Who Pissed on My Father's Head," Wayne Koestenbaum spells out the difficulty of analyzing desires and fantasies that conflict with political and moral judgment. Focusing on his father's childhood experiences in Nazi Germany, Koestenbaum argues that "tyranny" is an "everyday structure of feeling," but, despite its "mundanity," "everyone . . . pretends not to be friends with it" (53). Koestenbaum then impressionistically weaves together images of eroticism and political subjugation: his Jewish family's harrowing experiences in Nazi Germany, recollections of childhood bathtub autoeroticism, and pornographic golden shower scenes. Koestenbaum concludes with an anecdote about watching Leni Riefenstahl's *Triumph of the Will.* "I find many propagandistic images seductive," he confesses. "I expected I would find the near-naked Nazi boys attractive, showering in preparation for the rally; I'm relieved to find them scrawny" (56). That moment of relief reveals the fear of being betrayed by a visceral response and the anxiety that an erotic reflex will signal political complicity. While theoretical work in feminist and queer theory has opened discussions of "politically incorrect" fantasy, the "fascination" fascism exerts over the contemporary imagination has still been spoken of only falteringly.

The primary difficulty in interpreting eroticized fictions of fascism, then, is the ambiguous relationship they establish between fantasy and politics. As Fredric Jameson puts it in *Fables of Aggression*, "archaic fantasy and ideological commitment" are typically constructed as antithetical: as "distinct realms of the sexual and the political" (9). Fantasy is increasingly understood as politically inflected (nationalism and racism, for example, have been usefully read as structured by fantasy), and yet, as the example of the fascist modernists shows, sexual fantasy and politics are expected to have a mimetic relationship to one another. These hermeneutic problems are of central importance to eroticized fictions of fascism and present the reader with the most basic challenge of deciding what it means when an author simultaneously eroticizes fascism and repudiates it politically.

In its common usage, "fantasy" designates a subjective, individual process, but, as Teresa de Lauretis argues in "On the Subject of Fantasy," it can also be "a collective event, public, spectacular, and of enormous social consequence, as when an entire nation or social group is said to be the subject of a fantasy of domination, a fantasy of imperialistic, racial, religious, or sexual mastery" (63). Images of eroticized fascism encompass both kinds of fantasies, individual associations and more widely shared "social fantasies" (Spackman) or "public fantasies" (Cowie)—for example, the sadistic German depicted in both propaganda and fiction. In "The Stubborn Drive," de Lauretis proposes that we think of the process of fantasy as "the psychic mechanism that governs the translation of social representations into subjectivity and self-representation by a sort of adaptation or reworking of the social imaginary into individual fantasies" (865–66). The metaphor of translation is useful; however, unlike in the translation of languages, there is no clear, consistent key to how contingent elements are taken up in fantasy. In *By Force of Fantasy*, Ethel Person characterizes the exchange between fantasy and external or material "reality" as a "two-way loop between the inner and outer worlds" (68), but the precise nature of that "loop" has not been well defined, even in fantasies that have more neutral political content than does fascism.

I will examine how political and historical referents and social or collective fantasies of fascism are drawn into individual fantasy structures and crafted into fiction. Literary representation is not pure fantasy or a raw unconscious impulse but is subject to secondary processes and mediation. The authors I examine show a strong awareness of the significance of their provocations—they constantly reference and often criticize public fantasies of fascism, such as those articulated by propaganda—and their fictions cannot therefore be treated as unmediated reveries. Indeed, the more important dynamic is the tension in these texts between the historical referent of fascism and an imagined eroticized fascism. I do not mean to position history as a stable discourse, free of bias, in contrast to fantasy but rather to suggest that there is a collectively agreed-upon and recognizable set of historical referents associated with fascism around which fictions of eroticized fascism are organized. Throughout the following chapters, Hitler as he is depicted in the texts I discuss always looks like the Hitler of photographs, with the trademark mustache, the paunchy body, the pasty skin, and the unctuous side-parted hair. The SS wear the usual uniforms; boots, belts, and helmets appear constantly, as does the swastika. Fascism as an object in fantasy, then, is consistent with historical fascism: violent, oppressive, and easily recognizable by its iconography. It is in the action, or verb, of the fantasy that fascism is distorted in the service of individualized fantasy.

Writers portray fascism in an erotic light for a variety of reasons, many of them specific to the author, the author's nationality, and the historical period. There are, however, some dynamics shared by the different authors I consider: prohibition, fetishism, and sadomasochism. First, these texts explore an erotics of prohibition. Propaganda plays a large role in defining the fascist enemy and the prohibitions that then become eroticized in the fictions. I do not read propaganda as a perfectly conscious, deliberate mode of manipulation impressed on the unthinking masses but rather as a form of communication that can express its creator's inadvertent or unconscious investments (and fantasies) and that can also be read many ways and have unintended effects in its reception. In *Mothers in the Fatherland*, the historian Claudia Koonz puzzles over the manner in which "the symbolic language of propaganda" resurfaces in "erotic culture" (4). This "perverse" reading effect, by which political propaganda is adapted to erotic fantasy, is one of many unintended effects of propaganda I will examine. These fictions transpose the language and images of prohibition to erotic scenarios. As Judith Butler remarks in "The Force of Fantasy," "limits are, in a sense, what fantasy loves most, what it incessantly thematicizes and subordinates to its own aims. [T]he very rhetoric by which certain erotic acts or relations are prohibited invariably eroticize that prohibition in the service of fantasy" (111). These authors literalize the most lurid metaphors of propaganda, turning the discourse of prohibition into one of provocation. The particular motivations behind such transformations vary from author to author, but, inevitably, eroticized images of fascism touch on prohibitions around nationalism, political partisanship, and sexual politics (specifically, prohibitions surrounding homosexuality, sadomasochism, and gender stereotypes).

Second, the depictions of fascism in most of these texts function according to the logic of fetishism. Following the psychoanalytic pattern of fetishistic denial and asseveration, these authors suggest that they know very well fascism's murderous history, but still they imagine fascism as erotic. Third and most important, the fantasies in these fictions are sadomasochistic. The representation of sadomasochism, however, is quite different from how sadomasochism is commonly understood, as a pathology conflated with fascism. My interpretation of sadomasochistic fantasy, drawn from these texts, will emerge through particular readings over the course of the book, but let me suggest a few preliminaries. Not all the writers discussed have exactly the same response to sadomasochism: some treat it enthusiastically, while others look upon it as one among many propagandistic stereotypes of fascism. Nevertheless, all these authors depict sadomasochism as an erotics rather than a pathology. Most centrally, in these texts, erotic sadomasochism is distinguished from fascist violence. In terms of the model of fantasy outlined above, the historical referent "fascism" is characterized as violent and dangerous, but the erotic sado-masochistic action of the fantasy is distinguished from fascist violence.

Sadomasochism is a particularly modern erotics. The tone of crisis that is one of the most constant features of modern literature finds expression in the erotics of sadomasochism: the oppositional compulsions of restraint and re-lease, the building of tension, the creation of scenarios in which pain and pleasure are pushed to their extreme. The literary pedigree of sado-masochism can be traced to the Marquis de Sade and Leopold von Sacher-Masoch, whose works depict eroticism as intimately tied to cultural prohibi-tion and conflict. Sade's "sadistic" fictions are cornerstones of Enlightenment philosophy and address political questions in the course of their pornographic sequences (for example, the political treatise, "Another Effort, Frenchmen, If You Would be Republicans," is inserted into the middle of strenuous sexual sequences in *Philosophy in the Bedroom*). Sacher-Masoch, the Austrian author of *Venus in Furs* and of an extensive cycle of sto-ries protesting Slavic antisemitism, uses fantasies of domination and submis-sion to explore questions of women's power, the social contract of marriage, and the role of men in relation to modern feminism.[12] Both Sade and Sacher-Masoch collapse the distinction between a "private" world of desire and the "public" world of politics. The authors of eroticized fictions of fascism con-tinue this literary tradition, casting the most urgent political predicament of their time—fascism—as fantasies of sadomasochistic eroticism. These writ-ers suggest that erotic literature has sociopolitical significance that extends far beyond sexuality itself, as do fantasies of nonnormative sexualities. In *Creativity and Perversion*, the psychoanalyst Janine Chasseguet-Smirgel ar-gues that "man has always endeavoured to go beyond the narrow limits of his condition. I consider that perversion is one of the essential ways and means he applies to push forward the frontiers of what is possible and to unsettle reality. . . . [P]erversion and perverse behaviour are particularly present at those times in the history of mankind which precede or accompany major so-cial and political upheavals" (1). The rise of fascism is one of those monu-mental historical moments in which sexual "perversion" is enlisted by many different cultural institutions: by politicians and propagandists who develop an image of deviant fascism and by writers who seek to unsettle dominant paradigms of politics and sexuality.

In chapter 1, I explain how British renderings of eroticized fascism engage with fantasies drawn from the earlier propagandistic cultural "scripts" regarding German authoritarianism. Throughout this book, I focus my analysis on representational continuities: for example, the continuities between the propaganda of World War I and that of World War II, and between perceptions of Germany under the Kaiser's authoritarianism and under Nazism. In positing such continuities, I counter the tendency to read all images of Germans in World War I as mere preludes to Nazism, or as Nazism in utero. I agree with the contention of the historians John Horne and Alan Kramer in "German 'Atrocities' and Franco-German Opinion, 1914" that "the complexity" of "the relationship between event, perception, and contemporary interpretation" of German conduct in World War I "has been buried by the inter-war pacifist reaction to wartime propaganda and by the history of genocide in the Second World War" (1–2). In this chapter, I argue that there was a libidinal, sexualized trope of German authoritarianism that predated German Nazism. I show how World War I propaganda and the theorization of authoritarianism established the terms by which fascism would subsequently be associated with libidinal deviance.

Chapter 2 traces a response to propagandistic discourse and contemporary theories of authoritarianism in D. H. Lawrence's "leadership novels." Lawrence explores the possibility that authoritarianism lifts the libidinal repression required by democracy, but, instead of condemning authoritarianism as regressive and uncivilized, Lawrence perceives it as both potentially liberative and destructive. Lawrence's resulting "libido/power" theory anticipates fantasy-infused eroticized representations of fascism.

Chapter 3 moves from interwar Britain to France before the Occupation, and to two artists loosely affiliated with surrealism. Displaying an interest in the unconscious that is similar to Lawrence's, both Bataille and Bellmer explore fascism as an irrational libidinal force and as an aesthetic opportunity. Both link the most striking symbol of Nazism, the swastika, to uncannily erotic automata and dolls. While Bataille's and Bellmer's deployments of the swastika are predicated upon that symbol's significance, they also experiment with the possible distance between the historical referent and transgressive eroticism.

Chapter 4 focuses on a text that directly treats the Occupation, Vercors's *Silence of the Sea* (*Le silence de la mer*). Vercors critically engages a major trope of World War II deployed by both the political right and the left: the metaphorization of the Occupation as a sexual encounter. In his novel of resistance, Vercors sexualizes the Nazi enemy but through a narrative of seduction rather than rape. Against the Manichean structures of propaganda, Vercors challenges his readers to resist an "exceptional" fascism that is all the more alluring in that it shows a handsome human face.

Chapter 5 moves to a later period in French history, the days immediately following the Liberation. Genet's erotic treatment of the SS and their collaborators in his novel *Funeral Rites* challenges the hypocrisy and prejudices of the patriotic French press and of the Resistance during and following the

Occupation. The novel evokes, only to collapse, the Third Reich's mythic constructions of masculinity and virility.

If Genet rehearses cultural clichés of the Nazi as an object of gay eroticism, Marguerite Duras and Sylvia Plath address a corresponding cliché regarding women's masochistic attraction to fascism. In chapter 6, then, looking at how feminists have responded to gendered theories of fascism, from Virginia Woolf's *Three Guineas* to postmodern theory, I identify a persistent rhetorical strategy in feminist theory: an analogy that posits fascism as a correlative of patriarchy. Inherent in this analogy is the assumption that women are not erotically complicit with patriarchy and the demand for a sexuality free from power fantasies and certainly free from female masochism. In contrast, Marguerite Duras and Sylvia Plath explore fantasies of an erotic, masochistic relationship to Nazism and in so doing work toward a more capacious understanding of female desire.

While these fictions undermine nationalist, patriotic conflations of fascism and deviant sexuality, they cannot be neatly classified as progressive or conservative. They are politically engaged even as they imaginatively distort fascism in politically inflammatory ways. They cannot be easily recuperated for a particular politics without their contradictory implications being truncated. They are not therapeutic exorcisms of desire. They make violence even more problematic because they lay claim to its seduction, bringing fascist destruction close to eroticism but without conflating the two. I will strive to keep these paradoxes in play rather than minimizing them. Obviously, these are sensational texts. While I hope not to reproduce that sensationalism uncritically or irresponsibly, I am committed to exploring their provocations and outrages in order to understand how and why these authors imagine fascism in the ways they do. A reading that condemns, champions, or apologizes misses these authors' central contradiction, their insistence on both eroticized fascism and on antifascism. These fictions demonstrate that, for democratic twentieth-century culture, fascism marked the limits of what is human, moral, and right. The fact that sexuality and fantasy have been and are still drawn into this discussion to secure fascism's position as the epitome of barbarism—a position that hardly needs such bolstering—suggests that antifascist, democratic culture has substantial, unacknowledged libidinal investments in fascism that need to be explored.

Chapter 1
Fascism and Sadomasochism:
The Origins of an Erotics

Jung hardly went far enough when he said, "Hitler is the unconscious of every German"; he comes uncomfortably near to being the unconscious of most of us.

—W. H. Auden

Sexualized images of fascism are commonly assumed to be the creation of postwar and postmodern culture: How could anyone who had lived through fascism have such a mistaken understanding of it? In *Political Inversions*, Andrew Hewitt suggests that images of eroticized fascism are drawn from "a store of representational fragments that are constantly recycled in popular culture, where they acquire an erotic charge they never really exerted the first time around" (1–2). On the contrary: many fictions written at the height of fascism crackle with just such an erotic charge, which can be traced to cultural preoccupations that were well in place even before the historical rise of fascism. While the idea of a prefascist construction of fascism may seem anachronistic, what I am suggesting is that British, French, and U.S. fictions of fascism are part of a cultural strategy, established in World War I and extending into World War II, to align the political enemy with sexual deviance. There are two important components of this strategy—propaganda and libido theories—which I will outline in this chapter.

During World War I, British, French and U.S. critiques of authoritarianism depicted Germany under the Kaiser as a violently atavistic nation that had abandoned the civilized practices of democracy. This discourse made use of popularized psychoanalytic theories of the unconscious and repression. Specifically, it viewed authoritarianism as unleashing unruly libidinal impulses and credited democracy with enacting the libidinal repression necessary for social management. This notion of authoritarianism flinging open the floodgates of erotic energy and violence persisted with the rise of fascism. The formulation appears in a range of cultural discourses—print and visual propaganda, reportage, speeches, art, and fiction. While I concentrate primarily on propaganda in this chapter, I do so not to give it a special status in relation to fiction but because propaganda is one of the clearest expressions of the discursive patterns I am tracing here, and because the fiction writers I examine suggest that propaganda played a central role in the construction of a sexualized enemy.

In the second part of this chapter, I will demonstrate how this discourse of uncivilized impulse and libidinal deviance became the bedrock of two competing readings of the libidinal apparatus of German authoritarianism (and subsequently, of fascism) as, respectively, repressive and sexually enabling. The fictions I will examine in the following chapters are strongly linked to this World War I discourse of democracy and the normative democratic libido, in contrast to a perverse authoritarian libido.

"Germany Puts the Clock Back": Authoritarianism and the Ethics of the Jungle

Freud is often invoked by theorists who explain fascism as a function of Oedipal attachments to the father, the "herd mentality," repressed homosexuality, and so on. I too will begin this portion of my story with Freud but will consider him a participant in the formulation of eroticized fascism rather than its detached analyst. Although a broad conception of the unconscious was in place by the late nineteenth century, Freud's particular characterization of it as a repository of uncivilized desires entered popular discourse around World War I, in the decades just before the rise of fascist and totalitarian regimes. In his 1915 essay, "Reflections upon War and Death," Freud proposes that "war neuroses" stem from a psychic conflict between the aggressive behavior the soldier is expected to display in wartime and his social inculcation. Noting that "civilization is the fruit of renunciation of instinctual satisfaction," Freud writes that war "strips us of the later accretions of civilization, and lays bare the primal man in each of us."[1] The aggressive and violent drives that are systematically repressed and sublimated in society are stirred up during wartime. This idea of an instinct-extinguishing civilization (democracy), with its sources in Jean-Jacques Rousseau and Thomas Hobbes, is, of course, an overstatement, since those ostensibly repressed aggressive impulses are constantly apparent in subdued forms in everyday life.[2] Freud's understanding of the mechanism of repression is far more nuanced than this crude hydraulic model indicates, but the simplifications of the repression/liberation model fit well with propaganda's Manichean methodology. The images of the primal man dormant inside the civilized man and of a tinderbox of archaic instinct in each of us were quickly taken up as paradigms for what was happening in Germany.

Freud suggests, in both "Reflections upon War and Death" and "Psychoanalysis and War Neuroses" (1919), that the peaceful ego is fragile and tenuous and is constantly in danger of being overwhelmed by the more instinctual and seductive regressive ego that manifests itself in war, for example. Freud implies—and this idea returns throughout theories of fascism—that the borders of peaceful, democratic culture are delicate and must be vigilantly patrolled for any signs of regression. If the fruit of civilization comes at such a high price, and the warlike ego is so exhilarating, we might well expect even more frequent lapses into savagery. Indeed, in *Civilization and Its Discontents* (1930), Freud pessimistically insists "that men are not gentle creatures who want to be loved, and who at the most can defend themselves if they are attacked; they are, on the contrary, creatures among whose instinctual endowments is to be reckoned a powerful share of aggressiveness," including the desire to exploit their fellowman, "to use him sexually without his consent, to seize his possessions, to humiliate him, to cause him pain, to torture and to kill him. *Homo homini lupus*" (69).

For Freud, this is not a national impulse but rather the universal condition of people in "civilized" culture. In propaganda, however, this becomes a nationalized, racialized battle between the civilized (the British, French, and Americans) and the uncivilized: that is, the warmongering German "Huns" (and the nefarious *boches* in France), a regressive lawless race living out the primal impulses forbidden by civilized democratic society. Dr. E. J. Dillon's *A Scrap of Paper: The Inner History of German Diplomacy and Her Scheme of World-Wide Conquest*, published during the early years of World War I in the British *Daily Telegraph* War Books series, exemplifies the way that British propaganda portrayed German barbarism.

> The name of Germany, whose love of wanton destruction, delight in human torture, and breach of every principle of manly and soldierly honour are now become proverbial, will henceforward be bracketed in history together with that of the Huns. (xxv)

> Brutal force, in the form of jackboot tyranny, then, is the amended formula of social life which is to be forced upon Europe and the world. (vi)

One central narrative in this propaganda is the insistence that contemporary Germany descends directly from an ethnically, racially tained stock: "Prussianism." "Decades before Hitler was ever heard of," George Orwell observed during World War II, "the word 'Prussian' had much the same significance in England as 'Nazi' has today."[3] Dillon, for example, claims that "the characteristic traits of the old Prussians . . . are brutal arrogance towards those under them, and cringing servility towards their superiors." Dillon traces these "Prussian" traits to the current "submissiveness of the [German] masses" (xv) and German soldiers, who are similarly "slavishly submissive" to the Kaiser (xxiv).[4] Peter E. Firchow argues that before the Franco-Prussian War, Germany was represented in British literature as a "cousin"—and that even Queen Victoria claimed German ancestry. After 1870, Britain adopted a Darwinian view of Germany as a degenerate nation.

There was a strong Prussian tradition of rigid hierarchy, discipline, masculine domination, and ritualized violence. Leaders such as Frederick William I were harsh disciplinarians, and anecdotes about public flogging surely contributed to the image of a traditional Teutonic cruelty.[5] As Daniel Pick points out, the propagandistic notion of "Prussianism" was driven less by historical reality than by a specious pseudoanthropological logic.[6] For example, J. H. Morgan, a British professor of law writing on German war atrocities in 1916, proposes that German "moral perversion" is a problem "for the anthropologists rather than for the lawyer, and [that] there may be some force in the contention of those who believe that the Prussian is not a member of the Teutonic family at all, but a 'throw back' to some Tartar stock."[7] William S. Sadler's 1918 *Long Heads and Round Heads: or What's the Matter with Germany* takes the cultural atavism argument even further. Sadler bases his "study of the spectacle of a highly civilized nation suddenly becoming war-mad and so unbelievably atrocious" (vii) on a series of phrenological comparisons of Neanderthal and Cro-Magnon heads with those of Paul von Hindenburg (Germany's military leader during World War I and the president of Germany from 1925 until his death) and Ludendorff (a World War II military strategist who served under Hindenburg in World War I). Sadler claims that the "German Alpine" type descended from the Neanderthal, while the "Teutonic" type developed from the Cro-Magnon, which marked the beginning of the period when "man's intellect began to assume domination over his brute instincts" (23). Sadler argues that the intelligent Teutonic strain, represented by Ludendorff, is disappearing from German stock and is being replaced by the Alpine type: "A subtle and persistent race substitution . . . has resulted in an unmistakable intellectual and moral deterioration" (45) and an exacerbation of "the brutal German joy of battle, the love of atrocity, and delight in suffering and torture" (54). This superseding of a "civilized" type by a regressive type exemplifies the propagandistic narrative that saw authoritarianism overwhelming democracy in Germany. Teutonic repression (which, like democracy, is able to discipline its own "brute instincts") is forced out by Alpine lawlessness: "force personified, dominant, brutal" (57). As a "race" and nation, Sadler warns, Germans are collectively regressing to previous stages of human evolution. Germany is what happens when the bonds of civilization are loosened.

The same words—"regression," "wantonness," "barbarism," "lack of respect," "slavishness," "domination," "tyranny"—are used again and again in British descriptions of Germany from the period, whether they are written by professional propagandists, historians, or amateurs publishing screeds about the Hun. Of course, German authoritarianism was much more socially repressive than British democracy. My point is that, in this racialized, nationalized discourse, the German enemy becomes a caricature: not the best form, I will contend, for accurate political analysis and one that can obscure the most significant threats of the enemy.

Underpinning these writers' warnings about Germany is an implied argument, like Freud's dark declaration that "man is a wolf to man," that primitive or atavistic societies—nondemocratic societies—allow the innate wolf to run rampant. But unlike Freud in *Civilization and Its Discontents*, who suggests an inevitable need for outlets for such impulses, propagandists agree that civilization, represented by Britain, France, and other democracies, is marked by necessary restraint. Moreover, whereas for Freud the desire to "use" others "sexually without . . . consent" was only one of many repressed drives, the sexual aggression of the enemy is significantly emphasized in wartime propaganda. Germany's sexual practices are imagined to be as aggressive and undemocratic as her politics: Germany is a nation of rapists and sadomasochists. In *Long Heads and Round Heads*, for example, Sadler warns that Germany "did not blush to carry hundreds of young and defenseless girls away with her retreating armies, to serve the base passions of her lustful and bloodthirsty warriors" (155)—a claim that can be found in almost any piece of popular propaganda of the period. This image of the German beast abducting British women for unspeakable sexual outrages—elsewhere, explicitly defined as rape—is a staple of atrocity stories. One of the most popular U.S. posters from World War I was a 1917 image depicting the silhouette of a German soldier in a pickelhaube leading a girl by the hand. This poster by Ellsworth Young urges, "Remember Belgium," casting a girl opposite Germany's male soldier to evoke sexual danger, a recurring theme in U.S., British, and French anti-German propaganda.

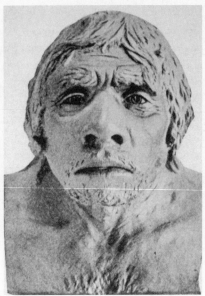

William S. Sadler, *Long Heads and Round Heads: Or What's the Matter with Germany* (1918). Courtesy of the General Research Division, The New York Public Library, Astor, Lenox and Tilden Foundations

The discourse of sexual violation is most striking in propaganda from the early years of the war and, specifically, in the atrocity stories from Belgium.[8] In both Britain and France, as Allyson Booth notes in *Postcards from the Trenches*, "the penetration of national boundaries was articulated as rape, both literally and figuratively" (70). The "rape of Belgium" is only the clearest example of how British, U.S., and French World War I propaganda disproportionately emphasized "sexual-sadistic" violence in the wartime atrocity stories. "Time and again," writes Nicoletta F. Gullace in "Sexual Violence and Family Honor," "the British press, along with those who recounted atrocities to official boards of inquiry, selected sexual crimes as the centerpiece of their accounts of war" (735). The historians Trevor Wilson, John Horne, and Alan Kramer defy the common inter- and postwar pacifist debunking of atrocity stories and instead attempt to substantiate them wherever possible. Although German executions of civilians can be amply corroborated, the extensive stories of German "sexual-sadistic crimes" do not hold up to historical scrutiny. In "German 'Atrocities' and Franco-German Opinion, 1914," Horne and Kramer review the influential pamphlets on Belgian atrocities by Joseph Bédier, *Les crimes allemands d'après des témoignages allemands* and *Comment l'Allemagne essaye de justifier ses crimes* (both published in Paris in 1915 and translated into English the same year as, respectively, *German Atrocities from German Evidence* and *How Germany Seeks to Justify Her Atrocities*). The reports were based on German diaries that were subsequently lost or destroyed. Horne and Kramer do not dispute the truth of the diaries or contemporary depositions but rather seek to show how "value laden and culturally relative stances . . . informed the whole question of German 'atrocities.'" Corroborating the evidence of German executions of civilians, Horne and Kramer assert that "some topics, although they were important in more popular forms of propaganda (such as sexual and sadistic crimes) did not figure prominently in the diaries or in Bédier's pamphlets" (7). They note one case of rape, and they show one example of mistranslation that serves to present "the Germans as sadists" (12). Wilson's *The Myriad Faces of War* reaches similar conclusions about the Bryce Report on Belgian atrocities, which had the same impact on the British understanding of German military conduct as Bédier had in France. While a 1922 Belgian commission did not confirm any of the Bryce Report's specific allegations, Wilson defends the report for the most part. However, he points out that Bryce's evidential depositions "do not contain accounts of the sexual-sadistic outrages against women, children and the aged that feature so largely" in the Belgian atrocity stories (182), and that "after the war . . . the tales of sexual-sadistic actions committed by the Germans in Belgium were discredited" (190). Wilson can only chalk this up to a "strange quirk of human psychology" (190); people were "eager to seize on tales in which the pathological and the mysterious figured prominently. Members of the respectable classes found themselves free to verbalize sexual-sadistic fantasies under the guise of patriotic warnings" (740). Wilson's language of "respectable" and "pathological" resonates with Mosse's argument that modern national identity is constructed around a contrast between abnormal and respectable sexuality. The point here is not that atrocity stories are simply wrong but rather that actual casualty figures of civilians, for example, were de-emphasized or paled in importance next to the more sensational tales of sexual sadism.[9]

Psychologists have long understood the varying degrees of aggression and violence underlying everyday life and nonpathological behaviors, but the anti-German propaganda of World War I disavowed the aggression of its own nation and projected it on Germans, where all aggression was transformed into pathological sadism. The propaganda attempted to shore up the distinction between the aggressor and the home nation by invoking clear-cut oppositions and effacing any possible identification across national lines. The rhetoric of monstrousness served to further increase the difference between the politically righteous self and the demonic, inhuman other.[10] While this would seem to be a ubiquitous feature of propaganda, German propaganda did not produce exactly the same tropes as anti-German propaganda. For example, in the early World War I propaganda of Belgium, Germany's major claim was that the civilian population was dangerous (made up of "francs-tireurs" or snipers). The nature of acts of national invasion accounts for this difference: Germany needed to justify its territorial advances, a situation that did not lend itself to the same sexual metaphors as the French experience of invasion.[11]

At the end of the war, and in the interwar period, British consumers of Great War propaganda grew suspicious, especially of the hyperbole regarding German sexual voraciousness in the atrocity stories.[12] Vera Brittain's and Robert Graves's memoirs of the war, for example, both consider the potency and influence of atrocity stories. In *Testament of Youth*, Brittain wonders why the characterization of Germans as "rapists" does not match her experiences during the war. Nevertheless, the very same tropes linking German authoritarianism to primal instincts resurfaced in World War II propaganda. In "Inside the Whale" (1937), George Orwell notes that during the interwar period, "all the familiar [World War I] war-time idiocies, spy-hunting, orthodoxy-sniffing . . . the retailing of incredible atrocity stories, came back into vogue as though the intervening years had never happened."[13] The association of Germany with the unconscious also returned, as W. H. Auden's remark that Hitler "comes uncomfortably near to being the unconscious of most of us" demonstrates.[14] Dorothy Sayers, best known for her popular detective fictions, wrote a 1941 treatise, *Begin Here: A Statement of Faith*, in which she describes fascism as harnessing unconscious impulses. Citing Stephen H. Roberts's claim, in his popular *The House that Hitler Built* (1938), that Hitler's "triumph was that of emotion and instinct over reason; it represented a great upsurge of the subconscious in the German people," Sayers argues that Hitler was "largely governed by the unconscious [and was] able to express the unformulated desires of the masses" (107). Leonard Woolf's 1935 *Quack, quack!*—a study of "fascist quackery"—also revives the tropes of World War I propaganda. Repeating the claim that "civilization consists largely in the repression and suppression of all kinds of savage instincts" (84–85), Woolf maintains that "psycho-analysis explains too clearly for Nazi mental comfort from what submerged layers of the savage and primitive mind Herr Hitler's social and racial message and Nazi political practices really spring." Woolf borrows Sadler's format in *Long Heads and Round Heads* twenty years earlier and juxtaposes photographs of the enemy with those of "primitive" people, hence continuing the theme of regression. Where Sadler displays Hindenburg and Ludendorff opposite Neanderthals and Cro-Magnons, however, Woolf shows Hitler and Mussolini alongside effigies of the Hawaiian war-god Kukailimoku. The fascist leaders share "the savage emotions of the savage's mask" (47), and German and Italian fascism show "the process of undoing the work of civilization and of recalling to consciousness and activity the savage instincts which several centuries of civilization have repressed" (86). Even as social progress is marked by "repression and suppression," such readings of fascism suggest, the taste for the primal forbidden fruit lingers, and it actually takes very little to awaken that taste.

And so the associations between Germany and sadomasochism and sexual deviance returned. Edgar Mowrer's 1933 *Germany Puts the Clock Back*, for example, maintains that Germans are "a people conditioned to obedience. . . . Such is the law of the jungle. . . . This people is formless and therefore craves a form so strong that it cannot be broken" (13–27)—a claim that comes directly from World War I analyses of "civilized" democratic cultures and authoritarian barbarism and sadomasochism. The "rape of Belgium" was replaced by the "rape of Austria." Orwell captures the spirit of juxtapositions of democracy and fascism as poles of good and evil, a recasting of democracy and authoritarianism, in *Coming Up For Air* (1939), set in Britain at the beginning of World War II. The man-in-the-street narrator attends a Left Book Club lecture by a "well-known anti-Fascist" (170). His voice is a mechanical "burr-burr-burr," from which a few phrases emerge that catch the narrator's attention:

> "Bestial atrocities . . . Hideous outbursts of sadism . . . Rubber truncheons . . . Concentration camps . . . Iniquitous persecution of the Jews . . . Back to the Dark Ages . . . Democracy . . . Fascism . . . Democracy . . . Fascism . . . Democracy." . . . Just like a gramophone. Turn the handle, press the button and it starts. . . . If you cut him open all you'd find inside would be Democracy-Fascism-Democracy. (172)

In this speech, a mixture of legitimate fears about Nazism—concentration camps and the persecution of Jews—is bolstered by the familiar theme of regression ("Back to the Dark Ages") and the inevitable references to "bestial atrocities" and "outbursts of sadism." In unearthing clichés from World War I to describe Nazism, Orwell implies, the urgently specific threats of Nazism are diminished. Moreover, democracy and fascism are played off each other with such mechanical repetition that democracy's position as the bastion of civilization begins to wear thin. Orwell accuses both the British right and the left of sheer laziness, of failing to identify and expose the specificity of fascism, of falling back on "the Hun."

The images of Germans with whips, of Germans as atavistic, sadomasochistic masters, and of Germans dragging half-naked women out of their

Leonard Woolf, *Quack, quack!* (1935). Courtesy of the Rare Book and Manuscript Library, Columbia University. Hawaiian god figures (VAN 231 and HAW 80) © Copyright The British Museum

homes became the tropes of eroticized fascism. The lavish sexualized language and sadomasochistic dynamics that propaganda attached to German authoritarianism may have worked too well, far outlasting and certainly distorting its purpose. The propaganda of World War I, and subsequently of

World War II, is significantly gendered, as many critics have pointed out, with Germany as a male aggressor who seeks to dominate a feminized Britain or France. The images are often highly suggestive sexually. Scholars of World War I frequently characterize Allied propaganda as "lurid,"[15] suggesting that these images could elicit sensational responses or could titillate. Visual propaganda regularly positioned the male German aggressor standing upright, phallically erect, over a horizontal British (or U.S. or French) woman collapsed on the ground, sometimes bound. In an image from the *New York Tribune* called *Made in Germany*, the German, dressed as a gladiator, stands over a woman with his sword drawn. He has the physique of a bodybuilder, and his skimpy clothes reveal most of his body: a loincloth hangs down over his crotch and his legs are spread over the curvaceous woman in a thin dress. The muscles of his thighs are especially detailed, each cord carefully shaded, whereas his face is crudely drawn. From the ankles up, this image is quite suggestive, while the face reverts to the rough outlines of caricature. I will analyze this pattern of a dominant, erect German with a threatening—and highly sexualized—body and a generic face more closely in chapter 4.

These fantasies in which Britain, France, and the United States cast themselves as the feminine victim of a virile Germany are often given romantic or erotic overtones. A French World War I poster called "Les Monstres" depicts a German soldier leaving a woman on the floor beside a tousled bed; the caption exclaims, "He might at least have courted her!!"[16] It is odd to see courtship invoked in this picture of sexual violence. A British World War I cartoon by Louis Raemaekers titled *Seduction* shows a dark-skinned German slumped in an easy chair, legs crossed, with a pistol pointed toward a kneeling woman, whose dress is pulled down to expose one breast, as in depictions of Liberty. The caption: "Germany to Belgium: 'Aren't I a lovable fellow?'"[17] These images, and many others like them, broadly imply sexual violence, but they also have what Ruth Harris calls an "almost pornographic" tone, since the terms of seduction, courtship, and romance hint at eroticism in Germany's imagined relationship to France and Britain.

This Manichaeanism and absolute prohibition are essential generators of eroticized images of fascism, which foreground the propagandistic construction of the enemy, questioning and sometimes parodying such representations and, above all, showing political prohibition—especially when based on sexual voraciousness—to be sexually exciting. This "perverse" reading effect is anticipated by Rudyard Kipling's 1915 story "Mary Postgate" (printed in *Selected Stories*). In this story Kipling, who contributed to the World War I British propaganda effort with comments such as "there are only two divisions in the world

Henry Wood, *Made in Germany* (1914). Courtesy of the Yale University Library

today, human beings and Germans,"[18] writes an unusual account of libidinal British patriotism. Mary Postgate is a forty-four-year-old single live-in maid. She is "thoroughly conscientious, tidy, companionable, and ladylike" (472)—and not a little repressed. When she finds a wounded German soldier in her backyard, Mary coldly watches him die, thinking of "horrors out of newspapers" (483). As the German expires, a "rapture," which Kipling describes as particularly physical, takes hold of her: "She gave herself up to feel." With the soldier's death rattle, "her long pleasure was broken" (485). She drew her breath short between her teeth and shivered from head to foot. "That's all right," she said contentedly, and went up to the house, where she scandalized the whole routine by taking a luxurious hot bath before tea, and came down looking, as Miss Fowler said when she saw her lying all relaxed on the other sofa, "quite handsome!" (484)

The sadistic libidinal energies Kipling shows in Mary resemble the kinds of "horrors" ascribed to Germans at the time. Mary's violation of the British righteousness and moral superiority so central to propaganda produces a sexual frisson that enacts the sexual "sadism" of which British propaganda accuses Germany.[19] Kipling's story is not intended to question British righteousness but is rather, as Sandra M. Gilbert and Susan Gubar suggest in *No Man's Land*, more of an anxious response to women's empowerment during the war. However, Kipling's story strongly echoes the terms of contemporary Belgian atrocity stories, with a crucial switch in gender and nationality: here the German is the prone victim and the British woman stands menacingly over him.

The authors I examine take such libidinal readings in a different direction. Instead of luxuriating in the enemy's death, they eroticize a typically masochistic encounter with the enemy. World War I propaganda and its "lurid" discourse of the sexually dangerous enemy opened the door to the imaginative creation of eroticized fascism in World War II. In some cases (Vercors, Marguerite Duras), a sexualized or romanticized fascism challenges the version of the enemy given in propaganda; in others (Jean Genet, Georges Bataille), the eroticized fascist literalizes and changes the tone of propaganda images. Lytton Strachey's infamous quip, when asked by a military tribunal, "What would you do if you saw a German soldier trying to violate your sister?"—"I would try to get between them"—was only a more witty version of this idiosyncratic reading of national and propagandistic discourse.[20] These alternative images of fascism declare an erotic interest in the object of political prohibition and the libidinal dynamics associated with the enemy rather than a rejection of them.

"The Dregs of Sexual Misery": Fascism and Sexual Repression

The sexual act, successfully performed, was rebellion. Desire was thought crime.

—George Orwell, *1984*

Hitler got the fascists sexually aroused.
—Gilles Deleuze and Félix Guattari, *Anti-Oedipus*

The description of fascism as sadomasochistic becomes explicit in theorists analyzing the rise of the Third Reich, but the character of sadomasochism changes in these accounts. Whereas, for World War I propagandists, authoritarian sadomasochism was primal and libidinally liberative (albeit dangerous), fascist sadomasochism is a sign of psychological degeneracy. The view of authoritarianism as libidinally liberative has unfortunate political implications. The "discontents" that supposedly accompany the curtailment of aggressive impulses do not speak well for the future of democracy. Nevertheless, the discourse of repressive fascism that supersedes the liberative discourse never quite overcomes the notion that democracy or socialism must stifle seductive libidinal impulses to arrive at its correct form of sexuality, based on complete equality, respect, and freedom.

Wilhelm Reich is perhaps the most influential theorist of fascist libidinal repression. The contradictions of his work, and his location of the sexual energies of fascism in repression shared by nonfascists, mirror the eroticized fictions of fascism. In 1933, the year Hitler officially took power, Reich wrote, in *The Mass Psychology of Fascism:*

> The effect of militarism is based essentially on a libidinous mechanism. The sexual effect of a uniform, the erotically provocative effect of rhythmically executed goose-stepping, the exhibitionistic nature of militaristic procedures, have been more practically comprehended by a salesgirl or an average secretary than by our most erudite politicians. (33)

Reich's talent for perceiving the libidinal within the political realm shifts the discussion of fascism away from strictly economic, historical, or political grounds and articulates the dynamics that are dormant in propagandistic critiques of fascism. The very features that render militarism (and fascist display) oppressive and sexless—restraint, rigidity, uniformity—can also render it erotic, depending on the viewer. Reich's assertion that the same movement, iconography, or activity can signify in different ways is central to fictions of eroticized fascism. Like the authors of such fictions, Reich contends that fascism can be libidinally provocative to nonfascists.

If fascism is politically repressive, how does it then liberate desire? Reich modifies the earlier theories of fascism to suggest that the desires fascism cultivates are not those of humans in their primal state, before the instinct-extinguishing sacrifices of civilization have set in, but are rather distorted—the

desires of the oppressed: " 'Fascism,' writes Reich, "is the basic emotional attitude of the suppressed man of our authoritarian machine civilization and its
mechanistic-mystical conception of life" (xiii). In a major change from most
theorists of fascism, who argue its political specificity, Reich claims that " 'fascism' is only the organized political expression of the structure of the average
man's character, a structure that is confined neither to certain races or nations
nor to certain parties, but is general and international." Democracy is no
longer the foil of fascism but rather one more flawed form of capitalism. The
basic structure of contemporary civilization, the family itself, requires constitutional repression and, most important for Reich, "a damming up of sexual
energy, which later breaks out in various ways" (89). Unlike the World War I
theorists, who believed that authoritarianism allowed instincts to run rampant,
Reich argues that the fascist individual is fiercely repressed and must "armor
himself against the natural and spontaneous in himself" (341). Fascism offers a
few channels—military display, the leader's cameo appearance, war—for libidinal release, but they are highly controlled. "One does not have to be a psy-
chologist to understand why the erotically provocative form of fascism offers a
kind of gratification, however distorted, to a sexually frustrated lower middle-
class woman. . . . Hitler conquers power with his negation of statistics and by
making use of the dregs of sexual misery" (202–3). Here Reich extends the
World War I depiction of cruel masters and subservient slaves in enthusiastic
symbiosis to articulate a gendered and sexually perverse model of the male fascist and the female masses.[21] The "sexually frustrated" woman (Reich sees sexual frustration as a condition of capitalist culture as well as fascist culture) has
a sadomasochistic encounter with a man who seeks to "conquer." Hence, the
sadomasochistic erotics that fascism offers are feeble simulations of healthy,
positive libido.

Subsequent work on fascism continues Reich's emphasis on the perverse
or twisted, rather than liberative, libidinal dynamics of fascism. In *Escape
from Freedom* (1941), Erich Fromm posits a "sadomasochistic personality"
type that describes fascist and capitalist subjects alike, and the *Authoritarian
Personality* project (Adorno et al, 1950) builds on this sexual pathologizing in
its "F-Scale" ("F" for fascist), a set of characteristics that may be used to cal-
ibrate an individual's susceptibility to fascism. Norman O. Brown's *Life
Against Death* (1959) and Herbert Marcuse's *Eros and Civilization* (1955) both
call for the lifting of repression, but they have trouble explaining how this
might happen. Brown cryptically calls for the "resurrection of the body," and
Marcuse heralds the "release of a repressed body, instrument of labor and of
fun in a society which is organized against its liberation." Within a field of
theorists asserting fascism's perverse and demoralizing libidinal appeal, no

one makes democratic or socialist sexuality sound very enticing. Instead, democracy is like bitter medicine that must be swallowed for one's own good, while fascism is an intoxicant that must be avoided.

In "'Pleasure, Sex, and Politics Belong Together,'" Dagmar Herzog usefully details the reading of sexually deviant fascism in German theorists of the right and left, where "sexual dysfunctionality" is thought to be "at the heart of the most important and gruesome political events of the twentieth century" (432). But is fascism's sexual deviance—for example, its sadomasochism—an established historical fact? In his best-selling 1960 study *The Rise and Fall of the Third Reich*, William L. Shirer emphatically states that "many of [the SA's] top leaders . . . were notorious perverts . . . men of unnatural sexual inclinations" (172). Shirer singles out Julius Streicher, editor of *Der Stürmer*, as "a noted pervert" and a "depraved sadist": "I never saw him without a whip in his hand or in his belt" (48–50). At the other end of the sadomasochistic spectrum, according to Shirer, stood Hitler, whose "masochistic inclination" produced a yearning "to be enslaved by the woman he loved" (187). Shirer is not an anomaly: a great deal of even the most respected historical scholarship on fascism alludes to the sexual aberrations of Nazism and the general sadomasochistic appeal of fascism. Robert O. Paxton's groundbreaking study of the World War II Occupation, *Vichy France: Old Guard and New Guard* (1972), notes a "yearning for discipline's chastising hand" in the French population that "led directly to a father figure" (34). Paxton calls the Occupation a "stunning shock of defeat, which turned a proud and skeptical people briefly into self-flagellants craving the healing hand of suffering and discipline" (48). Sadomasochism—either in the form of anecdotal evidence or in metaphors—creeps into even the most rigorous histories of fascism.

But how convincing is the case that fascism—fascist movements and their participants—is inherently sexually perverse? The argument is largely built upon profiles of individual fascist figures and especially profiles of Hitler. In *Hitler: A Study in Tyranny*, Alan Bullock observes that "much has been written, on the flimsiest of evidence, about Hitler's sex life" but that only two hypotheses about Hitler's sexuality are "worth serious consideration"—his syphilis and his impotency (392–94). Bullock does not entertain the sadomasochism hypothesis that persists in biographical works on Hitler and in general studies of fascism. (For example, in *Fascism: Past, Present, Future*, Walter Laqueur joins Paxton in proposing that there was "a curious sadomasochistic ingredient" in French fascism [64].) Significantly, the most recent scholarly biography of Hitler, Ian Kershaw's careful two-volume work, dismisses the claim that Hitler was a sexual sadist—or any kind of a sexual deviant—because of lack of convincing evidence. Indeed, much of the evidence of Hitler's sadomasochism comes from fellow Nazis. Ultimately, both psychoanalytic and historical discourse participate as much in the sexualization of fascism as the propagandists and literary figures I will discuss. If we want to know why fascism was and is construed as eroticized, the prevailing psychoanalytic and historical explanations are not sufficient.

What exactly is fascist about sadomasochism? Or sadomasochistic about fascism? Marcuse's view of totalitarianism and sadomasochism is representative: "Pleasure in the abasement of another as well as self-abasement under a stronger will, pleasure in the manifold surrogates for sexuality, in meaningless sacrifices, in the heroism of war are false pleasures, because the drives and needs that fulfill themselves in them make men less free, blinder, and more wretched than they have to be."[22] Reconciling the characterization of fascism as erotically provocative but socially and politically repressive, Marcuse must argue that the erotics fascism produces or appeals to are inauthentic, "false," or distorted. (This changes the logic of World War I antiauthoritarianism, which reads these pleasures as all too authentic.) This account of sadomasochism as a "false pleasure" is unsatisfying for a number of reasons. First, it assumes that fantasies of violence and power are pathological—or fascist. Second, it uses "masochism" and "sadism" to denote simple characterizations of very complex relations (the "masochistic masses" or the "sadistic leader") and personality disorders ("the sadomasochistic personality type") without any precise definition of these terms or their actual applicability to fascist practices. Instead, they remain all-encompassing terms of denigration that do not lend themselves to explanation or exploration. More seriously, the relationship between fascism and sadomasochism has become tautological: fascism is sadomasochistic and sadomasochism is fascist. This tautology has the function of obscuring both of its terms.

In "Sade sergent du sexe," Michel Foucault asserts that "Eros is absent" in Nazism. "It's a complete historical error":

> Nazism wasn't invented by the great erotic madmen of the twentieth century but by the most sinister, boring, disgusting petite bourgeoisie you can imagine. . . . It's the infected petit bourgeois dream of racial propriety that underlies the Nazi dream. (5, my translation from the French)

Nevertheless, Foucault concedes, "that said, it's not impossible that in a localized way there might be, inside the structure, erotic relations that would bind the executioner and the supplicant in their confrontation. But that's incidental" (5). In *Homos*, Leo Bersani takes issue with Foucault's dismissal: "I suspect he [Foucault] knew that it [Eros] was very much present, but he had good reason to insist on its absence" (88). Bersani asserts that "the polarized structure of master and slave, of dominance and submission, is the same in Nazism and S&M, and that structure—not the dream of racial 'purity' or the strictly formal dimension of the game—is what gives pleasure" (88). Bersani's observation is useful in that it is not based on an unexamined definition of sadomasochism as simple cruelty or evil but rather acknowledges a central term that is usually lost in theoretical discussions of sadomasochism: pleasure. Nevertheless, the radically different character and context—historically specific Nazism versus nonspecific sadomasochism—of the relationships between the Nazi and his victim and the partners in an erotic sadomasochistic scene or fantasy are strong arguments against Bersani's conclusion. The dynamics of sadomasochistic fantasy—domination and submission—are structurally similar to that of fascism, but these similarities must be qualified. For example, to speak of "submission" to fascism is a grotesque distortion of those who were victimized by it. Sadomasochistic fantasies (and it bears repeating that my subject here is fantasy, as expressed in literary form) have no inherent relation to fascism. However, the questions raised by the aforementioned interpretations of fascism—Is it repressive or liberative of desire?—are also raised by sadomasochism. Sadomasochistic fantasy is characterized by an opposition between restraint and release, submission and domination, dynamics that are analogous to the repressive/permissive opposition at work in characterizations of the fascist libido. The authors examined in the following chapters understand sadomasochism quite differently from its usual characterization as a pathological sexuality. In a culture that defines positive, appropriate sexuality as tranquil, tender, and promoting equality—a reflection of democratic values—these authors suggest that fantasies of power and violence can be an arousing component of sexuality. They make that point by eroticizing the politics most strongly associated with oppression but then go on to distinguish between erotic sadomasochism and fascist violence.

These texts consistently mark a difference between the violence of enacted historical fascism and sadomasochistic eroticism. In sadomasochistic fantasy, the characters are engaged with one another's desires and move, however circuitously, toward pleasure. In scenes of fascist violence, consent, recognition, and exchange among the characters are missing, as is erotic pleasure. These distinctions are lost when we read purely for thematic content, that is, when we note merely the fascist images in sexual scenarios. These texts must be read with an attention to erotic investment and incitement, for shifts in agency, and for the differences between historically faithful representations of fascism and a clearly distorted fantasy of fascism. For example, authoritarian power is most seductive to D. H. Lawrence when it stimulates erotic energies. These energies are sadomasochistic: one character seeks submission and another seeks domination. In his novel *Kangaroo*, for example, the protagonist sends a painted wooden heart to the leader of a protofascist movement, along with a note: "I send you my red heart. . . . You may command me" (168). When this power relation turns to political violence or "bullying," it is no longer attractive. Similarly, Vercors and Genet contrast romantic, erotic relationships in fantasy with fascist rape. In Genet's scenes of Nazi violence, one character exercises power over the other without consent or recognition that the other is human. In Genet's scenes of sadomasochism, the Nazis and their victims are attentive to each other and often switch roles—the scenes are even romantic. For these authors, eroticism is never free of power dynamics and tension, but erotic assertion never reaches the point of destructive violence. Jessica Benjamin's observation in *Like Subjects, Love Objects* that "what makes sexuality erotic is the survival of the other throughout the exercise of power"(206) is explicitly thematized in these fictions, in which the characters in the sadomasochistic drama do survive, and the characters subject to fascist violence do not. In psychoanalytic terms, these texts provide an erotic intersubjective relation between characters who historically had no such relation.

Georges Bataille's essay "The Psychological Structure of Fascism" (published in *Visions*) gives a similar definition of the relationship between fascism and sadomasochism, which will prove heuristic for the depictions of fascism in the following chapters. Bataille makes a distinction between the experience of "erotism," sexuality that violently shatters the subject and permits a rapturous desubjectivization, and fascist "sadism." For Bataille, the (fascist) master's or sovereign's exercise of power "initially presents itself as a clearly differentiated sadistic activity": namely, cruelty. Cruelty is quite different, for Bataille, from eroticism: "No erotic activity can be associated with cruelty" (146). Eroticism requires a complementary, interconnected recognition, whereas fascist cruelty seeks to exclude, reject, and obliterate the other. Bataille distinguishes fascist "sadism" from sadomasochistic eroticism as a form of sexuality that does not literally destroy. In *At the Mind's Limits*, Jean Améry, writing on his survival of Nazi imprisonment and torture, directly addresses the question of whether the Nazis were "sadomasochists" in the conventional sense. He asserts that Bataille's explanation of sadism/cruelty is resonant with his own experience with the SS. "[The Gestapo] were bureaucrats of torture. And yet, they were also much more. I saw it in their serious, tense faces, which were not swelling, let us say, with sexual-sadistic delight, but concentrated in murderous self-realization" (35–36).[23] As I have argued in the context of propaganda, the most relevant crime of fascism is not "sexual sadism" but murder.

In fictions of eroticized fascism, historical violence—fascist cruelty—is marked by a polarization of the aggressor and the victim and by a failure of recognition on the fascist's part, whereas sadomasochistic scenes undo this rigid distribution of power with disorienting shifts in perspective and position. These texts often slip from a non-Nazi to a Nazi voice, and characters switch from positions of domination and submission, narratively achieving what is precisely, according to Jessica Benjamin's *Like Subjects, Love Objects*, the goal of non-coercive sexual experience: a "dizzying loss of self in erotic experience" (186). These representations might be contrasted with the protofascist writings Klaus Theweleit studies in *Male Fantasies*. The fantasies of men in the Freikorps (the German forerunner of the SA) work to shore up the distinction between the self and the (female, communist) other as a means of preserving the male self from dangerous dissolution. Conversely, the authors discussed here eagerly court that dissolution in eroticism. Similarly, the clear-cut lines of propaganda that freeze the enemy into caricature are reproduced in the sadomasochistic tableau (the fascist and victim), but then this arrangement is taken apart and thrown into disarray in the erotic moment. Instead of increasing the distance from the other, these fictions bring the other (the enemy, the Nazi) into the author's sphere of fantasy in a way that specifically violates the dictates of fascist cruelty and violence. These texts derive their narrative vigor from the sadomasochistic encounter and shifting narrative identification with both sides of the erotic partnership, from fascist to victim and with positions ranging from "masochistic" to "sadistic."

There is a great deal of theoretical confusion about whether sadomasochism is an entity unto itself, or whether this term must be split into the separate impulses of sadism and masochism, which may then join together or remain apart (at one point, Freud describes sadomasochism as one impulse turning back on itself). In *Coldness and Cruelty*, Gilles Deleuze distinguishes the two component syndromes on the basis of Sade's and Sacher-Masoch's works and concludes that "the sadist and the masochist might well be enacting separate dramas, each complete in itself, with different sets of characters and no possibility of communication between them" (45). To take up Deleuze's distinction, the erotic universe of the authors discussed in this book have more in common with Sacher-Masoch than with Sade. The masochistic relation (on the model of Sacher-Masoch) depends on the masochist and torturer agreeing on how the erotic encounter is to be enacted. (The fact that the masochist draws up a contract for his own domination, which is then signed and acted out by his "torturer," suggests that the masochist is in control.) In contrast, sadism, for Deleuze, is an institutionally sanctioned violence exerted by the sadist over the victim, who is forced to participate against his or her will.[24] "Sadism" is a particularly fraught term in the context of this book, since it is often (mistakenly, I argue) used as a synonym for fascism. For the sake of precision, I will call fascist acts "aggression" or "violence" rather than sadism. (Bataille too rejects the usual understanding of "sadism" as inevitably sexual; a more appropriate word for fascist "sadism" would be "violence" or "cruelty," which could also be sexualized, but not in the sense of consensual eroticism.) In the same way that rape is more an act of violence and power than of eroticism, nonerotic "violence" is to be distinguished from sadomasochistic fantasy, and I shall make this distinction when the authors under discussion do so.

The fantasies of fascism in the texts of nonfascists are primarily cast from the victim's point of view, but that victim manipulates his or her oppressor in fantasy. For all these authors, the fascist is initially positioned as the historically identifiable enemy and aggressor. In scenes of eroticism, however, the fascist figure undergoes transformations, often switching from aggression to submission. This almost never happens in pure literary masochism on the Sacher-Masoch model: when the masochist's manipulations are unmasked or the "torturer" is submissive, the scene is over. There are other important differences between the Sacher-Masoch model and masochism in the texts I will consider here. For example, in Sacher-Masoch's texts, the "tormentor" must always be coaxed into playing her role; in fictions of eroticized fascism, the fascist figure is historically circumscribed as unremittingly cruel. However, in the fictional erotic scenarios I discuss, a passive or a sexually compelling fascist can be imagined. There remains an essential distinction between the historical referent "fascism" and an imaginatively distorted fascism. As fantasy, these texts play masochistically with fascism; outside these fantasies, fascism is always a historically real threat. The tension between the world outside the fiction—the fascism of cruelty and prohibition—and the sexualized fantasies inside is at the heart of these texts. Fantasy makes possible a sexually responsive fascism and can transform enacted political violence into erotic sadomasochism. These textual transformations of historical fascism entail resistant, and, in some cases, "perverse" reading strategies that produce masochistic pleasures as well as the pleasure of undermining or challenging dominant cultural paradigms of sexual politics.

I do, however, want to qualify the meaning of these textual resistances. In *Masochism in Modern Man*, Theodor Reik imbues the masochist with a spirit of subversive rebellion: "The masochist is a revolutionist of self-surrender. The lambskin he wears hides a wolf. . . . Beneath his softness there is hardness; be-hind his obsequiousness rebellion is concealed" (156). Reik's example is a masochist who, against his will, is sent to a military academy. He subsequently builds his erotic life around the act of dressing up in a tight uniform for sexual pleasure. For Reik, this man's gesture anticipates a threatening situation and turns it to his own erotic advantage: "If I am put in the military college, even if I am forced into the tightest costume, so that I can scarcely breathe and can-not reach my genitals at all, if my trousers are sewn up and my body almost in-accessible to my hands—even then I will get the sexual gratification you for-bade" (162). Eroticized fictions of fascism similarly recast prohibition, turning the oppressive scenario or prohibited object into a pleasure-producing fantasy. These authors convert historically repressive and politically prohibited fascism into pleasurable fantasy for a variety of reasons. Reik suggests that the masochistic ritual of eroticizing prohibition is a clear gesture of resistance:

[Does] no one see the expression of wild revolution in a ritual of this kind? Does it not reveal a rebellious, independent mind? . . . It surprises me that there are psychoanalysts who still think that masochists are in search of pain and discomfort from the start. Every case of masochistic behavior contradicts such an assumption. (162)

Although localized political protests can be extrapolated from fictions of eroticized fascism, the context in which these protests are delivered, eroti-cized fascism, puts up a serious obstacle to such politically rehabilitative readings. These masochistic fantasies provoke more than they constructively critique; any traces of a "wild" cultural revolution are confounded by images that are hostile to productive, organized politics.

At this point in history, it is perhaps difficult to imagine a nonsadomasochistic fascism, but sadomasochism and fascism must be distinguished from each other in order to understand how they become conflated. In the next chapter I will show that distinction in D. H. Lawrence's "leadership novels," where sado-masochistic literary fantasy is attached to a prefascist politics, authoritarianism. Lawrence was directly influenced by contemporary discussions of democracy, the unconscious, and the authoritarian libido, as I outlined them in the first part of this chapter. Lawrence's rejection of the democratic libidinal economy, which in his view mistakenly rejected political "masters" and cultivated an overly cere-bral approach to sex, impelled him to seriously consider authoritarianism. Al-though Lawrence's novels anticipate the linkage between sadomasochistic erotics and nondemocratic politics, they also show how fantasies of power and aggression, and the libidinization of politics, predate the rise of fascism.

Chapter 2
The Libidinal Politics of D. H. Lawrence's "Leadership Novels"

Of all the writers treated in this book, Lawrence's relation to fascism is most subject to critical debate. Since my analysis is predicated on the tension between an author's nonfascist politics and his or her eroticized fictions of fascism, and since Lawrence's politics are perhaps less clear than authors treated subsequently, I will begin by addressing this issue. Lawrence's literary engagement with authoritarianism in the early years of Mussolini's rule has led some critics to pronounce Lawrence a fascist ideologue or as William York Tindall puts it, a "theocratic fascist."[1] Lawrence never supported a fascist regime, and, in fact, wrote quite strongly against Italian Fascism and the beginnings of Nazism in texts such as *Movements in European History* and "A Letter From Germany."[2] Nevertheless, Lawrence's so-called leadership novels—*Aaron's Rod* (1922), *Kangaroo* (1923), and *The Plumed Serpent* (1926)—do explore the attractions of authoritarian and protofascist ideology.[3] It is important to realize that the novels were written before Mussolini began to model his social policies on Hitler's. *Aaron's Rod*, Lawrence's most realistic treatment of contemporary politics, was written from 1917 to 1921, in the context of Italy's turbulent factionalism. As Victoria de Grazia notes in *How Fascism Ruled Women*, Mussolini's movement was "an authoritarian regime with shallow roots in civil society through the late 1920s" and then "became a mass-based state with totalitarian pretensions in the 1930s" (8). Thus, the political movements in the leadership novels are based on Lawrence's understanding of authoritarianism. Lawrence shows, more clearly than almost any writer of his generation, what motivated the rejection of democracy in the interwar period.

All three leadership novels are set in motion by the protagonist's crisis, which is both personal and political. The disillusioned British or U.S. protagonist leaves his (or her, in the case of *The Plumed Serpent*) democratic home country for a foreign nation (Italy, Australia, Mexico) that is in the midst of a struggle among authoritarian, socialist, and democratic movements. The protagonist meets a charismatic male leader who is nationalistic, anticommunist, and antidemocratic, and who champions a reversion to a society built on gender and class hierarchies. Lawrence's positioning of authoritarianism and democracy against each other in terms of their libidinal structures anticipates statements such as Sontag's observation in "Fascinating Fascism" that "left-wing movements have tended to be unisex, and asexual in their imagery. Right-wing movements, however puritanical and repressive the realities they usher in, have an erotic surface. . . . Certainly Nazism is 'sexier' than communism" (102). Lawrence's distinctive contribution in the leadership novels is the way he connects authoritarian leaders and their movements to a sadomasochistic erotics that is, for Lawrence, an expression of instinctual libido. Arguing that the greatest ill of modernity is the repression of the libido and its aggressive and sexual drives—what I will call Lawrence's "libido/power theory"—Lawrence proposes that the way to correct this problem is to develop a politics that will allow these drives to be expressed. But whereas later theorists such as Reich and Marcuse will argue that noncapitalist, socialist politics will make people most libidinally free, for Lawrence—in a twist on the propagandistic construction of authoritarian sadomasochism—authoritarianism is erotically liberative.

Each of Lawrence's authoritarian or protofascist leaders appeals to the disillusioned protagonist in two ways, offering an antidemocratic politics and an enticing erotics: homosocial desire in *Aaron's Rod* and *Kangaroo*, and female submission and male dominance in *The Plumed Serpent*. Throughout Lawrence's novels, homoeroticism is either placed in a punishing context, such as the lesbian affair in the "Shame" chapter of *The Rainbow*, or isolated as a glorious erotic eruption that the narrative then contains, such as, in *Women in Love*, the excised "Prologue," the "Gladiatorial" chapter, and the unfinished conversation that concludes the novel, when Ursula tells Birkin that the "eternal union with a man" that he desires is "an obstinacy, a theory, a perversity." Lawrence also struggles with the character of sexuality in general, shuttling between the romantic, tranquil and, for Lawrence, stagnant language of contemporary heterosexuality and the supercharged struggle of sadomasochistic sexuality (for example, the mating cats who cuff and fight each other in *Women in Love*). The authoritarian and protofascist movements of Lawrence's leadership novels generate and make possible fantasies of homoerotic and homosocial bonds as well as sadomasochistic eroticism.

In his fiction, Lawrence is not a systematic thinker, and the leadership novels are perhaps his weakest in this respect, as they hoarsely shout the inadequacies of democracy and the need for masters to save the swarming masses from themselves—masters whom the narrative encourages readers to both admire as charismatic saviors and reject as tiresome posturers. The protagonists of the leadership novels ambivalently appreciate and dissent from authoritarianism. One of Lawrence's clearest articulations of his understanding of democracy, socialism, and fascism is *Movements in European History*, a textbook for schoolchildren commissioned by Oxford University Press that, in predictably Lawrentian fashion, careens off course in ways that render it useless as a history primer. Nevertheless, *Movements*, written between 1918 and 1924, is helpful for interpreting the leadership novels since it is relatively direct. The major flaw of democracy, Lawrence writes in an epilogue to *Movements* that Oxford decided not to include in its initial printing, is that its elected representatives are "forced, obviously, to be the *servants* of a huge, discontented mob, who all want more money and less work" (264). Democracy—and this view is strongly articulated throughout the leadership novels—is the rule of the lowest common denominator "herd," "vulgar, common, ugly, like the voice of the man in the crowd" (259). Lawrence's repugnance for the general populace is a key factor in his interest in authoritarianism, as it was for other British intellectuals who rejected democratic principles (and parliamentary politics in particular) after the war. Some of them, such as T. S. Eliot, Wyndham Lewis, and W. B. Yeats, subsequently embraced fascist ideology to various degrees, while others, such as Shaw, championed radical forms of socialism. In Lawrence's case, this turn against democracy was motivated by his experiences during World War I and the propagandistic climate in Britain, as I described it in the previous chapter.

Lawrence fictionalized these experiences in a chapter in *Kangaroo* called "The Nightmare." From mid-winter of 1915—a year numerous critics have identified as crucial for Lawrence, and which marked his turn from "optimistic socialist revolutionary" to "a paranoid antidemocratic misanthrope"[4]—Lawrence and his German wife, Frieda, lived in an isolated Cornwall cottage and, in application of the newly established Defense of the Realm Act (DORA), were put under surveillance once their antimilitaristic views became known. Suspected of passing messages and food to German submarines on the coast, harassed by neighbors and government spies who accused them of espionage, Lawrence and Frieda were forced to leave Cornwall, and then England. The protagonist of *Kangaroo*, who shares this history, speaks of the war years with bitterness:

No man who has really consciously lived through this [war] can believe again absolutely in democracy. No man who has heard reiterated in thousands of tones from all the common people during the crucial years of the war: "I believe in *John Bull*. Give me *John Bull*," can ever believe that in any crisis a people can govern itself, or is ever fit to govern itself. During the crucial years of the war, the people chose, and chose Bottomleyism. (240)

Horace Bottomley was the editor of *John Bull*, a reactionary newspaper that championed English jingoism during the war. Bottomley spearheaded the anti-German (or "Germhun," as Bottomley preferred) sentiment that swept Britain after the invasion of Belgium. In *John Bull* (15 May 1915), he called for "a vendetta against every German in Britain—whether 'naturalized' or not. . . . You cannot naturalize an unnatural abortion, a hellish freak. But you can exterminate him." Bottomley proposed that all Germans wear badges signaling their nationality and that their children be banned from British schools. An all-out assault was launched on Germans in the United Kingdom: in 1914, all male Germans, Austrians, and Hungarians who were old enough to serve in the military were sent to internment camps around the country, German-owned businesses were destroyed, and German employees fired (Haste, 119). For Lawrence, who had a great respect for German culture, the British populace's embrace of Bottomley was one more symptom of the degraded state of interwar Britain and democracy. Throughout the leadership novels, Lawrence shows not just contempt for the proletarian mass but a tangible fear of it.

In *Movements in European History*, Lawrence maintains that a "good form of socialism, if it could be brought about, would be the best form of government" (262), but he looks to the living example of socialism in the Soviet Union and finds it lacking. "Communism, sovietism," is admirable for its attention to its people's basic needs, but it is ruined by the insistence "that all existing *masters* shall be overthrown, and that men shall be 'free,' which means, there shall be no authority over the people" (261). For Lawrence, socialism fails because its leaders do not recognize that power and hierarchy are inevitable and desirable: "Because, if there is not power there will be force" (263). The "force" that develops in a power vacuum is, for Lawrence, the third political alternative, fascism. As with his treatment of socialism, Lawrence looks to the clearest instantiation of fascism to date: Mussolini's Italy. He recalls a trip to Florence in the early 1920s when he found the city "in a state of continual socialist riot," and another trip, slightly later, when the Fascisti had appeared with their processions and banners:

When I went to Naples, to the big main post office to send a telegram, there were white notices pasted over the doorways: "We, the mutilated soldiers, have turned out all the young women employed in this office, and have taken their place. No woman clerk or operator shall enter this office etc." . . . This was the beginning of Fascism. It was an anti-socialist movement started by the returned soldiers in the name of Law and Order. And suddenly, it gained possession of Italy. . . . The Fascisti seized [the socialist mayor] and stood him against the wall of his house and shot him under the eyes of his wife and children. . . . That is Fascism and Law and Order. Only another kind of bullying.

Now one *must* have Law and Order. . . . We *must* have authority, and there *must* be power. But there must not be bullying, nor the worship of mere Force. . . . A certain group of men in Italy intend to *force* their will on all other men. Earlier, socialists tried to force *their* will. In Russia, the communists succeed in forcing *their* will.

The forcing of one man's will over another man is bullying. . . . It de-grades both the bully and those who are bullied. (262–63)

On one hand, Lawrence argues, democracy and socialism fail to pose viable solutions to the interwar crisis because they disavow the importance of hier-archy and authority. On the other hand, if power is exaggerated, it turns to "force" and "bullying." Where exactly does Lawrence draw the line between "masters" and fascist "bullies"? In *Movements* the distinction turns on the re-sponsible exercise of power versus irresponsible acts of violence. The lead-ership novels continue to grapple with this essential question of the rela-tionship between authority and violence, adding to it an exploration of the libidinal properties of authoritarianism. In each of the leadership novels, the authoritarian power dynamic is initially erotic, but then an act of violence— a politically motivated bombing in *Aaron's Rod* and *Kangaroo*, a human sacri-fice in *The Plumed Serpent*—tips the balance and the protagonist's attraction to authoritarianism turns to contempt for bullying.

The bridge between a political and a libidinal reading of authoritarianism is articulated in Lawrence's idiosyncratic essay, "Fantasia of the Unconscious" (1921). Like *Movements in European History*, "Fantasia" is heuristic for the lead-ership novels, which champion an eroticized exercise of power and a submis-sion to it, and denigrate other kinds of power as bullying. "Fantasia" begins with Lawrence's insistence that psychoanalysis is one of the greatest evils to be-fall humanity, since it fosters "crippling self-consciousness." Nevertheless, many of Lawrence's theories echo Freud's, particularly in terms of the uncon-scious, repression, and the developmental model of libido set forth in "Fantasia," a libido that begins, as in Freud's model, with the polymorphous perversity of infancy. For Lawrence, the child starts life with a particular attribute of "will," a positive instinct, stemming from primary infantile impulses, to separate from others in order to define the self. This "will" manifests itself in

> the violent little pride and lustiness which kicks with glee, or crows with tiny exultance in its own being, or which claws the breast with a savage little rapacity, and an incipient masterfulness of which every mother is aware. . . . The child is self-willed, independent, and masterful . . . maintaining his proud independence like a little wild animal. From this centre he likes to command and to receive obedience. (36, 48)

Lawrence follows Freud in emphasizing the infant's sense that the world revolves around him, but Lawrence intensifies Freud's metaphor of royalty ("His Majesty the Baby")[5] to that of authoritarianism, of "commanding" and "receiving obedience." This early, spontaneous form of self-will that follows the dictates of libido rather than reason gives way to secondary forces of rationality and self-consciousness: the compromise of civilization to which Freud attributes our "discontents," and which Gustave Le Bon characterizes in *The Crowd* as "a passing from the instinctive to the rational state" (18). The onset of the rational and intellectual faculties is a tragedy for Lawrence, since people then become overly conscious and are crippled by what he calls "sex in the head." In combating these ostensible disasters of civilization, Lawrence makes one of his most startling claims in "Fantasia": "The supreme lesson of human consciousness is to learn how not to know" (76). The leadership novels strive for a political system founded on this irrationality and even idiocy.

Lawrence's language in "Fantasia of the Unconscious" echoes the British propaganda I discussed in the previous chapter. The tyranny and arrogance that propagandists attribute to authoritarian Germany are not far from the "savage little rapacity" and "incipient masterfulness" (in Lawrence's terms) of the child who acts with "proud independence like a little wild animal," demanding and "receiv[ing] obedience." Both Lawrence and British propagandists agree that authoritarianism enacts an atavistic return to a premodern and nondemocratic state, but for Lawrence authoritarianism offers a liberation from the crippling rationality that, for the propagandists, is the saving grace of civilization. In his essay "Blessed are the Powerful," Lawrence distinguishes instinctual "will" or "power" from a culturally constructed "will-to-power"[6] that consists in "bossing, or bullying, hiring a manservant or Salvationizing your social inferior, issuing loud orders and getting your own way, doing your opponent down" (*Phoenix II*, 439). Although there is some slippage in terms, Lawrence introduces the same ideas in his earlier fiction. "Bullying" is at work when Gerald Crich whips his horse in *Women in Love*, or when the female conductors in "Tickets, Please" tear John Thomas to pieces.[7] Mrs. Bolton's bossiness is described as the "endless assertion of her own will."[8]

"Fantasia" and *Movements* suggest that the distinction between instinctual, libidinal will and bullying is clear-cut, but all Lawrence's novels blur that line, particularly in their treatment of sexuality. Lawrence almost always describes sexual desire and practice in the sadomasochistic language of struggle and conflict. Even in Lawrence's rare descriptions of sex as a tender encounter (such as Clara and Paul's scene by the river in *Sons and Lovers*), the central dynamics of sexuality for Lawrence are not harmony or stasis but tension, struggle, and release. Even at its best, sex in Lawrence's novels amounts to two individuals fighting to keep themselves autonomous even as they merge. The struggle itself is eroticized throughout his work: for Lawrence, sexuality is essentially sadomasochistic. With the leadership novels, as libidinal dynamics spill over into political dynamics, sadomasochism takes a political form: authoritarianism.

Lawrence's translation of sadomasochistic sexuality into an erotic authoritarian politics in the leadership novels is anticipated in "Fantasia." After asserting that the libidinal aspects of aggression and power are repressed or sublimated in democratic society and subsequently turned into a desire to bully, Lawrence proposes that true "power" and "will" should dictate a new relationship between the "mass" and their leaders, a power structure that allows and encourages instinct and expressions of primal libido, including aggression and exertion, so that they do not emerge in the cruel forms of "will-to-power" and bullying. It is here, when Lawrence tries to imagine such a politics, that his philosophy most resembles fascist ideology:

> The secret is, to commit into the hands of the sacred few the responsibility which now lies like torture on the mass. Let the few, the leaders, be increasingly responsible for the whole. . . . Leaders—this is what mankind is craving for. But men must be prepared to obey, body and soul, once they have chosen the leader. (88)

> Men have got to choose their leaders, and obey them to the death. And it must be a system of culminating aristocracy, society tapering like a pyramid to the supreme leader. . . . And the polarizing of the passionate blood in the individual towards life, and towards leader, this must be the dynamic of the next civilization. (182–83)

Lawrence imagines political domination as consensual and natural—the people crave a leader, and a leader is born to rule. The leadership novels attempt to imagine a political movement appropriate to this social arrangement of "passionate" unconscious impulses. Authoritarianism, for Lawrence, is erotically liberative: but that is only half the story.

Aaron's Rod: Smashing the Matrimonial Cart

The struggle between individualism and collectivism that Lawrence introduces in his earlier novels (*The Rainbow* and *Women in Love*, for example) as a conflict between individual autonomy and the bond of love or marriage, becomes, in the leadership novels, a conflict in political structures. In *Aaron's Rod*, Lawrence begins with a localized struggle between a couple: its protagonist miner/flutist, Aaron Sisson, and his wife, Lottie, whose "strange woman's will . . . stronger than steel, strong as a diabolical, cold grey snake" (158) drives Aaron to abandon her and their children. Dramatizing Aaron's departure from the stifling heterosexual family at Christmastime, Lawrence pits Lottie's overdeveloped will-to-power against Aaron's opinion that a marriage must be based on two powerful individuals who do not try to control each other and remain in their "singleness."

Like all the leadership novels, *Aaron's Rod* is set just after the Great War. Although none of the protagonists fought in the war, returning soldiers are central to each of the novels, just as, historically, ex-soldiers played a major role in the formation of Italian and German fascism, and in the British Union of Fascists, led by the returned soldier Oswald Mosley. In *Kangaroo*, Lawrence suggests that the war was a glorious time for men, and that soldiers are "dying for another scrap" (178) as a means of reinvigorating their manhood. Aaron, like the protagonists of all the leadership novels, feels at odds with his countrymen. A secretary to the Miners Union in his colliery, he wants to feel solidarity with other workingmen, but he is disconnected and alienated from them. "He never went with the stream. . . . There was a hard, opposing core in him. . . . It remained hard, nay became harder and more deeply antagonistic to his surroundings, every moment. He recognised it as a secret malady he suffered from: this strained, unacknowledged opposition to his surroundings, a hard core of irrational, exhausting withholding of himself. Irritating, because he still *wanted* to give himself" (10–18). In holding himself apart from the "stream"—or the proletarian "mob"—Aaron is the typical leadership novel protagonist. A man apart, he is also searching for a worthy idol to bow down before.

Upon leaving his family, Aaron travels to London and joins an orchestra, in which he plays the flute, an instrument that carries several symbolic associations. In the Old Testament, Aaron (Moses' brother) had a "rod" that "budded and brought forth buds and blossoms" and led the Israelites out of Egypt, sustaining them through forty years of wandering in the desert. Lawrence suggests a parallel to the degenerate state of interwar England—dazed from war and in search of leadership.[9] Aaron's "rod" also obviously has a phallic form, which is of particular importance to Lawrence; the project of each of the leadership novels is to discover a new form of phallicism that will reinvigorate contemporary life. In all three novels, Lawrence contrasts the deadening democratic life between the wars to a foreign authoritarianism that reawakens primal libido.

In London, Aaron falls ill and is nursed back to health by a man called Rawdon Lilly, who has also separated from his wife. The two men live together while Aaron recovers. Their relationship is both domestic and erotic: they are described in feminine terms and refer to each other as "wife." The substitution of a same-sex male relationship for heterosexual marriage is a feature in both *Aaron's Rod* and *Kangaroo*, and an extension of the theme of "Blutbrüdershaft" in *Women in Love*. The turn in Aaron's illness comes about in a reprisal of "Gladiatorial," the erotic wrestling scene in *Women in Love*. Upon finding that Aaron's "bowels don't work," Lilly rubs Aaron's lower body with oil: "He saw a change. The spark had come back into the sick eyes" (91). Although this is a brief scene, the "mindless," intimate, healing contact stands in sharp contrast to the intellectual battle of wills between Aaron and his wife. This is the apex of the sexual connection between Aaron and Lilly, and throughout the novel homosocial desire surfaces from time to time as a seductive alternative to heterosexual marriage, only to be repressed once again.

Lawrence attaches a homoerotic charge to authoritarian politics, first, through Lilly, who is not part of any political movement but is a mouthpiece for authoritarian ideas, and then through Italy, a country that celebrates male camaraderie and beauty. Upon arriving in Italy, Aaron feels "a new self, a new life-urge rising inside himself. . . . It was a town of men . . . packed with men: but all, all men. And all farmers, land-owners and land-workers. . . . But men! Men! A town full of men, in spite of everything" (208). In Florence, Aaron is delighted to see glorious statues of nude men. Also in Italy, he befriends a homosexual couple. This male intensity is obtained through the rejection of women. Aaron lounges in a café with other men who have left their wives. One man advises Aaron to "smash the shafts, and the whole matrimonial cart" (237), and another man chimes in: "Terrible thing, the modern woman" (239). There must always be an excuse, an alibi, for homosociality or homoeroticism in Lawrence's novels. In *Aaron's Rod*, the pretext is a trip abroad to a country in a state of civil war, where women are rarely seen on the streets. In Italy, Lilly reappears and continues his aggressive pontifications on power, authority, and sexual politics. He insists that heterosexual love and marriage must be adjusted:

> There must be one who urges, and one who is impelled. Just as in love there is a beloved and a lover: The man is supposed to be the lover, the woman the beloved. Now, in the urge of power, it is the reverse. The woman must now submit, but deeply, deeply, submit. Not to any foolish fixed authority, not to any foolish and arbitrary will. But to something deep, deeper. . . . We must reverse the poles. The woman must now submit—but deeply, deeply, and richly! No subservience. None of that. No slavery. A deep, unfathomable free submission. (288)

Lilly echoes Lawrence's theory in "Fantasia" of an original "urge of power" but adds that the initial power structure has a natural order of male domination and female submission. Similarly natural to Lilly is the designation of "inferior beings" and the "superior being" to which they will submit: he insists that this code is "written between a man's brows." In the absence of "voluntary acceptance," Lilly recommends a "permanent and very efficacious" military power (272).

As he spouts racist and misogynist theories that become increasingly extreme over the course of the novel, we might well wonder what is so attractive about Lilly. Jim, a former army officer, announces to Lilly: "I suddenly saw that if there was a man in England who could save me, it was you" (73). Elsewhere Lilly is described as "maddening and fascinating." This combination of compelling and repellant qualities and the resulting erotic dynamic—being drawn toward the leader in an act of submission, then pushing him away in defiance—constitutes an erotic pulse in all the leadership novels. This pattern is underscored in *Aaron's Rod* through the constant quarrelling between Aaron and Lilly, Aaron's continuous questioning of Lilly's philosophies, and his pursuit of Lilly across continents. Aaron's challenges to Lilly take on more weight in the novel as Lilly's theories become increasingly severe. This is typical of the leadership novels, in which the most bellicose characters are almost always undercut either by other characters or by the narrator, and their strident political speeches are shown to be dangerously extreme. (In *Kangaroo* and *The Plumed Serpent*, it is women, and specifically wives, who reveal that the urge to dominate is the will-to-power and the will to bully.) This constant shifting of ground makes the political sympathies of the narrative difficult to determine. These crosscurrents have often been read in terms of Bakhtinian dialogism, but they also echo the pulse of eroticism throughout the novels, with their back-and-forth assertions and retractions, acts of aggression and of submission.

When the scene changes from Britain to Italy, *Aaron's Rod* shifts its focus from a would-be savior, Lilly, to a real political power struggle. The Italy Lawrence portrays in *Aaron's Rod* is in a state of postwar chaos—many shops are closed, soldiers are camped out everywhere, and various political factions stage protest marches. *Aaron's Rod* captures the turbulent period of civil war and economic crisis, strikes and riots between 1920 and 1922, which Lawrence describes in *Movements in European History*, when socialists, communists, and anarchists clashed with Fascisti. Aaron perceives the civil unrest, but he is unable to see the larger picture of what is happening. In the final scenes of the novel, as Socialists and Anarchists clash with government troops in Florence, Lilly reappears and assesses the political situation. "You've got to have a sort of slavery again," he tells Aaron and a group of men in a café. "People are not *men:* they are insects and instruments, and their destiny is slavery. They are too many for me, and so what I think is ineffectual. But ultimately they will be brought to agree—after sufficient extermination—and then they will elect for themselves a proper and healthy and energetic slavery" (272). Earlier in the novel Lilly specified that his ideal form of government would require "no subservience" and "no slavery," but now his fear of the mob has transformed people into insects to be stamped out. The group in the café starts to argue with Lilly, when, suddenly, an Anarchist's bomb explodes. Amidst the blood, the broken glass, and the panicked crowd, Aaron feels for his flute in his pocket. It has been split in two. Lawrence punctuates his novel with Lilly's bullying rhetoric and political violence, leaving his reader with serious doubts about extreme politics.

Lawrence's portrait of the early stages of Italian Fascism is quite different from that of George Bernard Shaw, for example, who asserted in 1927, in several letters published in British newspapers, that "Mussolini, without any of Napoleon's prestige, has done for Italy what Napoleon did for France. . . . Are we going to give him credit for his work and admit its necessity . . . or are we to go on shrieking that the murderer of Liberty and Matteotti is trampling Italy under foot?"[10] In *Aaron's Rod*, Lawrence underscores violence as the point beyond which his protagonist will not follow Lilly or any political movement. Aaron is symbolically castrated by an Anarchist's bomb, but the critique of violence also extends to the authoritarian ideology that Lilly expounds, suggesting Lawrence's dissatisfaction with any of the answers he generates in the novel. Just as Lawrence expresses his worry, in "Fantasia of the Unconscious," that instinctual power may become distorted into "will-to-power" in democracy, Lilly's bullying politics of authoritarianism, by means of which he purports to have solved the war of the sexes and the inter-war crisis, is associated with violence and "slavery," which, the novel asserts, are not adequate answers.

"Every Man Should Have a Mate": *Kangaroo*

The political climate in Australia at the beginning of Lawrence's second leadership novel is one of "real democracy" (27): Australia is "absolutely and flatly democratic," ruled by the "will of the people" (27). There, "authority was a dead letter" (28). The novel's protagonist, Richard Somers, a writer who has left England with his wife, Harriet, perceives Australia as alterna-tively "terrifying" and "treacly" (75). "Without any core or pith of mean-ing . . . no inner life, no high command. . . . Power . . . had no real signifi-cance here" (33), he muses, and then defensively asks, "What is more hopelessly uninteresting than accomplished liberty?" (33). The democratic rejection of authority and hierarchy is complete in this Australia, embodying all the flaws of democracy as outlined in *Movements in European History*.

Harassed by authorities in England during the war, Somers, who is based on Lawrence's World War I experiences, is predisposed to admire countries such as India, where "the joy of obedience and the sacred responsibility of authority" (120) are respected. Hence, upon settling in Australia, Somers is receptive to a group of veterans called the "Diggers,"[11] who are reviving a new system of authority led by a man known as "Kangaroo," who is implausibly Jewish (a detail that clashes with the antisemitism throughout the novel). Somers's neighbor, Jack Calcott, introduces him to the Diggers' plan "to have another sort of government for the Commonwealth—with a sort of Dictator: not the democratic vote-cadging sort" (110). When Somers meets the mystical, Buddha-like Kangaroo, this man's credo resembles Lilly's in *Aaron's Rod*: "The secret of all life is in obedience" (126), the obedience, that is, of the "mob" to the authority figure. But Kangaroo is gentler than Lilly. "Man," Kangaroo tells Somers, "needs to be relieved from this terrible responsibility of governing himself when he doesn't know what he wants. . . . Man again needs a father—not a friend or a brother sufferer, a suffering Saviour. Man needs a quiet, gen-tle father who uses his authority in the name of living life" (126). Authoritari-anism is presented as paternal protection that offers an escape from the exhausting choices of democracy. It is also pointedly presented as an affair be-tween men and takes on homosocial qualities. Jack Calcott, one of Kangaroo's supporters, tells Somers that "every man should have a mate—like most of us had in the war" (117). Having a "mate" is more complex than friendship and supplants the usual social ties because, as Calcott tells it, when a man's "mate calls," that man "turns away from his wife, children, mother." Somers responds to Jack with "the thrill of desire" (117) and is "tempted to give Jack his hand there and then" (118), but he hesitates: "Did he want to mix and make with this man?" (119). Although compelled by Kangaroo and the Diggers, Somers "had a fright against being swept away, because he half wanted to be swept away" (172). Struggling with these political desires, he counters them with his determination "to be cold, cold and alone like a single fish" (140). Lawrence returns to the oceanic rhetoric of *Aaron's Rod* (Aaron "never went with the stream, but made a side current of his own") to establish the tension between individuality and an alluring political collective.

Employing the rhetoric of "mating" and marriage, Lawrence depicts the authoritarian male relationships in *Kangaroo* as romantic but still based on domination and submission. When Calcott tells Somers, "we want a man like you . . . like a sort of queen bee to a hive" (107), Somers decides he must keep this a secret from Harriet, telling himself that "the pure male activity should be womanless, beyond woman" (108). Without knowing about Somers's proposition to be Kangaroo's "queen," Harriet herself gently mocks Somers's utopian and romantic desire to "move with men and get men to move with" him, comparing his "attempts with men" to affairs with women (78). Somers's desire and reluctance, attraction and repulsion, body forth the sadomasochistic dynamic that characterizes the leadership novels. In *Kangaroo*, the homoerotics of this authoritarian temptation are more pronounced than in *Aaron's Rod*, but the other political group that courts Somers in Australia—Willie Struthers's Socialist and Labor Party—makes a similar appeal to male intimacy. Struthers explains that it is his intention to build "a new bond between men" (218), and Somers is impressed when he quotes Walt Whitman and expresses his ideas about "Love of Comrades," "mate-trust," a "new tie between men, in the new democracy . . . the new passional bond in the new society" (219).

But the ecstatic thrill of Whitman can only go so far. Eventually, Somers must grapple with the politics behind the male bonding. Struthers asks Somers to write a column to rally the emotions of Australian people and interest them in the socialist cause. He thinks

all this theoretical socialism started by Jews like Marx, and appealing only to the will-to-power in the masses, making money the whole crux, this has cruelly injured the working people of Europe. . . . All this po-

litical socialism . . . has conspired to make money the only god. . . .
[Somers] wanted men once more to refer the sensual passion of love sa-
credly to the great dark God, the ithyphallic, of the first dark religions.
And how could that be done, when each dry little individual ego was just
mechanically set against any such dark flow, such ancient submission?
(223–24)

Just as *Movements in European History* asserts that socialism is incapable of
recognizing hierarchy and the need for masters, Somers suggests that
Struthers's socialism will not allow a place for the "ancient submission"—the
atavistic regression to "the first dark religions"—but will instead leave him
"dry" and alone.

Kangaroo's authoritarianism, in contrast, does call exactly for an atavistic
worship of "older gods, older ideals . . . nearer to the magic of the animal
world" (229). Lawrence makes use of the same metaphors of regression and
atavism seen in propaganda, such as William S. Sadler's *Long Heads and
Round Heads*, with its comparisons of authoritarian Germans to Neanderthal
and Cro-Magnon men. But rather than fearing this regression, Somers
craves it. Lawrence also establishes two metaphors to reflect the allure of authoritarianism: the dry separateness of socialism and the wet mergings of authoritarianism. Kangaroo's authoritarianism is described as a sea that seductively offers the comforts of union and fusion with one's fellowmen—in this
respect, it is like the "oceanic" quality of love and religious merging that
Freud describes in *Civilization and Its Discontents*. Using a metaphor that
Elias Canetti suggests is a specifically British crowd symbol,[12] Lawrence
translates Freud's "oceanic" desire to be overwhelmed into Somers's desire
to be "swept away"—and the fear of being so.[13]

The sea and flood imagery also evoke those Klaus Theweleit finds
throughout Freikorps diaries. For these protofascists, the flood symbolizes
feminine and sexual engulfment (as well as fear of the Communist masses),
which they both fear and desire. In *Kangaroo*, the sea is the "horrible flood"
of the masses and female engulfment and *also* a pleasurable—and anxiety-
producing—male bonding. The pulse of attraction and repulsion, assertion
and passivity, operate in this metaphor just as they do in Lawrence's eroticism. In *Kangaroo*, homosocial and homoerotic bonding are expressed eva-
sively, when compared to similar scenes in Lawrence's other novels. However, at a crucial point, when Somers is pondering mass movements and
whether to support Kangaroo, Lawrence returns to sea imagery. Prompted
by an item in the paper that calls into question the theory that "bullocks"
(whales) have "telepathy," Somers meditates on the sperm whale, exclaiming

over "the marvellous vivid communication of the huge sperm whales. Huge, grand, phallic beasts! Bullocks! . . . [He] wished he could take to the sea and be a whale, a great surge of living blood" (307). Here it is a phallically masterful mammal rather than the isolated "cold" fish (33) Somers longed to be previously, that navigates the sea. The whale permits an individuality that resists merging with the viscous, "treacly" mass. This leads into an exceedingly strange pseudoscientific description of the habits of sperm whales, whose feeding patterns are contrasted to "the herd instinct" in humans—the "mass-spirit" or "the mob"—which is "a collection of all the weak souls, sickeningly conscious of their weakness" (323):

> The mob has no direction even in its destructive lust. . . . And it is no good trying to reason with them. The mass does not act by reason. A mass is not even formed by reason. The more intense or extended the *collective* consciousness, the more does the truly reasonable, individual consciousness sink into abeyance. (328)

The mob instinct threatens to drown individual consciousness. *Sperm* whales, on the other hand, are described as having achieved "the highest form of vertebral telepathy":

> They are lounging, feeding lazily, individually, in mid-ocean, with no cohesion. Suddenly, a quick thought-wave from the leader-bull, and as quick as answering thoughts the cows and young bulls are ranged. . . . This is what makes the magic of a leader like Napoleon—his powers of sending out intense vibrations, messages to his men, without the exact intermediation of mental correspondence. It is not brain-power. In fact, it is, in some ways, the very *reverse* of brain-power: it might be called the acme of stupidity. (329)

This "marvelous reversion to the pre-mental form of consciousness" (330) is exactly what Lawrence valorizes in "Fantasia of the Unconscious" ("the supreme lesson of human consciousness is to learn how not to know") and what he seeks in a new form of politics. Here authoritarianism is rationalized as a natural, organic hierarchy that counteracts man-made democracy. The sperm whale, elevated to an authoritarian leader, has a "magical" ability to organize and lead the masses, who could not possibly lead themselves. This style of "leadership" is based on uniform obedience to the great, powerful individual and claims to be the best solution to failed democracy and to "the pretensions of Labour or Bolshevism" (334).

Lawrence's choice of a sperm whale as a model of erotic leadership strongly evokes *Moby Dick* (1851). In his 1924 essay on Herman Melville's novel, Lawrence writes that Moby Dick "is our deepest blood-nature . . . the last phallic being of the white man. Hunted into the death of upper consciousness and the ideal will. Our blood-self subjected to our will. Our blood-consciousness sapped by a parasitic mental or ideal consciousness."[14] Reinforcing the contrast in "Fantasia" between "blood-consciousness" and modern degeneration ("parasitic mental or ideal consciousness"), Lawrence reiterates the battle between the deathly "upper consciousness" and the proud, deep "blood-self." The sperm whale as a model of human authoritarianism joins the ostensibly natural relationships of domination and submission with a celebration of male eroticism. The evocative sperm-squeezing scene in *Moby Dick* may also have inspired Lawrence's intense focus on this rather random creature.

As seductive as Somers finds the promise of a virile masculine order, he ultimately rejects Kangaroo, in great part because of his "clinginess," his "will-to-love." There is a pivotal scene in which Kangaroo suddenly grabs Somers and pulls him to "his breast," pleading, "Don't thwart me . . . Don't—or I shall have to break all connexion with you, and I love you so" (231). In contrast to the stereotype of the removed, hard authoritarian leader (or the grand phallic sperm whale with Napoleonic leadership skills), Kangaroo is rather androgynous, even feminine.[15] Somers tells him, "You're such a Kangaroo, wanting to carry mankind in your belly-pouch, cosy" (233). Although his movement marginalizes women, Kangaroo has a maternal quality that irritates Somers. He tells Kangaroo that he is "against your ponderousness . . . your insistence," and Kangaroo's "whole sticky stream of love. . . . It's the will-to-love that I hate, Kangaroo. . . . It's a sort of syrup we *have* to stew in, and it's loathsome. . . . Let's be hard, separate men" (233). Somers fears being bullied into love, and he fears losing himself in the "sticky stream" or "syrup" of male love that Kangaroo offers. Somers rejects Kangaroo for the same reason men throughout Lawrence's works reject women—because, while women try to impress their "will-to-power" on men, men want to remain autonomous. The erotic allure of Kangaroo's all-male authoritarian movement is ultimately rejected, since Somers fears that Kangaroo's regime may lead to the overwhelming sea of "sticky" feminine demands.

As in *Aaron's Rod*, the volatile political climate in *Kangaroo* eventually degenerates into the violence that will break the "spell" these movements have cast over Somers. When Struthers gives a speech at an International Labour meeting, the Diggers interrupt him: "The hall was like a bomb that has exploded," splintering the audience into a frenzied "mob with many different centres" (346). The "crash," identified (rather vaguely, like the explosion at the end of *Aaron's Rod*) as "a bomb of some sort" that sets off a brawl, convinces Somers that he must break with both groups, particularly after a conversation with Jack Calcott following the skirmish. Calcott tells Somers that he probably killed some people: "Cripes, there's *nothing* bucks you up sometimes like killing a man—*nothing*. . . . Having a woman's something, isn't it? But it's a flea-bite, nothing, compared to killing your man when your blood comes up" (352). Here Lawrence contrasts the sadomasochistic erotics to which his characters are drawn with Calcott's brutality, which leaves Somers with a "torn feeling" in his abdomen. He resolves that he cannot support either Struthers or Kangaroo: "I can't be on either side. I've got to keep away from everything" (348).

Somers retreats from his political comrades and returns to his home with Harriet. They spend a symbolic three days in a flood together; the stormy sea is no longer the oceanic suspension of sperm whales in perfect harmony but "venomous," lashing a cliff and encroaching as if "to cut a man off." To Somers, back with his wife, the sea is now "female and vindictive" (388), castrating; and, as he and Harriet depart Australia on a passenger ship, the sea "seemed dark and cold and inhospitable" (394). As seduced as he is by the powerful male bonds and natural hierarchies of authoritarianism, Somers cannot embrace this politics of bullying. Yet heterosexual marriage and democracy are no sea of bliss. Lawrence is no closer to finding a desirable libidinal politics.

The Plumed Serpent: The Repudiation of the Modern

The last of the leadership novels, *The Plumed Serpent*, focuses on female subjectivity. The erotic dynamic of the protofascist movement Lawrence depicts shifts from male homoeroticism to female masochism; significantly, this shift leads Lawrence to come closer to endorsing authoritarianism than he does in the other novels. Instead of a wandering male protagonist, the heroine is Kate Leslie, a "liberated woman" who was once married to an Irish political radical and now lives in the United States. She travels to Mexico and immediately goes to a bullfight, in a scene foreshadowing the political themes of the novel. In the stands, the "degenerate mob of Mexico City" is physically separated from "the Authorities' section," which is composed of "a few common-looking people, bourgeois with not much taste." Meanwhile, in the ring below, the toreadors are described as "effeminate looking men . . . like eunuchs, or women in tight pants. . . . These were the darlings of the mob!" (19). Mexico's government is weak, Lawrence suggests, and its testosterone level is dangerously low. The country is overrun by bandits, and there is talk of a new president, Montes, but meanwhile the papers are reporting a growing underground movement calling for the return of the gods of antiquity: the Aztecs' plumed serpent Quetzalcoatl, the god of culture, and Tlaloc, the god of fertility.

The Quetzalcoatl movement of *The Plumed Serpent* could be read as a parody of Leonard Woolf's *Quack, quack!* if Lawrence's novel had any humor. Woolf's crude comparison of Mussolini and Hitler to primitive Hawaiian war gods is matched in Lawrence's novel by deadly earnest, similarly clumsy portraits of Quetzalcoatl leaders Don Ramón and Cipriano, who promise to bring "The Gods of Antiquity" back to Mexico. Where Woolf condemns sociopolitical atavism in Mussolini and Hitler, Lawrence's enthusiasm is most evident in the erotic charge exerted by the Quetzalcoatl men. Of the mysterious general Cipriano, Kate thinks that "there was something undeveloped and intense in him, the intensity and the crudity of the semi-savage. She could well understand the potency of the snake upon the Aztec and Maya imagination. Something smooth, undeveloped, yet vital in this man suggested the heavy-ebbing blood of reptiles in his veins" (74). As Kate contemplates her scheduled return to the United States, this reptilian imagery reappears: "She felt like a bird round whose body a snake has coiled itself. Mexico was the snake" (79). The dynamics of colonial domination and imperial conquest are masochistically erotic to Kate, particularly as the scenario is reversed and she, the "conquering" race, finds herself squeezed by the potent "semi-savages" of Mexico. Reiterating the association, in propaganda, of authoritarianism with regression and cultural atavism, Lawrence's racist exoticization of Mexicans as virile and closer to nature explains, for him, Kate's "willing submission" to the swarthy men of Quetzalcoatl. Indeed, Kate's masochistic enthrallment to Quetzalcoatl anticipates Reich's observation that salesgirls and secretaries better understand the eroticism of authoritarian display than politicians.

Kate decides to embrace the snake and moves to the remote town of Sayula. She begins to hear more about the movement of Quetzalcoatl and witnesses a gathering in which followers sing traditional songs and perform dances that are "heavy, with a touch of violence" (125), which Lawrence compares to flappers' "wincing" style of dancing. Just as in "A Propos of *Lady Chatterley's Lover*" Lawrence accuses the modern jazz-age flappers of treating sex like a cocktail, and posits the loutish gamekeeper Mellors as a sexual antidote (310), Quetzalcoatl is a "repudiation of the modern spirit" (125). Its atavistic rituals, with just a "touch" of exciting violence, will thrillingly disrupt modern ennui. The Quetzalcoatl movement speaks to Kate's rootlessness, and she finds herself in the middle of the rapidly growing revival movement. She meets the leader, Don Ramón, who preaches pride in Mexican heritage, individual potency, and the proper place for men and women. Kate is skeptical but is brought under the spell of his physical charisma, which Lawrence describes as some radioactive pheromone: "He emanated a fascination almost like a narcotic, asserting his pure, fine sensuality against her. The strange, soft, still sureness of him, as if he sat secure within his own dark aura. . . . He emitted an effluence so powerful, that it seemed to hamper her consciousness, to bind down her limbs" (196). Ramón declares himself "the First Man of Quetzalcoatl," and Cipriano is appointed the "First Man of Huizilopochtli" (261),the god of war and sacrifice. When Cipriano asks Kate to marry him, at first she resists, repulsed by Cipriano's philosophies of male suprematism. He coaxes her, seduces her, and she "swoon[s] prone beneath . . . the ancient phallic mystery. . . . Submission absolute, like the earth under the sky. Beneath an over-arching absolute. Ah! what a marriage! How terrible! and how complete!" (325). She is sold. Yet the practices of Quetzalcoatl are far from orgiastic. Cipriano insists that he and Kate must maintain emotional and sexual distance: he will not allow her to have "spasms of frictional voluptuousness" (one of Lawrence's odder euphemisms for female orgasm, along with Mellors's curse, in *Lady Chatterley's Lover,* against women who "grind their own coffee" [55]). The men of Quetzalcoatl insist that their women must give up this kind of "willful" sexuality, and, to Kate, "succeeding the first moment of disappointment, when this sort of 'satisfaction' was denied her, came the knowledge that she did not really want it, that it was really nauseous to her" (439).

Whereas, for Lawrence, the authoritarian movements of *Aaron's Rod* and *Kangaroo* offer homoerotic libidinal energies that are repressed elsewhere, and are hence aligned against the democratic status quo, the sexual politics of *The Plumed Serpent* seem to be merely an exaggeration of those of patriarchal culture. According to Lawrence's view of British and U.S. gender politics, however, powerful women are the status quo. Lawrence's postwar novels are populated by threateningly liberated women and weakened men.[16] Lawrence writes of female masochism out of a fear of female power—and with a wishful thinking that women might really be naturally submissive.

As the bride of Quetzalcoatl, Kate is required to dress in the antiquated uniform of Quetzalcoatl women and attend gatherings, including one in an old church that is "hung with red and black banners" (396). Kate is "shocked" to witness Ramón and Cipriano performing executions at one of these meetings. These human sacrifices "seemed to her all terrible *will,* the exertion of pure, awful will. And deep in her soul came a revulsion against this manifestation of pure will" (401). However, the executions are not condemned in the same way as the violence in *Aaron's Rod* and *Kangaroo;* they are, to Kate, "fascinating also. There was something dark and lustrous and fascinating to her in Cipriano, and in Ramón. The black, relentless power, even passion of the will in men! The strange, sombre, lustrous beauty of it! She knew herself under the spell" (401–2). While Lawrence initially draws a distinction between the "dark and lustrous" power of life that Ramón and Cipriano summon forth in the people, and the "pure, awful will" that leads to human sacrifice (a reiteration of "Fantasia of the Unconscious"), libidinal self-will and bullying will-to-power often merge in *The Plumed Serpent.* The narrative is not in complete sympathy with the authoritarian order of Quetzalcoatl, but it goes further than the previous novels in advocating authoritarian politics, most likely as a result of Lawrence's closer alliance with the novel's sexual politics. In *The Plumed Serpent,* men are encouraged to cultivate their instinctual will, but women are already too willful. Hence, Kate thinks that "without Cipriano to touch me and limit me and submerge my will, I shall become a horrible, elderly female. I ought to *want* to be limited" (457). Whereas Ramón and Cipriano are glorified for cultivating their masculine egos and for appointing themselves saviors of Mexico, women are warned that they will turn into "grimalkins" (456)—a particularly monstrous breed of old maid—if they do not submit. Lawrence wants to have it both ways: a female protagonist who is a New Woman (Kate, Ursula in *Women in Love*, Constance Chatterley in *Lady Chatterley's Lover,* Lou Witt in *St. Mawr,* and so on) but who is also on a quest for a powerful man to whom she will subjugate herself.

The conclusion of *The Plumed Serpent* illustrates important contradictions in Lawrence's thought. Kate's belief that the individual must be autonomous, and that, in a relationship, each party must remain separate while at the same time together, expresses Lawrence's philosophical ideal of "balance" between individuals as they appear in *The Rainbow, Women in Love*, and throughout the leadership novels. But this ideal is contradicted by authoritarian systems, for, in such an order, individual autonomy is only available to the leaders. Lawrence proposes a liberation of desire that anticipates progressive theorists such as Reich and Marcuse, and he champions the autonomy of the individual while he valorizes male supremacy, maintains an elitist attitude toward the "mob," and urges the necessity of a strict social hierarchy. Nevertheless, Lawrence's conception of authoritarianism as a libidinal phenomenon set the stage for later fictions of fascism.

In the following chapters, the forms of fascism represented in fiction will shift from the imagined movements of Lawrence's novels to the historically specific movements of Mussolini, Franco, and Hitler. Characters like Lilly, Kangaroo, and Don Rámon disappear and are superseded by real fascist leaders. The massive changes between the early years of Mussolini's rule, which coincided with the leadership novels, and the period when Hitler came to power (and Mussolini subsequently began to model his social policies on Hitler's) result in equally remarkable changes in the fictional representations of fascism. After the mid-1930s, "fascism," for U.S., British, and French fiction writers, comes increasingly to mean Nazism, as the Third Reich overshadows other fascist movements in Europe and the Mediterranean. Once Nazism's nationalist invasions, systematic antisemitism, and social repression become known, fascism acquires a particular political and discursive status in fiction, and a distinct set of expectations for the proper representation of fascism appears. Many of the elements that influenced Lawrence's postwar fictions carry over to French writers between the wars and during the early years of World War II. Propaganda, for example, remains a powerful influence, with its conception of the sexually deviant German enemy, which, in the case of Britain, was forged during World War I, and was drawn even earlier in France, during the Franco-Prussian War. From this point of view, British, French, and U.S. nonfascist writers are always working in relation to the expectation that Germans should be portrayed as oppressive, monstrous, and uncivilized. When writers stray from these expectations, they do so self-consciously and with an eye toward provocation. How this provocation is negotiated in relation to the authors' antifascist political resistance—how these fictions are both sexually "treasonous" and antifascist—will be of central concern in the chapters that follow.

Chapter 3
The Surreal Swastikas of Georges Bataille and Hans Bellmer

Many of the artists and writers associated with surrealism, a movement born in the wake of World War I, shared Lawrence's fascination with the unconscious, primitivism, and eroticism. The common understanding, in Allied World War I nations, of authoritarianism and totalitarianism as particularly connected to cultural regression, the unconscious, and taboo libidinal drives coincided with the surrealists' fascination with eruptions of the irrational. Like Lawrence, many artists who aligned themselves with surrealism (and many who never considered themselves part of any organized artistic group but are nevertheless categorized as surrealists) imagined fascism as a politics that mobilized libidinal forces in ways that democratic or socialist politics did not—as a rapturous vacillation between the twin poles of Eros and Thanatos.

In his 1924 *Manifesto of Surrealism*, André Breton defines surrealism as a practice of "psychic automatism in its pure state," with an "absence of any control exercised by reason, exempt from any aesthetic or moral concern" (26). Throughout the 1920s and early 1930s, Breton promoted automatic writing and states of dream, reverie, or fantasy as methods for releasing psychic repression and sublimation. By ripping words and objects out of their everyday contexts and allowing the play of coincidence, surrealism aimed at liberating the imagination and desire. In the *Second Manifesto of Surrealism* (1930), Breton writes that "the idea of Surrealism aims quite simply at the total recovery of our psychic force by a means which is nothing other than the dizzying descent into ourselves, the systematic illumination of hidden places, and the progressive darkening of other places, and the perpetual excursion into the midst of forbidden territory" (136–37). However, not every project carried out under the banner of surrealism had Breton's approval, and, in the *Second Manifesto*, Breton "expels" a number of rebel surrealists for activities deemed sexually "perverse" or politically "counterrevolutionary." It was, ironically, the deepest and darkest descents into the most "forbidden territory" that most angered Breton, those works that both explore "perverse" sexuality and treat fascism irreverently or without sufficient political critique or "moral concern." Breton's insistence that certain forms of sexuality are worthy of surrealist exploration and that others are perverse was an important prohibition against which other surrealists reacted, and it also takes a form similar to the normative/deviant dichotomy I have characterized as underpinning eroticized representations of fascism.[1]

The most notorious example of Breton's regulation of surrealist practice had to do with Salvador Dalí's "paranoiac-critical" treatment of Hitler as a libidinal object. "Hitler turned me on in the highest," Dalí muses in his *Unspeakable Confessions*. "His fat back, especially when I saw him appear in the uniform with the Sam Browne belt and shoulder straps that tightly held in his flesh, aroused in me a delicious gustatory thrill originating in the mouth and affording me a Wagnerian ecstasy" (125). Breton dealt with this confession, and with Dalí's irritating representation of Lenin as a limp phallus in his 1933 painting *The Enigma of William Tell*, by holding an inquisition meeting in 1934 and denouncing Dalí's "counterrevolutionary actions involving the glorification of Hitlerian fascism."[2] Dalí countered that Hitler, like "all those personalities who have a lot of authority," was "capable of rousing human phantoms,"[3] and was therefore an appropriate subject for surrealist treatment. In his *Diary of a Genius*, Dalí insists that his "Hitler-inspired vertigo was apolitical" (15), that he "had painted both Lenin and Hitler on the basis of dreams"—invoking a privileged surrealist state. And, in *The Unspeakable Confessions*, he added that "the master of Nazism was nothing more to me than an object of unconscious delirium, a prodigious self-destructive and cataclysmic force" (125). Breton rejected these explanations. In a sense, Dalí was right that, when Breton cordoned off Lenin and Hitler from "appropriate" subjects of surrealist representation, he was imposing "a censorship determined by reason, aesthetics, morality, to Breton's taste, or by whim" (127). However ridiculous and calculatedly outrageous Dalí's claim that Hitler could be dealt with like any other subject, such as a tree or a piece of cheese, Dalí's associations with Hitler (as a fleshly, eminently tasty body, as a wet nurse, as a masochistic masturbator) were theoretically fair game. Nevertheless, what sealed the case against Dalí was his explicit support of Franco after the Spanish Civil War.[4]

Hal Foster suggests that Dalí's expulsion from surrealism in 1934 "was defensive at least to the degree that Dalí . . . touched upon a secret sharing in the archaic between Surrealism and Nazism" (*Compulsive Beauty*, 188). If Dalí's history is a cautionary tale of an artist who followed surrealist principles too far, to the point of political naïveté or opportunism, Georges Bataille and Hans Bellmer present a different case. Bataille's work in the early 1930s teeters on the brink of a political/aesthetic appreciation for fascism similar to Dalí's, but by 1936 this theoretical position changed to an overt antifascism that was nevertheless accompanied by an eroticization of fascism. Hans Bellmer produced few explicit treatments of Nazism, but, in recent years, leading art critics have read him as staunchly antifascist. Less attention has been paid to the eroticism in these works, which, I will argue, is given as much elaboration by Bellmer as anti-Nazism.

In the *Second Manifesto*, Bataille is singled out for Breton's special invective: "M. Bataille professes to wish only to consider in the world that which is vilest, most discouraging, and most corrupted."[5] By 1930, Bataille had published a number of pornographic novels—*Story of the Eye*, *My Mother*, *Madame Edwarda*—that strove to be as shocking as possible. His characters delight in filth, commit sacrilege, and seek the most extreme sexual experiences. Breton is revolted by Bataille's obsessions and diagnoses his state of mind as "dishonest or pathological." Jeering at Bataille's work as a bourgeois pose that neglected the political (and more specifically, Marxist) mission of surrealism, namely, class struggle, Breton describes Bataille as a man who "wallows in impurities" (185). Bataille, in turn, objected to Breton's romantic and idealistic version of surrealism. He saw Breton creating a new hierarchy—Dalí dubbed Breton the self-appointed "Pope" of surrealism—while Bataille's own goal was to destroy such stratification and to examine those elements that had been cast out of society as "low" or "base." Even so, Bataille's work does adhere to many of the tenets of surrealism, such as the pursuit of shock and the privileging of the irrational and the erotic. Throughout his work, Bataille exalts what he calls, in *The Tears of Eros*, the "limit experience," a state of crisis that shatters the subject's boundaries and produces an "overcoming of reason" (20). Reason and logic inhibit the attainment of the limit experience, while blasphemy, sacrifice, mystical ecstasy, war, and eroticism are all potential routes to it. In *Erotism: Death and Sensuality*, Bataille writes that "erotism" is an exemplary means of achieving the limit experience; it "entails a breaking down of . . . the established patterns . . . of the regulated social order basic to our discontinuous mode of existence as defined and separate individuals" (18). Erotism provokes, disturbs, and challenges "established patterns" of bourgeois life and thought. Bataille's theories of erotism—including his famously hyperbolic pronouncement that erotism assents "to life up to the point of death" (11)—took the surrealist interest in sexuality to a new level of fervent obsession and bound it to a fascination with Thanatos.

Breton's claim that surrealism should be put "in the service of the Revolution" put restrictions on representation. Although not requiring anything as didactic as socialist realism, the expectation that this artistic movement, with the unconscious as its central inspiration, could be put "in the service" of socialist politics necessarily entailed some censorship. Bataille leaned heavily on Marxism but also tried to refine many Marxist concepts (for example, "use value" and "expenditure") for his iconoclastic antiphilosophy. In 1933, he published a controversial essay, "The Psychological Structure of Fascism," in which he criticized democracy for being a "homogeneous" politics and came close to endorsing fascism. Like Lawrence, Bataille takes up the theory that democracy disavows violence, aggression, and fantasies of power and casts them off as fascist; and, like Lawrence, Bataille is attracted to those ideological cast-offs. Bataille divides social systems into two categories. The first is the "homogeneous" system, which expulses all elements that violate "the laws of homogeneity." Bataille calls these excluded elements "heterogeneous," and includes in this group phenomena of "violence, excess, delirium, eroticism"—phenomena that particularly excite Bataille. These unruly elements are embraced by the "heterogeneous" system, of which fascism, Bataille argues, is an example. In *Visions of Excess*, he claims that "fascist leaders are incontestably part of heterogeneous existence," since "the simple fact of dominating one's fellows implies the heterogeneity of the master" (146). Bataille's position echoes Lawrence's critique of the democratic demand that "all existing *masters* shall be overthrown, and that men shall be 'free.'" Bataille focuses on a "*force* that situates" fascist leaders "above men, parties, and even laws; a force that disrupts the regular course of things, the peaceful but fastidious homogeneity powerless to maintain itself" (143). In contrast, democratic politicians, for Bataille, represent homogeneous society, symbolized by the crude exchange of money, which reduces man to "no more than a function" (138). And then, as if to palliate the socialist surrealist imperative, Bataille asserts that the homogeneous (democratic) "classical royal society . . . is characterized by a more or less decisive loss of contact with the lower classes," whereas fascism has "close ties with the impoverished classes" (154).

The years 1933 and 1934 were crucial for the consolidation of National Socialism: Hitler was sworn in as chancellor in 1933, the same year the Reichstag was burned and the Third Reich proclaimed a national boycott on Jewish-owned stores. By 1933, Mussolini had been in power for ten years in Italy, though he had not yet implemented his most extreme national and racial policies, including the persecution of non-Aryans, antimiscegenation laws, and the ban on women in the workplace. In France, right-wing protofascist groups were active and had even launched a specific attack on surrealist artists: in 1930, the Patriotic League and the Anti-Semitic League broke up a Paris screening of Luis Buñuel's and Dalí's *L'Age d'or*.[6] Nowhere in "The Psychological Structure of Fascism" does Bataille address any of this. Instead, he focuses on a highly speculative, abstract psychological structure of leaders and followers. As for Lawrence, Bataille's understanding of class relations and his investment in transgressive erotics determined his response to fascism. Just as Lawrence's contempt for the "masses" and interest in sadomasochistic power dynamics precipitated his advocacy of "masters," Bataille's "contempt for middle-class homogeneity," as Anthony Stephens observes, led him to "romanticize fascist modes of dominance."[7] Bataille's analysis of fascism suffers from its neglect of the specific policies of fascism and from its reliance on a vague concept of an unnamed "force" to explain the psychological "unification" of heterogeneous elements that fascism supposedly brings about—a "force" that would appear quite different if Bataille had attended more to the history of the fascist movements that were currently gaining political power.

Bataille's essay and its shortcomings bear comparison to an essay Dalí wrote in 1936 for *Cahiers d'art* entitled "Honneur à l'objet!" (Honor to the object!), which demonstrates the dangers of an aesthetic or fetishistic approach to fascism. The "object" in question is the swastika. Looking at the morphology of the cross in Christian symbolism, Dalí associates it with Western imperialism.[8] The double cross (*croix gammée*), the swastika, has doubled itself and atavistically "become again" what it was in the Chinese (and "antiplatonic") past. Dalí looks at the swastika in formal terms, as a figure perpetually chasing its own tail, perpetually in movement. "This sign, eminently irrational, coming out of climates of octagonal civilization, presents itself before all of us like an amalgam (this word is a bit ambitious) of antagonistic tendencies and movements. In fact, its movement tends simultaneously toward the right and the left" (82–83). Dalí's reading of the swastika as rotating in both political directions at once is reminiscent of Bataille's claim that the psychological structure of fascism resolves opposing social elements—the high and the low, the taboo and the sacred—and also of historical readings that see fascism combining ideology of both the right and the left (as Zeev Sternhell argues, for example). Dalí's insistently abstract analysis of the swastika leaves the reader wondering about Dalí's political intentions. Dalí predicts that "the swastika will be the emblem of action, antisculptural, that which bears in its own morphology the unequivocal intention to truly smash into pieces all that gains from the object . . . like the sun, that is to say, an object that is important but that doesn't interest us, that leaves us perfectly cold, we surrealists" (82). Again, the claim of political neutrality in the face of Nazism is chilling indeed.

The dangers of Bataille's similarly detached theory of fascism crystallized in his 1935 speech to Contre-Attaque, a leftist political group Bataille founded with Breton (an alliance that, predictably, did not last long). Speaking of the Popular Front, Bataille insisted on the necessity of force: "We address ourselves to the direct and violent drives which, in the minds of those who hear us, can contribute to the surge of power that will liberate men from the absurd swindlers who lead them" (*Visions*, 162). This "surge of power," like the "great surge of living blood" that Lawrence imagines in the sperm whales of *Kangaroo*, is an expression of irrational and unconscious forces that are repressed by the "swindlers" of organized politics. Arguing that the "learned" will never recognize the inherent power of angry people, Bataille urges that the debate be taken to another site, "the street . . . where emotion can seize men and push them to the limit, without meeting the eternal obstacles that result from the defense of old political positions" (163). Bataille's critics, including some among the surrealists, quickly pointed out similarities between Bataille's call for a riot of violence and the thuggish street violence of fascist squads—the kind of violence that was already beginning in Paris. Bataille's vision of a mob tearing violently through the streets was called *surfasciste*, and later Bataille himself admitted that there was a "paradoxical fascist tendency" in the Contre-Attaque stance (*Visions*, xviii).

Bataille began to reevaluate whether the "direct and violent drives" that he associated with fascism were actually liberative in his 1935 novel *Blue of Noon* (*Le bleu du ciel*). *Blue of Noon* takes its readers on a tour of European cities and sites of political conflict—in 1957 Bataille described the novel as a series of "portents" of the Spanish Civil War and World War II (*Blue of Noon*, 154). It is a sort of threshold text, marking the buildup of fascist power leading to civil war in Spain and Germany's occupation of the Rhineland in 1936. The novel follows the breakdown of the narrator, Troppmann, who is estranged from his wife and whose crisis of guilt is both political and sexual. Despite his apathy, he is coincidentally in Barcelona as the communists, anarchists, and fascists fight in the streets, and also in Vienna the day after Austrian chancellor Engelbert Dollfuss is assassinated in Hitler's infamous "blood purge" of 1934. *Blue of Noon* is, then, more attentive to the historical events of fascism than the 1933 essay, and accordingly produces a different rendering of fascism, though that fascism is still intimately connected to "violence, excess, delirium, eroticism."

The novel opens in London, in a squalid dive and then an expensive hotel where Troppmann and his lover, Dirty (Dorothea), are sick and drunk.

Bleeding, belching, and vomiting, they attempt to live out the most degrading, blasphemous fantasies they can imagine. Troppmann is impotent with Dirty, whom the narrator describes as "beautiful" but who smells like "armpit and crotch" and "cheap perfumes" (14). Despite Dirty's down-and-out demeanor, her bag is full of banknotes, and she wears a "sumptuous evening gown." At this point, Dirty's nationality is unclear, but later she is associated with Germany and throughout the novel her doubles—subsidiary characters in dream sequences and in the main narrative—are aligned with Nazism. Returning to Paris, Troppmann meets up with Lazare, a character unkindly modeled on the socialist philosopher Simone Weil. (Weil was a close friend of Boris Souvarine, a founder of the French Communist Party, when Collette Peignot, also called "Laure," left him for Bataille.) A Jewish, self-righteous, myopic Communist of "ridiculous appearance" (27), Lazare is, Troppmann pronounces, a "garbage-eating bird of ill omen" (36). Bataille sets up Dirty and Lazare as physical opposites. Dirty, despite her debauchery, is rich, blonde, and beautiful; Lazare is poor, dark, "ugly and conspicuously filthy" (29), with "grimy nails" and a "cadaverous hue" to her skin. Lazare, driven by the desire to "give her life and blood for the cause of the downtrodden," is mocked by her friends and by Troppmann; they laugh at her masochistic desire to have pins stuck into her to "prepare her" for withstanding torture (89). (Weil, who died of anorexia, was given to masochistic sacrifice, including a physically grueling stint as a factory worker that led to her nervous collapse.)

The two women represent conflicting political views and erotic systems. Dirty's deviant sexuality is associated with fascism and Lazare's asexuality with socialism. Dirty is decadent, perverse, abusive, and so rich that "she could spit in other people's faces" (37). Lazare is allied with the working class and political activism, and Troppmann is disgusted by her intellectual preoccupation with politics and martyrdom and her repellent virginity. Despite his distaste, Troppmann perceives that Lazare is responding to political events in the most "humane" manner possible, and he admires her "visionary powers of thought." In Barcelona, Lazare is in the middle of the action, leading a Catalan anarchist worker's raid on a prison.[9] Troppmann, an admittedly "rich Frenchman in Catalonia for his own pleasure," who wants to voyeuristically "witness" civil war skirmishes without becoming involved (97), cannot "evade [his] feeling of guilt toward the workers" (98). He wants to join them in the streets, but they make him feel that there is "no justification" for his life.

Troppmann vacillates between respect for Lazare's communist devotion and depression about socialism in general. This and his obsessive attraction to Dirty mirrors Bataille's evolving evaluation of the respective libidinal structures of socialism and fascism. Stumbling around Paris in Dirty's absence, Troppmann amuses himself by getting drunk in bars and discussing his "abnormal sex life" (67) and his "perverted love for corpses" (75), a taste he associates with Dirty. One night, while drinking and prowling, Troppmann meets a woman who has qualities similar to those of Dirty. She is "blonde, with strong patrician features"; when Troppmann threatens her with a belt, she "[spits] her contempt" in his face. Troppmann follows her into a bar, where they dance: "She was surely German—very bleached, with a haughty, provocative manner" (53). She produces a nude wax doll, which she manipulates obscenely; its "spread legs and the truncated little calves made you wince, but they were fascinating too."

The doll or automaton, associated here with German perversion, is a recurring image in modernism and particularly surrealism. Its prototype, the seductive automaton in E. T. A. Hoffmann's story "The Sand-man," links the doll both to the uncanny and to fetishism. In Hoffmann's story, Spalanzani, a professor of physics, has a glorious doll, Olympia, which the narrator takes for a live woman and with which he falls in love, despite her "stiffness and apathy" (202). Olympia is neither alive nor quite dead: she is animated and can dance, play the piano, and speak. The *unheimlich* (literally "unhomely") is, for Freud, in his 1919 essay "The Uncanny," "that class of the frightening which leads back to what is known of old and long familiar"[10]—ultimately, the mother's womb. The *unheimlich* is that which is concealed, kept from sight, obscure, dangerous, and inaccessible to knowledge. Noting that some definitions of *heimlich* are identical to those of their ostensible opposite, *unheimlich*, Freud concludes: "*Heimlich* is a word the meaning of which develops in the direction of ambivalence, until it finally coincides with its opposite."[11] In the realm of the uncanny, terror and lasciviousness—Thanatos and Eros—intermingle. This intermingling is demonstrated in the dream Troppmann has the same night he has been out with the German woman and her doll. He finds himself before an object that is both bed and hearse. He oscillates between fear and hilarity. A corpse of initially "indefinable shape" emerges as a mangled doll's body with the head of a mare's skull wearing a soldier's helmet. The uncanny doll, dead but animated in the costume of war, brings together Eros and Thanatos in a form Troppmann finds particularly confusing: it makes him anxious but also causes him to laugh (57). Oscillating between violence and eroticism, and, like the uncanny, between the dead and the alive, the doll/corpse/soldier keeps changing before Troppmann's eyes. It turns into "a Minerva in gown and armor, erect and aggressive beneath her helmet," leaving Troppmann "delighted" and "aghast." "There was no way of knowing if I was supposed to take her seriously." This phantom reflects the epistemological confusion of the uncanny and also Troppmann's uncertainty about Dirty, who "in this dream . . . had assumed the garb and likeness" of the "*Commendatore*" (57), Don Giovanni's escort to hell.

Dirty's oscillations, from dead to alive, terrifying to erotic, suggests the dynamic of fetishism. Freud's 1927 "Fetishism" (in *Sexuality and the Psychology of Love*, 214–19) (which posits a male fetishist) asserts unilaterally that "the fetish is a penis-substitute" and, more specifically, that the fetish is a substitute for the woman's (mother's) phallus (214). "What is possibly the last impression received before the uncanny traumatic one"—the "horror" of discovering that women are "castrated"—"is preserved as a fetish." In other words, the fetish object—a shoe, a piece of velvet, for example—is a relic from "the last moment in which the woman could still be regarded as phallic" (217), and the fetish remains "a sort of permanent memorial" (216) to this moment, a comfort that alludes to the moment before the "knowledge" of castration. Hence the fetishist refuses "to take cognizance of the fact that a woman has no penis" (215); however, at the same time—and this is the most important structure of fetishism—the fetish also "acknowledges" castration. As a talisman against castration anxiety, the fetish also allows that anxiety to be expressed. Thus, the dynamics of fetishism are denial or disavowal: "I know very well [the woman has no penis, and that I may be castrated too], but all the same [this fetish allows me to suspend that knowledge and obtain sexual pleasure nonetheless]." Fetishism and the uncanny involve similar defense mechanisms of anxiety and disavowal.

Troppmann knows very well that fascism is murderous and terrifying, but Dirty is erotic to him nonetheless. The discourse of socialist normativity that shapes Bataille's understanding of fascism is disturbed by this fetishism. By reproducing the fantasy of sexually deviant fascism without advocating fascist politics, the assumption that a political nonfascist would have only those sexual identifications/investments that are designated "nonfascist" begins to disintegrate. Troppmann's attraction to Dirty is set against his generalized repulsion and fear, and also against his pull toward leftist politics and his vacillating sympathy toward Lazare.

Dirty's fascist characteristics become stronger when Troppmann accompanies her to Germany. He gives this account of their visit to Trier, the oldest city in Germany (and the birthplace of Karl Marx):

[We] met a group of Hitler youth, children ten to fifteen years old wearing shorts and black velvet boleros. They walked fast, paid no attention to anyone, and spoke in abrupt voices. There was nothing that wasn't dismal—terribly so: a vast gray sky slowly turning into falling snow. We started moving fast. We had to cross a plateau of plowed earth. Freshly worked furrows proliferated. (142)

Crossing this bleak and morbid landscape, they turn into a graveyard lit by candles. Aroused, they fall on top of the graves. "The earth beneath [Dirty's] body lay open like a grave; her naked cleft lay open to me like a freshly dug grave" (144). Excited and stunned, they "make love over a starry graveyard" (144), coming close to combining the Eros and Thanatos of Troppmann's dreams. But from this point on, the exalted heterogeneous "violence, excess, delirium, eroticism" no longer deliver Troppmann to frenzied ecstasy. Everywhere they go, Troppmann notes the graveyards, and Dirty becomes more closely allied with Thanatos and the approaching war. Walking into a portentously "empty" town, Troppmann notices that, as in his dream, Dirty reminds him "of the soldier who fought the war in muddy trenches" (145). On the train from Coblenz to Frankfurt, where they spend their last hours together, Dirty tells Troppmann, "I know I'm a freak, but I sometimes wish there would be a war" (147). She tells him she has a fantasy of notifying "the man with the moustache" that his children were killed in the war. Although she never names the man, Troppmann is chilled by her words.

When he takes her in his arms, Troppmann notices that "Dirty was in a bright red silk dress—the red of swastikaed flags. Her body was naked under the dress. She smelled of wet earth" (148). This shade of red is equally evocative of passion and violence: nude flesh under the Nazi flag. This conflation of extreme emotions would seem to be a perfect Bataillean moment of erotism. Although Troppmann is aroused, he does not make love to Dirty but leaves her in the compartment and roams the train. He immediately runs into "a very tall, very handsome SA officer. He had porcelain-blue eyes that even in a lighted railways car were lost in the clouds, as if he had personally heard the Valkyries' summons" (148). The act of leaving Dirty leads straight to a Nazi officer; in Germany, Dirty merges with her surroundings. And as if by osmosis, her dress has absorbed the bloodred Nazi symbols around her. No longer an erotic incitement, the fetish character of fascism begins to collapse. The oscillation between Eros and Thanatos that so excited Troppmann is leaning more and more toward pure Thanatos, and he is not aroused but "frightened." Finally, as Dirty disappears onto her train (a vehicle that came to be a ghastly symbol of the Holocaust), Troppmann prophetically hears "the noise of wheel on rail, of wheels that crush, in crushed, bursting flesh" (149). The vague unease Troppmann feels in other countries now is given a clear reference:

Nazism is a "rising tide of murder" against which "it will be impossible to set anything but trivialities" (151). In the last scene of the novel, Dirty has left and Troppmann hears "a sound of fierce music, a sound of unbearable bitterness" (150), which he follows to a stage in a square. A group of Hitler Youth musicians stands "in military formation." The boys wear "short black velvet pants and short jackets adorned with shoulder knots; they were bareheaded. . . . They were playing with such ferocity, with so strident a beat, that I stood breathless in front of them . . . All these Nazi boys (some of them were blonde, with doll-like faces) seemed, in their sticklike stiffness, to be possessed of some cataclysmic exultation" (150).

The doll returns again, with its unsettling uncanniness: the Nazi boys, with their "sticklike stiffness," are terrifying to Troppmann. Rosalind Krauss asserts that "the eeriness of waxwork figures, artificial dolls, and automata can be laid to the way these objects trigger . . . confusion between the animate and the inanimate [which is related to] that class of the uncanny . . . involving a regression to animistic thinking and its confusion of boundaries" (L'Amour Fou, 85–86). This confusion of boundaries that characterizes the uncanny also operates in propaganda, where the boundaries between human and nonhuman are endlessly highlighted through depictions of Germans as bestial. Indeed, in the propaganda images I examine in chapters 1 and 4, Germans are often rendered doll-like, with stiff jointed limbs and without fully realized faces. As I will show in chapter 5, Genet refers to a Nazi sympathizer as a "clock-work . . . torture-machine"; and, thirty years later, the last image of the Nazi torturess in the film *Ilsa: She-Wolf of the SS* shows her as a hollow doll that shatters into pieces. These images take the propagandistic tropes of the inhuman fascist even further: not only is the fascist inhuman, he is inanimate, mechanical. Eroticized fictions of fascism, conversely, typically "flesh out" the fascist subject, just as Bataille sexualizes Dirty and the obscenely pink doll early in the story. In the frightening conclusion of *Blue of Noon*, however, Bataille returns to the monstrous image of fascism. No longer the eroticized doll of Troppmann's Paris nights, these "doll-like" boy soldiers are the frightening bugle corps of the war Troppmann has dreamt about. Krauss suggests that the uncanny—and fetishism—both work "to produce the image of what one fears in order to protect oneself from anxiety" (L'Amour Fou, 86). Converted into a manipulable doll, fascism is given another face. If Bataille's first fetishized doll is a way of containing the fearful recognition that fascists are not monsters but rather monstrously human, the Nazi boys at the end of the novel, "hateful automatons . . . in a trance," function differently, exposing rather than containing fascist violence:

In front of them, their leader—a degenerately skinny kid with the sulky face of a fish—kept time with a long drum major's stick. He held this stick obscenely erect, with the knob at his crotch, it then looked like a monstrous monkey's penis that had been decorated with braids of colored cord. Like a dirty little brute, he would then jerk the stick level with his mouth; from crotch to mouth, from mouth to crotch, each rise and fall jerking to a grinding salvo from the drums. The sight was obscene. It was terrifying. . . . Each peal of music in the night was an incantatory summons to war and murder. (151)

Elsewhere Bataille's characters strive for the "obscene" as a means of attaining a limit experience, but this "obscene" sight is far from the exciting indeterminability of the lurid doll in Paris. The doll boys are as grotesque as any propaganda; in fact, these boy Nazis might be read as exaggerations of propaganda images, which capitalize on the suggestions of sadism to conjure up an explicitly sexual Nazism, complete with "monstrous monkey's penis."

Troppmann's intuition that these young Nazis are "entranced by a longing to meet their death" (151) is not accompanied by the usual Bataillean enthusiasm. Troppmann finds the leader's masturbatory rhythms grotesque and obscene rather than erotic. As with Lawrence, erotic sadomasochism is markedly different from fascist violence. The sadomasochistic eroticism of Bataille's pornographic novels, even the most delightfully degraded and blasphemous, requires a complementary, interconnected recognition, whereas "sadistic fascism" excludes and obliterates. The "obscenity" of the Nazi conductor in *Blue of Noon* is not the obscenity of erotism but rather the obscenity of power (what Lawrence would call "bullying"): domination without recognition (the SA officer's eyes "were lost in the clouds"), the rule of automata with their dead, unreflecting eyes. With the character Dirty, Bataille portrays a fetishistic fascism, erotic and intriguing in its transgressive oscillations, its perverse sexuality, and its exciting charge of Thanatos, as opposed to the dully earnest, asexual leftist Lazare. With Dirty's dress in Germany, however, the fetishistic oscillation and irony begin to collapse. The "red of swastikaed flags" points to toward the "rising tide" of blood that Nazism will release, and even for Bataille, this is beyond the limits of any experience worth having. Bataille ultimately abandons the exciting oscillations when Nazi violence overpowers his constructed fantasy world of eroticism.

The grotesquely sexual dolls of *Blue of Noon* may well have been inspired by Hans Bellmer, whose work took French surrealism by storm in the mid-1930s. Best known for his photographs of jointed dolls—*poupées*—arranged in darkly eroticized sadomasochistic tableaux, Bellmer is often singled out by art historians as among the most violently misogynist surrealists. Recently, however, critics such as Hal Foster and Rosalind Krauss have proposed that Bellmer's oeuvre presents a rebellion against Nazism and patriarchy. Only a small percentage of Bellmer's work—perhaps two of the thousands of photographs and drawings—can be said to launch an explicit attack on Nazism, and the argument in favor of this view leans heavily on Bellmer's biography. Bellmer witnessed Hitler's rise to power in Germany; his father joined the National Socialists and Bellmer's Jewish friends were deported. In September 1939, after Germany invaded Poland and France declared war, Bellmer (along with Max Ernst) was interned as an enemy alien in Camp des Milles near Aix-en-Provence. Later, in Paris in 1944, Bellmer manufactured false identity papers for the Maquis (the Resistance forces). Although Bellmer was openly anti-Nazi, his representations of Nazism are not explicitly oppositional. I will look at the two images most relevant to this argument and evaluate the ways Bellmer negotiates the symbol of the swastika with the sadomasochistic eroticism he develops throughout his photographs. Although Bellmer's images have typically been read as "sadistic," I will suggest that his photographs illustrate the more complex sadomasochistic dynamic that characterizes fictions of eroticized fascism.

Bellmer was born in 1902 in Kattowitz, Germany (a town that was annexed to Poland after World War I), into a middle-class family. The most important biographical detail for most critics has to do with Bellmer's father, a strict, brutish Nazi engineer who was despised by his son.[12] Determined to "give up all work which, even indirectly, could be in any way useful to the State,"[13] Bellmer became an artist. And how better to infuriate his abusive Nazi father, whose party loudly condemned "degenerate art," and to dissent from economic production than to play with dolls? While living in Germany, Bellmer saw Max Reinhardt's production of *Tales of Hoffmann*, including the haunting story "The Sand-Man."[14] About 1933, Bellmer and his brother built a jointed, wooden doll connected by bolts. This first doll had a hollow abdomen in which was installed a series of panorama scenes that were supposedly "the thoughts and dreams of a young girl."[15] The viewer peered into a pinhole in the doll's navel and pressed a button on its nipple to change the scenes. In 1934, Bellmer published *Die Puppe*, a book of ten photographs of the doll's construction. The surface of her skin is ragged, her abdomen an open crater, and in some shots her half-shell mask face is covered by a hat or a wig. In many, one leg is missing and she is propped up by a series of connected wooden rods. She stands or leans in some of the photos; in others, her parts are disassembled and arranged on a flat surface.

Bellmer's next doll series, *Les jeux de la poupée*, published in 1949 but created more than ten years earlier, is significantly more sinister and dramatic than *Die Puppe*. Instead of the stiff joints of the first doll, this one was connected with ball joints, including a crucial joint at the stomach. This allowed for greater manipulation and permitted Bellmer to create the striking double configurations that characterize the series: a double-jointedness—two sets of interlocking legs—that Krauss reads as uncanny. Bellmer built two forms of the doll, mirror images from the pelvis down, and joined them around a single stomach piece, resulting in some of the most remarkable images in the series. Bellmer photographed the second *poupée*—wearing white socks and black Mary Janes—strewn down spiral staircases, tied spread-eagled to trees, hung in doorways like octopi, flattened against doors, behind iron carpet beaters, and twisted and recombined in unsettling tableaux in forests. These enigmatic narratives evoke rape, murder, pedophilia, bondage, religious martyrdom, and torture even as they conjure up a darkly erotic tension. Like Hoffmann's Olympia, Bellmer's *poupées* demonstrate the struggle between the repressed and the acknowledged, fantasy and consciousness, the living and the dead. One photograph shows the double *poupée* (two sets of legs connected at the pelvis) standing upright against a tree. A shadowy male figure (Bellmer's brother) in a long dark coat watches from behind a tree in the distance. At first it seems that the doll is bound to the tree, but the ropelike folds around her ankles are only the gathers of her white cotton socks. A piece of checked material—a tablecloth?—lies rumpled at her feet. What is she doing out here in the woods, "naked" and posing seductively—for now she seems to be leaning against the tree, her knee flexed for the camera? The woods stretch far into the background, sloping up a sharp hill. The doll is in the foreground and so close to the camera that the fabric at her feet is cut off by the frame. The setup repeats the voyeuristic spectacle of the first doll with a panorama in its stomach but self-consciously introduces a second voyeur in the tableau itself. The viewer experiences a split spectatorship, both looking at the doll as a voyeur and looking at the voyeur in the photograph. This image demonstrates the multiple identifications Bellmer's work can elicit.

Many of Bellmer's photographs suggest danger, dismemberment, and sexual violence despite their affectless—lifeless—material. Critics have often read Bellmer's *poupées* as having been manipulated and acted on violently, and as fundamentally sadistic pieces. Many critics, Xavière Gauthier and Susan Rubin Suleiman among them, have criticized the inherent misogyny in surrealism in general and in Bellmer's work in particular, as this figurative male violence is exercised on the "female" doll. In *Hans Bellmer*, Peter Webb speculates that "there is something intrinsically sadistic about the Surrealist object on account of the displacements that it perpetrates and the violence that it does to the identity and integrity of things" (51).[16] The surrealist object, and particularly Bellmer's work, does perform a decomposition of form and a wrenching disturbance of reality. However, I have been arguing that violence in fantasy should not be conflated with enacted violence; the term "sadism" is often used to blur this line. In *Like Subjects, Love Objects*, Jessica Benjamin describes sadism as "an inability to tolerate outsideness or otherness. . . . Aggression and its derivative, mastery, represent the effort to turn outward the invading stimuli, the unbearable tension" (192). If the female body is the other—and the mother's body is the originary "otherness"—then Bellmer's *poupées* can be read as the artist's defenses against femininity. But I maintain that the dynamic and mutable "sadomasochism" or "sadism" should not be fixed in that way, and that there ought to be no naturalized identification of gender with a particular erotic dynamic. Certainly, surrealism, like most avant-garde movements of the period, was male-centered and bore the traces of misogyny inherent in its culture. Bellmer's *poupées* can be read another way, however. Often an initial sense of victimization gives way, upon closer examination, to the perception that the doll is self-contained, stretching itself out before an unsettled viewer. In sequence after sequence, the doll's resiliency is displayed. An object of desire that is endlessly taken apart and recombined, it is an object that survives. This survival is a crucial component of sadomasochism. As D. W. Winnicott writes of the violence of identity formation, the object can be useful for the subject only if it survives.[17] The serialization of Bellmer's work—the fact that he worked with the same models over and over again—underscores the effect of the doll's resistance. Bellmer's *poupées* are both seductresses and doomed maidens, both desiring subjects and objects of manipulation. The spectatorship they invite is both voyeuristic (which some have called "sadistic") *and* masochistic.

In *Subversive Intent*, Suleiman maintains, following Deleuze, that sadism is "a paternal and patriarchal structure" (65), and, in terms of institutional structures and the exercise of social power, this seems to be true. But masochistic or sadistic drives in fantasy are much more pliant in terms of gender. Carol J. Clover has suggested this in her reading of horror films (*Men, Women, and Chain Saws: Gender in the Modern Horror Film*), perhaps the genre most open to charges of "sadism." Against the usual reading of horror films as "sadistic," Clover claims that critics' failure "to see beyond sadism . . . has everything to do with their stake in the dominant fiction" (230) that preserves masochism as the domain of women and sadism that of men. Bellmer's tableaux have many of the same features as the horror films Clover examines: their eerie sense of danger, their menacing atmosphere, and the suggestion of victimization and nefarious evil. And the *poupée* itself strongly resembles the brave beleaguered girl, the "victim-hero" of horror, who suffers but survives. Clover maintains that "horror is far more victim-identified than the standard view would have it" (9), and that the male viewer in particular, whose spectatorship and involvement are, in film theory, almost always assumed to be "organized around the experience of a mastering, voyeuristic gaze," actually identifies strongly with the female "victim-hero" (8–9). I suggest that the same dynamic can be read in the *poupées*. Although Bellmer takes the doll apart and perhaps terrorizes it, it is also the sympathetic star of the show. In viewing the *poupées*, as in viewing a horror film, "we are both Red Riding Hood and the Wolf; the force of the experience, in horror, comes from 'knowing' both sides of the story" (Clover, 12). Bellmer's photographs potentially implicate his viewers in both "sides" of the sado-masochistic drama. Like the reading of propaganda, a particular viewer's reading of Bellmer depends upon, and is determined by, that viewer's point of identification and interest—the narrative that viewer perceives over and above other possible narratives. In Bellmer's pieces, an ostensibly feminine masochistic identification is every bit as possible as a "sadistic" one.[18]

What does this have to do with fascism? In *Compulsive Beauty*, Hal Foster argues that Bellmer created the *poupées* as a way of refusing to participate in the National Socialist economy, and the sadism meted out on the bodies of the dolls takes apart the fascist psychic armor Klaus Theweleit describes in *Male Fantasies*. Foster maintains that the *poupées* are "second-degree" representations of sadism: representations of fascist sadism that is subverted from within. This is a convincing general reading, but what of Bellmer's images that explicitly take up Nazism? In one photograph, a doll composed of two sets of legs, joined at the waist, is splayed out on a dark lawn, one leg jutting into the foreground, its opposite pointing upward, and the other two perpendicular legs spread out on either side. In contrast to most of the photographs in Bellmer's second doll series, in which the doll is placed in a larger environment, this form fills the entire frame. Glaringly lit in the foreground and so dark in the background that it is an indistinguishable wash of blackness, the composition, like a crime scene photograph, is set at an angle so that the viewer seems to have stumbled upon a body with a flashlight. In some prints, the grass has been colored a jaundiced green, and the legs are sprinkled with a number of pink, measlelike contusions. Like the horror scenes Clover reads, this scene would seem to engender fear or masochistic identification more than delectation. At the same time, the scene replicates the quasi-pornographic tropes of Bellmer's other dolls, with their spread legs

Hans Bellmer, *La poupée* (1935–38). Courtesy of Ubu Gallery, New York, and Galerie Berinson, Berlin. © 2001 Artist Rights Society (ARS), New York/ADAGP, Paris

and ostentatious display of "skin" arranged for the viewer's consumption. But the doll is no more alive than the hay underneath it.

The image has a curious delayed effect. A pattern gradually emerges: these legs seem to be spread out in the shape of a swastika, thighs jutting out in four directions. But what does that mean? That the doll has been ravaged by Nazism? That the doll body represents Nazism? That this "crime scene" is an allegory of the violence of Nazism? There is no clear answer; moreover, the swastika is not self-evident. Those who know Bellmer's background and are looking for references to Nazism may find it, but the swastika shape is subtle, if present at all. If one views the photograph in relation to Bellmer's other work, this doll appears very much like the other photographs in the series, with their doubled legs, sadomasochistic aesthetic, and their uncanny pull between Thanatos and Eros.

One of Bellmer's images definitely alludes to Nazism. While living in Paris after the war, Bellmer no longer photographed the doll, preferring instead to produce drawings and works of decalcomania and gouaches, both of which permitted the play of chance more than the photographs did. Bellmer made several series of pornographic photographs. He staged and photographed scenes from Bataille's *Story of the Eye* with live models and, in the late 1950s, photographed his lover Unica Zürn naked and bound with rope so that her body bulged with the multiple breastlike protuberances. In 1946, he arranged what is undoubtedly a swastika composition in *La croix gamahuchée*, which plays, both in title (*croix gammée* means swastika) and composition on the infamous double cross of National Socialism. Here two tangled female bodies are arranged around a jolting center: one woman's hand is spread, fingers inserted into a vagina, alluding to the verb *gamahucher* (to perform oral sex). Like Bellmer's *poupées*, no faces are visible here. The strongest forms are four very white legs stretched out in opposite directions—north, south, east, and west—and bent at the knees. Background clutter suggests a domestic interior: a ledge, a wall, and a dresser on which the women brace themselves. A dresser drawer handle replicates the orifice in the middle of the composition. One woman wears nail polish, a ring, and a bracelet; the other wears a black sweater; a leg in the foreground wears a black wedge-soled shoe and a black stocking. These are live models (one is Nora Mitrani, a Bulgarian Jewish poet who was Bellmer's lover); although in the photograph they are configured like the dolls, there is no mistaking their flesh for lifeless plaster.

The women's bodies are cramped and contorted into a swastika shape. Bellmer shot the image from one angle and rotated the right side of the print to the bottom to sharpen the contours of the Nazi symbol. At first glance, the position suggests "sixty-nine"—a structural inversion of the *croix gammée* in that the interlocked figures of sixty-nine turn inward and cradle each other, while the axes of the swastika point outward. The penetrating fingers at the center of the composition are an aggressive punctuation mark between the legs, splayed like broken spokes forced into position. The awkward contortions and balance that were required to create the shape make the effect stagy and belabored—hardly a spontaneous eroticism.

The composition of Bellmer's image recalls Wilhelm Reich's chapter on "The Symbolism of the Swastika" in *The Mass Psychology of Fascism*. Like Dalí's "Honor to the object!" Reich investigates the pre-Nazi past of the symbol, tracing it to figures on ancient synagogue ruins in East Jordania that represented male and female forces, to Greece, where it symbolized and sun and the male force, and to a fourteenth-century Soest fertility symbol. "Thus

Hans Bellmer, *La croix gamahuchée* (1946). Courtesy of Ubu Gallery, New York, and Galerie Berinson, Berlin. © 2001 Artist Rights Society (ARS), New York/ADAGP, Paris

the swastika was originally a sexual symbol," Reich concludes (102). Elaborating, he suggests that the two interlocking spokes of the swastika show "a sexual act lying down" and "a sexual act in the standing position" (102). As if anticipating the delayed perception of the swastika in Bellmer's images, Reich maintains that "very few people fail to recognize the meaning of the swastika; most people divine its meaning sooner or later if they look at it for awhile" (103).

The play in Bellmer's image between its sexual charge and the embedded political symbol suggests the coupling of Eros and Thanatos. But, as with the earlier image of the doll on the lawn, this photograph is only a delayed critique of Nazi violence. The image initially solicits an erotic response—or, at least, titillation or shock—and Bellmer then redirects this response through the title of the piece or, in the case of the doll photographed on the lawn, only through a suggested shape in the composition. Bellmer puts before his viewer images that are sadomasochistic or pornographic and that also allude to Nazi iconography, inducing the viewer to share the oscillation of the fetish. Still, these images are not substantially different from others with no clear political message. The image of the doll sprawled on the lawn does not stand out from the other *poupées;* it does not represent a unique erotics. Apart from its swastika shape, *La croix gamahuchée* looks a great deal like other photographs Bellmer composed in the same period, including his photographs to illustrate Bataille's *Story of the Eye*. (Indeed, other photographs without such a clear swastika shape bear the same title.) What makes these images distinct in terms of fascism?

In his book *L'anatomie de l'image* Bellmer writes that the dolls "reveal scandalously the interior that will always remain hidden and sensed behind the successive layers of the human structure and its last unknowns."[19] The "scandal" is that the dolls reflect (according to Bellmer) "universal" fantasies, not particularized or pathological ones. Bellmer's photographs of humans are an extension of this theory, showing even more forcefully how the desires embodied by the dolls are ultimately inspired by human carnality. The true "scandal" of Bellmer's swastikas is that they reflect fantasies that appear throughout Bellmer's work, and not just in the few images that allude to Nazism. Erotic fantasies, including violence, will always be dormant, Bellmer suggests, within the universal "human structure," not just in the "authoritarian personality type."

Bellmer shows that the erotic body—a body of no particular political affiliation—can be configured to mirror the swastika. The body contains that possibility, just as Dirty's body becomes "swastika-ized" or Nazified depending on where it appears. The erotic female body is transformed into the symbol of Nazism through a shift in perception. Once one "sees" a swastika composition in the photograph of the doll on the lawn, it is difficult to read it any other way. *La croix gamahuchée* shows the oscillations of fetishism with the swastika shape and the pornographic arrangement competing with each other. Bellmer's works suggest that it is impossible to keep one apart from the other. Eros and Thanatos, sadism and masochism, antifascist desire and fascist desire, are figured as an intimately imbricated optical illusion, like an Escher drawing in which the black and the white pull at each other and constantly reverse the plane of perception. Bellmer never stabilizes those lines, thwarting the reading of a politically differentiated erotics.

Perception and propaganda are key terms in the next chapter, which moves from the surrealists' aestheticized, fetishistic depictions of fascism to Vercors, a French Resistance fighter who wrote about the Nazi Occupation that begun in 1940. Vercors's representation of fascism is much more realistic than Bataille's and Bellmer's and is more concerned with political verisimilitude than with provocation. Under the Occupation, the need for an active resistance to Nazism and Marshal Philippe Pétain's collaborationist Vichy government led to strong pressure from the French left on writers to portray the enemy in a prescribed way. This climate developed rapidly, in the course of about a year, in response to the emergence of the violent Vichy police state in 1941. Vercors is as resistant to representational restrictions as Bataille and Dalí were to Breton's demands. However, whereas Bataille and Bellmer imagine the general libidinal dynamics of fascism (for example, primitive impulses, unconscious desires disavowed by democracy) through fetishistic representations, Vercors's depiction of Nazism capitalizes on the erotic metaphors of courtship in propaganda produced by both the political right and the left.

Chapter 4
Beauty and the *Boche*:
Propaganda and the Sexualized Enemy
in Vercors's *Silence of the Sea*

In 1942, during the Nazi Occupation of France, a novella called *The Silence of the Sea* (*Le silence de la mer*) appeared under the pseudonym "Vercors," which was later revealed to be that of Jean Bruller, an illustrator known for his left-wing political satires. Most of the publishing houses in France were controlled by the Vichy government, busy turning out propaganda in praise of Deutschland.[1] As a result, this slim book by Vercors was distributed in France through the clandestine channels of *Les Editions de minuit*, the press Vercors had co-founded a year earlier.[2] The book circulated underground and abroad, where, curiously, it was simultaneously hailed as a document of French political resistance and condemned as an act of German collaboration. This controversy turns on two factors: first, the shift in Nazi Occupation policies in 1941 and the accompanying expectation that Resistance writers should portray Germans as uniformly evil; and second, Vercors's objections to such requirements and his attempts to dislodge the notion of a monolithic enemy.

The Silence of the Sea tells the story of a Nazi officer, Werner von Ebrennac, who is billeted in the house of a Frenchman (the narrator) and his niece for seven months. When von Ebrennac first arrives, the narrator describes him as "massive . . . huge," with "narrow shoulders and hips [that] were most striking." Von Ebrennac's face is "handsome" and "very masculine." Spontaneously, the narrator and his niece both fall silent. This silence, which "like the morning mist . . . was thick and motionless," becomes their gesture of resistance to the enforced occupation. "By a silent agreement," the narrator recounts, "my niece and I had decided to make no changes in our life, not even in the smallest detail—as if the officer didn't exist, as if he had been a ghost."[3] To their surprise, von Ebrennac accepts and even shapes his communication around their silence. Every night, von Ebrennac enters their living room and delivers what the narrator calls his "interminable monologues" (13). He tells them how uneasy he feels about the Occupation and how much he admires France's strength and beauty. The narrator observes that "not once did he try to get an answer from us, or a sign of agreement or even a glance" (13). When he first arrives, von Ebrennac limits his monologues to innocuous subjects such as the weather, but he gradually reveals more about himself to the narrator and his niece. He recalls marching into Saintes, where the French population "received us well. I was very happy. I thought: This is going to be easy. And then I saw that it was not that at all, that it was cowardice. . . . I despised those people, and for France's sake I was afraid" (16). He finds something quite different in the narrator's home. Confronted with "the unrelentingly expressionless face" of the Frenchwoman and her icy silence, von Ebrennac reiterates his love and his need for France: "Her riches, her true riches, one can't conquer; one can only drink them in at her breast. She has to offer you her breast, like a mother, in a movement of maternal feeling" (21). Invoking consent rather than force, von Ebrennac makes a bid for acceptance by appearing in civilian clothes instead of his uniform. The narrator speculates, "Was it to spare us the sight of the uniform of the enemy? or to make us forget it, to get us used to his personality?" (13). As von Ebrennac starts addressing himself more and more to the young woman, despite her wall of silence, his descriptions of France become less maternal and more matrimonial. In one speech he proclaims that this is the last war Germany and France will fight; instead, once he manages to "conquer" the dignified "silence of France," Germany and France will "get married" (15–16). Silence is a celebrated and doomed virtue to be "conquered" through marriage. Once there is marriage, there will be no need or use for silence, von Ebrennac implies, and its dissipation will please both parties.

Against his better political judgment, the narrator feels a growing respect and even admiration for von Ebrennac: "Nothing seemed to discourage him, and . . . he never tried to shake off our inexorable silence by any violent expression" (22). Most important, von Ebrennac does not conform to the propagandistic stereotypes of the barbaric *boche*. Courteous and apologetic, von Ebrennac is a cultured man, a composer who takes a laudatory inventory of his "host's" library, praising the French classics in particular.[4] Von Ebrennac is politely complimentary: "I feel a very deep respect for people who love their country," he remarks (5). By acting as a guest instead of a jailer—asking for France to "offer . . . her breast" rather than seizing it—von Ebrennac succeeds in partially winning the narrator over. But the Frenchwoman is "invariably severe and impassive" (8). She rigorously avoids von Ebrennac's eyes and concentrates on whatever project is at hand: she knits "with machinelike energy" (10), like Penelope desperately holding her suitors at bay. Her devotion to her uncle and France's independence makes the erotic attraction that develops all the more surprising. In the compressed economy of Vercors's *récit*, this mute romance develops through moments of visual revelation. The woman gives minute signs of her feelings for von Ebrennac, which are observed by the narrator: when von Ebrennac speaks, she drops her sewing, plucks at her needle, snaps her thread, unravels her ball of knitting wool, or quakes slightly. She never has a conversation with von Ebrennac, but the terseness of the story and her muteness magnify these moments.

The end of the story is striking: once, and only once, von Ebrennac's peaceful, carefully tempered character is shattered. He has returned disillusioned from meetings in Paris that he had hoped would herald the glorious "marriage" between Germany and France. Shocked and betrayed by the disclosure of Nazi plans, he tells the Frenchwoman, "Everything that I have said in these six months, everything that the walls of this room have heard . . . You must forget it all" (37). The other Nazi officers had laughed at his romantic ideas, telling him instead, "We have the chance to destroy France, and destroy her we will. . . . We'll have a groveling bitch of her" (39). Finally, the stereotypical German appears but only indirectly, further marking the distance between this stereotype and von Ebrennac, the "exceptional German." Von Ebrennac recounts that his colleagues told him of their strategies to "rid Europe of this pest . . . this poison" (40), and this disclosure of the Nazi campaign against Jews makes von Ebrennac distraught. " 'There is no hope,' " he states flatly, "as if to torture himself with the intolerable but established fact" (39). Rather than enacting this violence on the French populace, he turns it upon himself. He quietly says that he has requested reassignment to a fighting unit and is leaving the next day. "Off to Hell," he salutes them, exchanging his last glance with the Frenchwoman. The narrator describes his niece's face like a "Greek tragic mask" that suddenly gushes sweat. Her eyes are "moored" to von Ebrennac's (45). She is caught "in that prison which she had herself built" (22): the prison of silence, of resistance, of love. For his part, von Ebrennac nervously grips the mantelpiece "and [holds] his face towards the fire through his forearms, as if through the bars of a grating" (20). Both these characters, Vercors implies, are imprisoned by the circumstances of the Occupation. Both behave nobly within the circumstances: von Ebrennac acts humanely in the face of his regime's cruelty, and the Frenchwoman silently defends her country's liberty. Both are devastated by the way their shared story ends.

"The Subtle Provocation of a 'Collabo' "

The story of an erotic attraction between a Frenchwoman and a Nazi officer was unsettling to a nation living under Vichy rule. Although Vercors's novel protests Nazi subjugation, it also shows an attraction to the representative of that subjugation, von Ebrennac. When reminded in an interview some fifty years after the publication of *The Silence of the Sea* that "some have reproached you for making this German too likable," Vercors exclaimed, "But that was the real theme of my story!" He insists that he wanted to portray "the best German possible, with all his seductive qualities," thus challenging his readers "to not let themselves be seduced."[5] But to many readers, Vercors seemed to be trading in dangerously ambiguous politics. If the novella is, as Margaret Atack categorizes it in *Literature and the French Resistance*, a narrative of "persuasion," it was not clear to all readers in 1942 of what precisely it was seeking to persuade them. The central and most inflammatory proposition of *The Silence of the Sea* is that Vercors, an author politically committed to the Resistance movement, would write a story that explores a romance with a Nazi officer. Among those critics who attacked Vercors's work as treasonous, and who even suspected it was Nazi propaganda, many pointed to the lack of verisimilitude in the representation of von Ebrennac. In 1943, Arthur Koestler wrote, in *The Yogi and the Commissar*, that he was unconvinced by Vercors's Nazi, "who in spite of his versatile intelligence has apparently never read a speech of Hitler's, nor seen a newspaper in the ten years between the Reichstag fire and the attack on Poland" (20).[6]

The most crucial factor in the reception of Vercors's novel was the shift in the nature of the Occupation in 1941. In *Vichy France*, Robert O. Paxton characterizes the early rhetoric of the Occupation as paternal, with Vichy representing the German occupying forces as good fathers or older brothers who were trying to persuade France to cooperate. However, the climate turned quickly "from persuasion to constraint" in 1941, when the Communist resistance shot a Nazi soldier, and Germany retaliated by shooting fifty Resistance fighters for every German soldier killed. The violence of the Occupation escalated from that point on (221–28). Vercors reflects this tension between persuasion and force in von Ebrennac's statement that he would rather be "offered" France's treasures than be obliged to "conquer" them. But, as S. Beynon John notes in "The Ambiguous Invader," in the time between Vercors's completion of *The Silence of the Sea* (the summer of 1941) and its publication (August 1942), "the character of the German Occupation had become dramatically more severe" (196), with the forced labor laws and the order for the deportation of Jews. In *What is Literature?* Jean-Paul Sartre argues that the reception of Vercors's novel was largely determined by the political situation of its audience. He observed that readers far from the occupied territory conceived of the enemy as "a whole, as the incarnation of evil," and that a true *littérature engagée* would reinforce the idea that "all war is a Manichaeism." Speaking for many at the time, Sartre maintained that "at this turn of the war it was necessary to be either for them or against them" (67), and Vercors's novella seemed to be neither:

> As early as the end of '42, *The Silence of the Sea* had lost its effectiveness; the reason is that the war was starting again on our soil. . . . An invisible barrier of fire once again separated Germans and Frenchmen. We no longer wished to know whether the Germans who plucked out the eyes and ripped off the nails of our friends were accomplices or victims of Nazism; it was no longer enough to maintain a lofty silence before them. (66–67)

Using Vercors's metaphor of silence, Sartre asserts that Vercors's complex portrait of a "good" Nazi shirked its political obligations—even though Sartre admits that "in the occupied zone . . . nobody doubted [Vercors's] intentions or the efficacy of his writing; he was writing for us" (66). For Sartre, it was a political mistake to concede that the Nazis were anything less than evil.[7] Vercors's likable Nazi also seemed complicit with one of the German policies in the "persuasion" phase of the Occupation: that the occupying troops, in Henri Peyre's words, should "win the French over to esteem and admiration for the qualities of the victors."[8] Von Ebrennac does have some of these ingratiating qualities, but it is these very qualities that the narrator and niece must resist. Nevertheless, because Vercors never states this monologically (because von Ebrennac is never a stereotypically violent *boche* and because there is never a pure moment of Resistance victory), readers saw *The Silence of the Sea* as flirting with collaboration. Too much ambiguity seemed to be complicit with Nazism.

Many years after the publication of his story, Vercors recalled a review by Ilya Ehrenbourg "denouncing *The Silence of the Sea* as the subtle provocation of a 'collabo'. . . like well-disguised propaganda."[9] Instead, I will argue that *The Silence of the Sea* is exactly the opposite: it is a protest against the distortions and racializations of propaganda, including the sexualization of Germans. "What I wanted to attack with this story," Vercors once said, clearly responding to Sartre's dicta, were the "mental structures so strongly ingrained in us at that time . . . Manichean structures" of "black and white."[10] *The Silence of the Sea* shifts one of the dominant tropes of propaganda—Germany's rape of France—to that of romance, changing the nationalistic construction of a sexually deviant enemy to one that is all too human.

"Das Tier und die Schöne"

Those critics who praise *The Silence of the Sea* for protesting the German Occupation typically emphasize the narrator's and niece's tactics of defiance and
Vercors's Resistance credentials but are rather silent themselves about the sexual undercurrents throughout the novella, and about the fact that Vercors
bases the moral ambiguity of von Ebrennac not just on his nobility but also
on his erotic appeal.[11] The tension between libidinal attraction and political
subjugation in *The Silence of the Sea* is underscored by one of von Ebrennac's
oddest monologues to the Frenchwoman. "There is a very lovely children's
story which I have read, which you have read, which everybody has read," he
tells her (17). "I don't know if it has the same title in both countries. With us
it's called 'Das Tier und die Schöne'—'Beauty and the Beast.'" Claiming the
fable's universality, von Ebrennac narrates the story dramatically:

> Poor Beauty! The Beast holds her at his pleasure, captive and power-
> less—at every hour of the day he forces his oppressive and relentless
> presence on her. . . . Beauty is all pride and dignity—she has hardened
> her heart. . . . But the Beast is something better than he seems. Oh, he's
> not very polished, he's clumsy and brutal, he seems very uncouth beside
> his exquisite Beauty! But he has a heart. Yes, he has a heart which hopes
> to raise itself up. . . . If Beauty only would! But it is a long time before
> Beauty will. However, little by little she discovers the light at the back
> of the eyes of her hated jailer—the light which reveals his supplication
> and his love. She is less conscious of his heavy hand and of the chains of
> her prison. . . . She ceases to hate him. His constancy moves her, she
> gives him her hand . . . At once the Beast is transformed, the spell which
> has kept him in that brutish hide is broken: and now behold a handsome
> and chivalrous knight. (17–18)

"I loved the Beast," von Ebrennac concludes, "above all because I understood his misery" (18). Von Ebrennac has already shown himself to be a sophisticated reader of Montaigne, Balzac, and other classic French writers:
why then does he tell the Frenchwoman a fairy tale? And why this fairy tale?
Most obviously, Vercors—and von Ebrennac—uses the tale to analogize the
relationship between the Frenchwoman and the Nazi officer. The story of
"Beauty and the Beast" (specifics change from version to version) begins
with a man indebted to a Beast who is under a spell, from which he will be
delivered only when someone loves him. The Beast pins his hopes on the

man's daughter, Beauty, and wants her as payment.[12] Out of obligation to her father and love for him, Beauty agrees to live with the Beast. At first, she is repulsed by his ugliness and terrified by his temper but becomes fonder of the Beast as he tries to please her. The Beast reluctantly allows Beauty to visit her father and misses her presence so much that he falls ill. When Beauty discovers this, she rushes back to the castle. With the Beast on his deathbed, Beauty declares her love and he is transformed into a handsome prince. The subtitle of an 1804 version of the tale implies the moral that "a rough outside" may conceal "a gentle heart."[13] Von Ebrennac similarly encourages the Frenchwoman to see beyond his affiliation with the beastly *boche*.

In most fairy tales, there is a character who embodies evil: the wolf, the cruel stepsisters, the witch. By identifying with the hero, the reader is rewarded at the end of the story for having conquered or outsmarted the evil character. In *The Uses of Enchantment*, Bruno Bettelheim concedes that "evil is not without its attractions—symbolized by the mighty giant or dragon, the power of the witch, the cunning queen in 'Snow White'" (9), but he is adamant in his conviction that "the figures in fairy tales are not ambivalent—not good and bad at the same time, as we are all in reality. . . . A person is either good or bad, nothing in between" (9). The fairy tale characterization is remarkably close to Sartre's insistence that during wartime individuals necessarily think in Manichean terms, and that the conflict should be represented as such. Didactic models of childhood inculcation operate according to the same logic as propaganda that aims to mobilize a population for war: they eliminate the ambiguities and exceptions of a psychologically and politically fraught situation.[14] However, "Beauty and the Beast" is, in many ways, an anomaly among the classic tales, since there is no resolutely evil force. At the beginning of the story, when the Beast demands that Beauty's father give her to him, the reader confronts the typical structure of good and evil, but this arrangement quickly breaks down. The Beast is hideous and exercises brute power, but he is vulnerable to love, also a disposition of Vercors's von Ebrennac. "Beauty and the Beast" discourages the reader from partitioning the world into good and evil (and appearance and essence), for it shows that a malevolent character can become good. The story rewards Beauty for loving the Beast, a "terrifying and also magnetic" character, as Betsy Hearne writes (*Beauty and the Beast*, 139). Vercors replicates the test of Beauty's loyalty in *The Silence of the Sea* in the Frenchwoman's confused response to von Ebrennac. The Nazi's identification with the Beast is consistent with Vercors's sketch of him as an intelligent and sensitive man who is not morally aligned with Nazi philosophy, despite being its political representative. The parallels between the Nazi Occupation of France and the Beast's "oppressive and relentless presence," which he "forces" on Beauty are clear. Yet von Ebrennac's descriptions of the Beast's "heavy hand" and "the chains" of Beauty's "prison" borrow from the rhetoric of resistance and show his empathy for her position. Von Ebrennac uses the fairy tale to minimize his political affiliations and emphasize his personal qualities.

The fairy tale embedded in Vercors's story also gestures toward erotic metaphors that cast the Occupation as a marriage or courtship, which, as Kaplan points out in *Reproductions of Banality*, were usually gendered as "a (sexual) occupation by a phallic (Nazi) authority" (16). Both the French and the Germans used this metaphor. Sartre notes that Nazi sympathizers often described the Occupation in terms of a sexualized union with Germany. "One can pick out all over articles of Chateaubriand, Drieu, Brazillach [*sic*], curious metaphors which present the relations of France and Germany under the aspect of a sexual union where France plays the role of the Woman."[15] "Beauty and the Beast" is also a story about marriage and about coming to terms with sexuality. Von Ebrennac speaks of his hopes for a Franco-German "marriage." Hence he collapses when he hears the Nazi program to "destroy France, and . . . have a groveling bitch of her" (39). This shift from seduction, courtship, and marriage to figurative rape is parallel to the historical shift from "persuasion to constraint," from courtship to the "rape of Belgium" in World War I and again during the Occupation. But instead of telling another story of Germany's "rape" of France, Vercors tells a story about a romance. The interpolated fairy tale in *Silence of the Sea* does so as well. Furthermore, the appearance of "Beauty and the Beast" in Vercors's novella casts *The Silence of the Sea* in relation to a distinctive form of propaganda that would have been familiar to Vercors and anyone living in France during World War I.

Livres Roses

In interviews Vercors suggests that *The Silence of the Sea* was in great part based on the experience of a German officer billeted in his home in Villiers-sur-Morin. Vercors's memories of this soldier include several features that make their way into the portrait of von Ebrennac: he walked around carpets to avoid dirtying them, put up a mortuary mask of Pascal—one of Vercors's intellectual heroes—and read Victor Hugo.[16] The realization that this German did not seem much like the *boches* portrayed in propaganda was apparently unsettling to someone who had been raised on political caricatures. Radivoje D. Konstantinovic's biography, *Vercors écrivain et dessinateur*, describes "the young Jean, a student at the École Alsacienne in Paris," as "animated by sincere hate for the *Boches*." Twelve years old when World War I broke out, Vercors was a "fervent little patriot" who read the novels of Barrès and other committed authors and "believ[ed] each assertion of anti-German propaganda" (32). This political formation on the basis of pedagogical literature was typical of the period: as Judith K. Proud points out in *Children and Propaganda*, the French educational system of Vercors's youth included mandatory courses in *éducation morale et patriotique* (78). And, as Cate Haste writes, the anti-German propaganda that influenced Vercors's youth is particularly illustrative of how "the line between education and propaganda in wartime is a fine one" (111). Just as British writers such as Lawrence, Orwell, and Kipling orient their fictional representations of Germans around anti-German propaganda from World War I, *The Silence of the Sea* is discursively constructed in relation to French anti-German propaganda, and, in particular, the propaganda of Vercors's youth. From 1914 to 1918—Vercors's formative years—the children's imprints of French publishers had a particular and consistent character: almost all new titles were specifically about the war. These texts were known colloquially as *livres roses*, or "pink books." From February 1915 to 1919, Larousse published, in its *Livres roses pour la jeunesse* collection, a series about the war: *La série de guerre*. Many other French publishers (including Berger-Levrault, Hachette, and Floury) produced similar imprints. In the very slim volume of the *Catalogue général de la Librairie Française* for the war years, under the category *Guerre*, and under the subheading *Livres pour les enfants*, many entries appear with suggestive titles, including *En guerre!* (At war), *Eux et nous* (Them and us), *Histoire d'un brave petit soldat* (The story of a brave little soldier), and *Nos gosses et la guerre* (Our kids and the war).[17]

The primary function of the *livres roses* was to promote French nationalism and anti-German activism. Many tell "true stories" of French heroism in Belgium and celebrate small acts of bravery at home. Others are fictionalized versions of the same themes, but all include elements that underscore the pedagogical mission of moral and political inculcation. The cover illustration of *L'héroïsme français. Anecdotes de la guerre, suivies de réflexions et de questions pour les écoliers de France* (French heroism: Anecdotes from the war, followed by reflections and questions for French students) depicts *le boy-scout martyr* (27) calmly smiling, kerchief neatly tied, facing a firing squad of German soldiers. The stories inside urge their readers to emulate such audacity. One chapter focuses on the famous story of "Miss Cavell," who aided the French in Belgium and was murdered by German soldiers. Cavell appears constantly in French and British propaganda for both adults and children, as well as in memoirs from the period.[18] An illustration in *L'héroïsme français* shows Miss Cavell supine on the ground as a German in a pickelhaube stands over her with the proverbial smoking gun. The chapter concludes with a *réflexion* that presents several definitive statements about the story and asks a series of blatantly leading comprehension questions for students: "Even the cruelest war respects noncombatants and women. In murdering Miss Cavell, the Germans committed a crime against civilization. . . . Why was Miss Cavell admirable? What did she do in Belgium? . . . What do you think of the officer who murdered her?" (248).

All the *livres roses* include some gesture—a preface, a pedagogical tone, or a framing narrative—that guides their audience to view the war as one of "civilization against barbarity" (*L'héroïsme français*, 244). These moral signposts suggest a narrative form the *livres roses* often imitate: the fairy tale. *L'héroïsme français*, with its *réflexions*, replicates the structure of Charles Perrault's *contes*, each of which is followed by a moral. Other *livres roses* replicate the formula of the fairy tale—"Once upon a time . . ."—but render it historically specific: "Once upon a time there was a brave French boy-scout/a bad German soldier. . . ." As their titles demonstrate, these books borrow the fairy tale's posited opposition between good and bad characters: *Eux et nous*, *Petit-Bé et vilain Boche*, and so on. More directly, many *livres roses* use the narratives of famous fairy tales quite explicitly, inscribing them within stories of the war. In *L'Alsace heureuse*, which tells of "the great sorrow of the country Alsace" during the German invasion,[19] France is represented as Sleeping Beauty. In 1918, Berger-Levrault published *Contes de guerre pour Jean-Pierre* (Tales of war for Jean-Pierre) by Émile Moselly, which includes a story called "L'ogre et le Petit Poucet." This story rewrites Perrault's *conte* "Le Petit Poucet" in the terms of the conflict with Germany: "Once upon a time, in a Northern country, there was a very nasty ogre. . . . He ruled over a legion of docile subjects. . . . They had made war their industry. From ancient times . . . the young men, drunk on beer and heroics . . . struck out at each other with swords" (9–10). The "beast of the north" declares war on an unspecified country—though the hints that a "descendant of *Petit Poucet*" lives there, and that its inhabitants sing the "Marseillaise," leave little doubt of the country's identity (13).

Fairy tales provide propaganda with starkly drawn, overtly moral narratives of clearly delineated good and evil, and with a precedent of violent and erotic stories for children. The early versions of many fairy tales, in which death, dismemberment, and violence with sexual overtones (for example, "Bluebeard") are commonplace, sometimes shock readers brought up on the Disney versions. In the Brothers Grimm version of "Cinderella," for example, the wicked stepsisters do not just try to force their feet into the magic slipper: they carve off their heels and push their bloody stumps into the shoe. "Le Petit Poucet" is very violent, and it is only in reading these early versions of the stories that we fully understand why the fairy tale lends itself to use by propaganda. Throughout the classic fairy tales, violence is combined with sexually suggestive scenarios, which Judith Proud calls "other levels of 'hidden' or privileged reading, to be absorbed at a subconscious level or enjoyed consciously by those with greater perception." Proud cites examples ranging from the "slightly risqué asides incorporated into the seemingly innocents texts of *La Belle au bois dormant* (Sleeping Beauty) and *Le Petit Poucet*," expurgated from many editions of the *Contes,* to Little Red Riding Hood's great interest in the wolf "*en son déshabillé*" (34). Not surprisingly, these erotic and violent aspects of the classic fairy tales also find their way into the *livres roses.*

Just as the *livres roses* combine a moral tale with a specific historical and political moment, von Ebrennac's telling of "Beauty and the Beast" uses the tale's "timeless" structure to comment on the immediate situation. The *boche*—"an instantly recognisable literary and visual stereotype," as Proud puts it (17)—is virtually identical throughout the many kinds of *livres roses.* Whether the book is comic, melodramatic, or historical, the German soldier is a static and cruel type in a pickelhaube and heavy boots. One *livre rose, Carnet de route du soldat Fritz Bosch* (Soldier Fritz Bosch's travelogue), is the mock journal of a German soldier sent to France. Fritz Bosch's intelligence is exercised solely in his contemplations of beer and sausage; his chubby, blonde wife is similarly greedy and obsessed with gastronomy (she nags her husband to send her gourmet food and French lingerie). As Fritz blunders along with his troop, the young French reader is encouraged to see him as a fool, and as a representative of Germans in general. Another *livre rose, Petit Bé et le vilain Boche,* tells the story of a boy whose town is occupied and in whose house a German soldier is billeted—a common scenario among the *livres roses,* with obvious parallels to *The Silence of the Sea.* The book's text and illustrations emphasize the German's barbarity ("had there ever been such a cruel enemy?" [4]) and crudeness: *le vilain Boche* is slothful, rude, and forever guzzling beer. Throughout the story, Petit Bé tricks and mocks this villain, as, for example, when he places the family dog next to the German, revealing the "striking" physical resemblance between Germans and dogs. Even when presented as gentle domestic humor, the insinuation that the German is bestial is persistent.

The *livres roses* warn that beneath the brutal German exterior is an equally brutal national amorality—just the opposite of the moral of "Beauty and the Beast." Foolish Fritz, for example, recites the "Ten Commandments of Germany," a biblical parody that depicts Germans pillaging French towns and terrorizing their civilians, spitting on park benches, burning buildings, and looting homes. Rule 8 is, "Thou shalt massacre women, children, and the wounded"; the illustration shows a soldier thrusting his bayonet at two women and their babies. The tenth commandment in *Carnet de route du Soldat Fritz Bosch* demands the recognition of the supremacy of German civilization and depicts a winged monkey in a German uniform clutching the globe in its clawed, webbed paws. Responding to the Kaiser's chauvinistic vision of German supremacy, French propagandists countered with a chauvinism of their own. Behind Fritz's stupidity, the book warns, is a diabolical nation of monsters. Above all, the cartoon sequence presents Germany as a godless nation that thinks nothing of twisting the Ten Commandments to suit its own evil purposes (even as the French propagandist does the same).

Caricature is the primary mode of the *livres roses*. Exaggerated and mechanistic, the Germans in these books are drawn statically and crudely, their joints like those of puppets. Even when an illustrator draws realistically, as in *L'héroïsme français*, the images are usually split into spatially conflicting spheres, that of the *boche* and that of the French, the stark separations typical of propaganda. Generally, the figuring of the *boche* has phallic or sexual overtones: the *boche* usually stands erect and the French victim is supine (as in the illustration of Miss Cavell) and often partially nude. When the French hero is standing, the *boche* is usually pointing a gun horizontally at him or her. The French and German figures in propaganda are usually not on the same plane of representation, even though they occupy the same frame. For example, when French figures are realistically rendered, Germans are depicted with clichéd iconography (heaped with sausages, soaked in beer, and so on). German faces are often either distorted and animalistic or blankly featureless, when they are not concealed entirely.

Just as the British press depicted Germans as "The Evil Beast at Bay," much of the adult French press was no more sophisticated than the *livres roses* in the way it represented the Germans: the same mode of caricature dominates. In *Guerre, mythes et caricature*, Ouriel Reshef proposes that wartime caricature counters the radical uncertainty of a national crisis by reducing a complicated and random conflict into a neatly intelligible world of formulaic images (18). His study of Franco-Prussian War caricatures suggest they were a significant precursor to the World War I *livres roses*. The cartoons from the years surrounding 1870 established a specific iconography for Germans and Prussians that carried through to World War I: the

J. Robinet, from *Carnet de route du soldat Fritz Bosch* (1915). Courtesy of the General Research Division, The New York Public Library, Astor, Lenox and Tilden Foundations

helmet, eagle, beer stein, and pipe became codified as German and carried "*ipso facto* an anti-German charge" (161). The artists of this early period also used fairy tales to create a cultural chasm between the Prussians and the French: a cartoon from 1869 called *Le cabinet de Barbe Bleue* shows a Prussian soldier as Bluebeard, with the conquered states represented as young women strangled, hanging side by side in his closet (31). Reshef suggests that caricature serves a specific psychic function for a nation at war. "In times of crisis—

war, revolution, or civil war—the psychological underpinnings of thought (stereotypes, dreams, myths) . . . erupt in caricature" (210).

Like the metaphors of the Occupation, these caricatures are based on strongly gendered national types. Between 1871 and 1914, in French political caricatures, Germans were portrayed with exaggerated masculine attributes. This corresponded to an increasingly feminized image of France: a less militant and more damsel-in-distress Marianne. The nude female body appeared frequently, chained and violated. A political cartoon from the Franco-Prussian War called *La Poule* (The tart) shows a woman, naked except for her boots, tied to a pool table and surrounded by malevolent Prussian men (82). Libidinal energy and political aggression manifest themselves in these caricatures in what Reshef calls an "unbridled political pornography" (211).[20] The pattern continued in World War I propaganda, including the *livres roses*. In schoolbooks such as the best-selling *Tour de France par deux enfants*, the German invasion of Alsace-Lorraine is figured as a rape but unsettlingly, lasciviously so. "Feminized France," Resef observes, "is engaged in a sadomasochistic relation with Germany"—the *surmâle* (191). In two of the commandments in *Carnet de route du soldat Fritz Bosch*, the German soldiers are shown in suggestively sadomasochistic tableaux. Commandment 3, "Thou shalt passively obey all your commanders," is accompanied by a drawing of a uniformed soldier on his hands and knees before the tall, shiny boots of another standing over him, ordering him to sweep the floor—a stock threat in sadomasochistic pornography. Commandment 6 shows one German soldier flogging another with a cat-o'-nine-tails. In Commandment 8, two women lie at the feet of a German soldier, who shoves a phallic bayonet at them.

The implication of sexual violence permeates the *livres roses*, and they often include titillating images. The composition of these images (aggressor/victim, erect/supine, male/female) mirrors the structural tensions of sadomasochistic fantasy and roles (master/slave, top/bottom), but these images are supposed to produce a reading that remains strictly within the politicized us/them dichotomy. Interestingly, in World War II, the Vichy government returned to similar strategies of representation and to the same features—boots, whips, punishment—in its effort to arouse allegiance to the collaborationist government. A children's book called *Mon alphabet*, designed by F. Touzet and published by a Vichy government press, urges its readers "*C c c Châtions Les Traîtres!*" (Let's P-p-p Punish The Traitors!) and shows a blond boy in shorts, shiny black boots, and a cat-o'-nine-tails watching a traitor being pitched into the air.[21] Given the highly charged and conflicting elements of propaganda aimed at stirring up patriotism and volatile feelings about the enemy, it is no wonder that subsequent fictions echo propaganda and make use of its often startling images.

The ways that childhood reading influences a writer's later imagination are complex and often indirect; I am not claiming that *The Silence of the Sea* was a conscious rewriting of the *livres roses* but rather that the discursive structures of this propaganda echo in Vercors's story, and that the *livres roses*

F. Touzet, "C c c Châtions Les Traîtres!" (1940–45) from *Mon alphabet*. Printed by Éditions Centres d'Information et de Renseignements (C.I.R.). Photo: Bruce White. Courtesy of the Mitchell Wolfson Jr. Collection, The Wolfsonian-Florida International University, Miami Beach, Florida were powerfully pervasive in shaping this generation's understanding of Germany. A contemporary of Vercors's, Pauline Réage, the pseudonymous author of the sadomasochistic classic *The Story of O* (*Histoire d'O*, 1954), has even more directly suggested that the *livres roses* influenced her erotic imagination. Like Vercors, Réage came of age during World War I; she was born in 1907, thus sharing with Vercors a common national history, education, and culture, including the *éducation morale et patriotique*. Both Vercors and Réage participated in the French Resistance during World War II and moved in similar literary circles. Their respective novels, *The Silence of the Sea* and *The Story of O*, share the central irony that an author who is politically committed to the Resistance movement should write a novel based on an erotic identification with the dominator. When Réage discusses her creative process and the fantasies that led to *Story of O*, she remarks that "it was a way of expressing a certain number of childhood and adolescent fantasies that persisted into my later life, that not only refused to go away but came back time and again."[22] In particular, Réage emphasizes the influence of the wars on her imagination. "I'm a product of WWI, and it made a deep impression on me."[23] She proceeds to sketch her life in relationship to World Wars I and II. Réage recounts a recurring childhood dream of her own death at the hands of German soldiers, which stemmed from "the ridiculous little books they made us read in those days, called 'pink books,' frightfully chauvinistic books filled with evil Germans in their awful helmets."[24] Although *The Story of O* is not set during the war and is not explicitly political, it is discursively similar to the propaganda Réage invokes. The static dichotomies of Réage's novel—the empty female O, the powerful masters, the masochistic women, the sadistic men—reproduce the Manichean structures of the *livres roses*. (Indeed, these same qualities of exaggerated characters and timelessness suggest two other forms: pornography and fairy tales. Jean Paulhan remarks in his introduction to Réage's novel, "I advance through *O* with a strange feeling, as though I am moving through a fairy tale—we know that fairy tales are erotic novels for children" ["Happiness in Slavery" in Réage, *Story of O*, xxi–xxxvi].) The baroque world of the Roissy sadists/masters in *The Story of O* resembles the world of propaganda, with its language of sexual deviation—sadomasochism and rape. The language propaganda uses to describe Germans—slavery, tyranny, the love of masters and of submission—is literalized and writ large in the world of Roissy, as if the hypermasculine Germans of the *Carnet de route du soldat Fritz Bosch* had stepped off the page, transformed into "masters," and had found in the women of Roissy enthusiastic "victims." The translation of prohibited propagandistic images into erotic ones is comparable to the "luxurious" pleasure Mary Postgate takes in

Kipling's story. For Kipling, violating the British righteousness central to British propaganda (Mary watching the soldier die) produces a sexual frisson; for writers such as Genet, enacting the threats of propaganda produces masochistic pleasure. As in Reik's "uniform ritual," playing out and exaggerating the oppressive threat and obtaining pleasure nevertheless is the essence of these masochistic readings.

Obviously, Vercors's erotic images are very different from Réage's (and from Kipling's). Where Réage explicitly sexualizes domination and submission, Vercors changes these dynamics into romance. The Occupation in *Silence of the Sea* is not a rape but a seduction. Von Ebrennac strives to distinguish himself from the sadistic *boche* of propaganda by telling the Frenchwoman the story of a previous German girlfriend's cruel compulsion. He recalls walking outdoors with this "very beautiful and very sweet" girl (23). They were lying "on the moss in the midst of the bracken" when she was stung by a mosquito: " 'Oh, he's stung me on the chin! Dirty little beast, nasty little mosquito! . . . I have caught one, Werner! Oh, look, I'm going to punish him: I'm—pulling—his—legs—off—one—after—the—other" (24). Von Ebrennac concludes, "I was scared away for ever where German girls were concerned. . . . And that's what our politicians are like too" (25). Von Ebrennac distances himself from this Germanic/Nazi "sadism," suggesting he is an exception to the rule—the misjudged Beast.

The sexual metaphors of German invasion, in both World Wars I and II, varied depending on the political use to which they were put. In the hands of Vichy and German propagandists, the initially dominant metaphors were courtship and marriage; for the French Resistance, rape. Paul Eluard, Sartre, and other leftist writers used the old association of Germany and sexual deviance to conflate sexual and political alliances—a phenomenon I will return to in the next chapter. Vercors keeps Nazi cruelty in place with the reported speech of the Germans at von Ebrennac's meeting but undermines it with von Ebrennac himself. Vercors's allusions to sexualized discourses of Nazism produced by both the French right and the left demonstrate his complex politics. A Resistance fighter with strong affiliations to the Communist Party, Vercors never joined any political party. In his autobiography *L'Après-Briand* (*1932–1942*), Vercors recounts his increasing disillusion with leftist politics between the wars. Feeling that communism and socialism distorted political reality as much as conservative politics, Vercors was concerned about the quality of representation in the "clandestine journals" produced by the French left: "More 'anti-Boche' than anti-Nazi, more anxious to inspire hate than justice, their militant and bloody ardor is surely necessary to stimulate the combativeness of soldiers. I admire and approve of them. Nevertheless, my vocation is different" (230–31, my translation). Vercors declared his vocation to publish "precise" and "rigorous" reflections on situations that were ambiguous in many ways but were nevertheless "no less severe toward the enemy" than the *anti-boche* journals. In an interview some fifty years after the publication of *The Silence of the Sea*, Vercors explained that he wanted to portray "the best German possible, with all his seduction" (*A dire vrai*, 32)—and to challenge his readers to resist. Vercors's questioning of the focus of the underground press corresponded to a question the French Resistance (and the nation) struggled with: Are we at war with the Nazis or with the Germans? For propaganda purposes, the choice was clear: it was necessary to condemn an entire country and an entire nationality. But, in the case of art, Vercors argues in favor of "vicissitudes" rather than rigid positions based on hatred and false valorization.

Is anything worthwhile gained by arguing for the humanity of the Nazis? Is it possible to overstate their horrendous policies? Sartre makes a good case in *What Is Literature?* that Vercors's insinuation "that most of them [the Nazis] were 'men like us'" amounted to a tepid relativism (67), raising the important question of Vercors's political acumen in choosing Nazis to make a philosophical point about the left's call for conformity. However, we might consider the case of Jean Améry, who was arrested by the Gestapo in 1943 for distributing anti-Nazi propaganda. In *At the Mind's Limits*, he writes of when he finally faced torture at the hands of real Nazis—rather than distorted literary or propagandistic versions of them: "not 'Gestapo faces' with twisted noses, hypertrophied chins, pockmarks, and knife scars, as might appear in a book, but rather faces like anyone else's. Plain, ordinary faces" (25). Améry's description of his interrogation and physical torture is one of the most powerful condemnations of Nazi brutality, and his argument that "torture was not an accidental quality of this Third Reich, but its essence" (24) is far more specific and convincing than the racialized, jingoistic Allied propaganda that argued the Nazis were not human beings but beasts. An accurate news account of the atrocious Nazi war crimes would have made much more of an impact than images recycled from the Franco-Prussian War or fairy tales. Programmatic and simplistic propaganda risks banalizing evil. As Hannah Arendt famously wrote in *Eichmann in Jerusalem*, her report on the Adolf Eichmann trial: "The trouble with Eichmann was precisely that so many were like him, and that the many were neither perverted nor sadists, that they were, and still are, terribly and terrifyingly normal" (276). *The Silence of the Sea* works against the wartime ideology that expunges the contradictory details, impulses, and motivations that constitute history. Instead, Vercors asks his readers to resist Nazism without the spurious atrocity tales, to resist a fascism that may be alluring, that may show a human face.

In so doing, Vercors sets forth a recurring trope of eroticized fascism: the "exceptional Nazi." This persona appears throughout postwar fictions, for example, in Duras's *Hiroshima mon amour*, Bette Greene's 1973 young adult novel, *Summer of My German Soldier* (about a girl in the Southern United States who falls in love with a Nazi soldier), British writer Louis de Bernières's *Corelli's Mandolin* (1994)[25] and, perhaps most famously, Steven Spielberg's film *Schindler's List*. The "exceptional Nazi" narrative argues that not all fascists are monstrous, and that a critique of propaganda is a project in good political faith—that is, it does not compromise an antifascist political position. Although this narrative purports to be more realistic than the black-and-white strokes of propaganda, it remains tinged with the romantic rhetoric of the early Occupation, and it also continues to be invested in a sexually deviant fascism. Although these fictions focus on a Nazi who rises above perversity, the sexually "sadistic" Nazi still exists in them (for example, in Spielberg's film, the Schindler character is contrasted with the more typical Nazi "sadist" Amon Goeth, played by Ralph Fiennes). Vercors's Occupation scenario partially perpetuates the national stereotypes of a sexually normative France (heterosexual, romantic) and a cruel, perverse Germany, as represented by von Ebrennac's German girlfriend and the German politicians. It is only when von Ebrennac leaves the bucolic French household to rendezvous with his compatriots that he becomes "German" again.

As the Occupation went on, the careful political balancing of *The Silence of the Sea*—the exceptional German versus the German of propaganda—gave way to more extreme depictions of Nazism. To move from Vercors to Jean Genet is to move from a representation of Nazism that earnestly strives for accuracy to one that strives for maximum provocation, from a careful sketch of propaganda's lacunae and ideological distortion to a boldly drawn, inflammatory declaration that Nazism is just as terrible as propaganda suggests, and that it is erotic nevertheless.

Chapter 5
Horizontal Treason:
Jean Genet's *Funeral Rites*

In his best-selling 1960 history, *The Rise and Fall of the Third Reich*, William L. Shirer remarks of the SA, the precursors to Hitler's SS, that "the brown-shirted S.A. never became much more than a motley mob of brawlers. Many of its top leaders, beginning with its chief, Roehm, were notorious perverts. Lieutenant Edmund Heines, who led the Munich S.A., was not only a homosexual but a convicted murderer. These two and dozens of others quarreled and feuded as only men of unnatural sexual inclinations, with their peculiar jealousies, can" (172). Shirer highlights the "unnatural sexual inclinations" of certain high-ranking Nazi officers, but this information is then generalized as a broad psychological profile of Nazism in general. This, in turn, reinforces an already popular homophobic reading of Nazism as homosexual—either overt or repressed. Homosexuality is often pathologized in these accounts as sadomasochism. But how, given accounts such as Richard Plant's *Pink Triangle*, which documents the Third Reich's oppression of homosexuals, can the "homosexualization" of Nazism continue? As B. Ruby Rich observes in "From Repressive Tolerance to Erotic Liberation: Maedchen in Uniform," "the stereotype of Nazi campiness, of SS regalia as s-&-m toys, of the Gestapo as a leather-boy thrill, of the big bull dyke as concentration camp boss, etc., all seem to have a firm hold in our culture's fantasy life and historical mythology—this despite the facts of the Third Reich's large-scale massacre of homosexuals as pollutants of Aryan blood and a stain on the future master race" (119). It is possible to describe and analyze fascist doctrine without presupposing a characteristic homosexuality; Ian Kershaw raises the subject only in the context of "victims of social prejudice" (*Hitler*, 2:254). The perception of Nazism as both homophobic and homosexual is a further example of the confusion about fascism's libidinal character and the recourse to sexual scapegoating as a means of defining fascism.

In his 1949 novel *Funeral Rites (Pompes funèbres)*,[1] Jean Genet reveals the cultural stakes for both the political right and the left in conflating fascism and homosexuality—a conflation that Andrew Hewitt, in *Political Inversions*, calls "homo-fascism." For Hewitt, Adorno's infamous declaration in *Minima Moralia* that "totalitarianism and homosexuality belong together" is based on a consolidation of two anxieties: "the liberal fear of becoming fascist and the heterosexual, homosocial fear of becoming homosexual" (9). I would add that there is also the fear of sadomasochistic impulses. Hewitt's explanation accounts for homophobic formulations such as Shirer's, but Genet adds another dimension to "homo-fascism": namely, he inaugurates a tradition of a homoerotic figuring of fascism in which homosexuality is not reviled as a pathological sexuality but is rather the only relevant and meaningful sexuality in that textual universe. In imbuing fascism with a homoerotic charge, then, Genet both repeats and provokes fears about the idea that "totalitarianism and homosexuality belong together."

Although Genet allied himself with the far left (he participated in the Paris student revolts in 1968 and supported the Black Panthers and the rights of French immigrant workers), his fiction affronts both the political right and the left, transposing and recasting the values that each holds sacred into the anarchic laws of fantasy. One of the best illustrations of this is the article Genet wrote for *Esquire* on the U.S. Democratic Party's Convention of Chicago in 1968, entitled "Members of the Assembly." The article begins with a description of protesters at the convention decrying the murder of a seventeen-year-old boy of color who was "killed two days before by the Chicago police." In the days of the Vietnam War, a crooked government, and televised police assaults, Genet was on the side of those who swore to "trust no one over thirty." Yet the next part of the article is a thrilled paean to the "superb thighs" and "muscled torsos" of the police force that subdued the crowd. Just when he is supposed to be most committed to progressive politics, Genet proclaims his erotic response to the conservative opposition, swooning under the towering man in riot gear, a posture that would please neither the policemen nor Genet's political compatriots on the left. Nearly every piece of Genet's writing stages an openly declared sexual fascination with a politically inappropriate object (according to the values of the bourgeois reader Genet constantly posits and addresses). His boldest work in this respect is *Funeral Rites*, in which the scandalous objects of desire are Nazis. For the narrator of *Funeral Rites*, the Nazi soldiers in their tight, stiff uniforms, ornate decorations, and high black boots are figured and fetishized as cruel and alluring executioners, simultaneously objects of eroticism and agents of death.

For four years, Paris and the other occupied zones had been ripped apart by the presence of SS soldiers and the Militia (or *Milice*), the force formed by French premier Pierre Laval and recruited from the French population to po-lice its own citizens,[2] while the Resistance forces (FFI: Forces Françaises de l'Intérieur) fought from barricades all over the city. As Pierre Assouline points out in *Gaston Gallimard*, given the sensitive political climate of postwar France, Gallimard initially refused to publish a novel in which Nazi soldiers, militia-men, and Hitler himself are sexualized. When *Funeral Rites* did appear, just three years after the Liberation, it provoked scathing responses from critics. Jean-Jacques Gautier called Genet's prose "the kind that feeds on the carcasses of crawling meat and the leprosy of souls."[3] François Mauriac wrote that Genet "simply makes us sick."[4] On the other side of the ocean, John Leonard's review of *Funeral Rites*, "Portrait of the Artist as a Narcissistic Hitler," deems it "the proclamation of an esthetic of fascism. . . . Unless we refuse this vision, we de-serve it. To be neutral about it is to flirt with our own personal fascism; it is ei-ther a failure of nerve or . . . immoral" (43).

Critics championing *Funeral Rites* have, with a few exceptions, been rather queasy in their handling of the scenes of eroticized fascism around which the novel is structured. When, for example, in *Jean Genet*, Bettina Knapp de-fends Genet's literary accomplishments in *Funeral Rites*, she makes no men-tion of Hitler or the most sexually explicit scenes in the novel, thus defusing its most troubling and powerful aspects (44). Jean-Paul Sartre and Susan Sontag similarly downplay the political implications of *Funeral Rites*. In *Saint Genet*, Sartre claims that "Genet lives outside history, in parentheses. . . . He deigns to take notice of the circumstances of his life only insofar as they seem to repeat the original drama of the lost paradise" (5), suggesting that the Nazi Occupation of Paris was simply a convenient historical pretext for Genet to tell the story of his personal traumas. In "Fascinating Fascism," Sontag cred-its Genet for contributing "one of the first texts that showed the erotic allure fascism exercised on someone who was not a fascist" (103). Sontag carefully separates Genet from artists she finds guilty of glamorizing fascism, as well as from "male homosexuals" who are "regulars of sadomasochistic sex"—an elision of the gay sadomasochism in *Funeral Rites*, which is no more neces-sarily linked to fascist political sympathies than Genet is automatically exon-erated of having them.

In *Glas*, Jacques Derrida emphasizes the fetishistic substitutions that shape Genet's imagination, focusing on the malleability of the fetish object in the imagination: "The reference can always, but this is never indispensable, be turned inside out like a glove" (141). These reversals and oscillations of fetishism are characteristic of sadomasochism in *Funeral Rites*, in which the characters' relations to domination and power are constantly being reversed: sadistic Nazis become tender lovers and Hitler becomes a shy "Madame." However, Genet develops a detailed cultural context around the sexualized objects in *Funeral Rites*, a context that is not reversible. A passage from the opening page of *Funeral Rites* makes this clear. In the days following the Liberation of France, Genet writes, the newspapers "bring before us the Hitlerian massacres and the games, which others call sadistic, of a police that recruited its torturers from among the French. Photographs still show dismembered, mutilated corpses and villages in ruins . . . burned by German soldiers. It is within the framework of this tragedy that the event is set" (11). Although everything that enters the frame of Genet's fantasy can be reversed, this decisive historical framework of Nazi violence remains steady: "The swastika contains not only the particular exaltation of dangerous banners, but also devastation and death" (81). The juxtaposition of the historical frame and the sadomasochistic fantasy within it forms the basic dynamic of *Funeral Rites*. Like Vercors's *Silence of the Sea*, *Funeral Rites* rehearses and revises mainstream representations of the *boche*; Genet, however, focuses on the atmosphere of patriotism that pervaded France after the Liberation and the cultural anxieties around sexual collaboration.

The narrator—who calls himself Jean Genet—explains that the impetus for writing the novel was the desire to exhume the spirit of his lover, Jean D., a member of the Communist resistance who was shot on the Paris barricades in 1944.[5] Early in the novel, the narrator is shocked at the flatness of the rituals of Jean's Communist funeral: "The blood-red moiré ribbon on which was inscribed in gold letters: 'To our leader, the Communist Youth Movement,' the priest's remarks in French, these were all knives that slashed my heart" (75). The narrator's despondency at losing Jean is exacerbated by seeing his death absorbed into a political cause and inscribed in a generic political slogan on an official ribbon. Like Bataille's and Vercors's provocations of the French left, Genet also positions himself in relation to Resistance politics and particularly against the conflation of political and sexual treason. The reclamation of Jean D. is a "very grave role," and the novel itself is Jean's "grave," as the narrator imagines a private ceremony in which he cannibalizes Jean, wresting him away from the Communists and incorporating him into a fantasy that eroticizes the SS and the Militiamen who may have killed Jean D. Hence, playing on the connotations of "grave," the narrator remarks, "the gravest erotic image, that toward which everything tended . . . was offered me by a German soldier in the black uniform of the tank driver."

The political frame for the reclamation of Jean D. is established in the opening paragraphs of *Funeral Rites*, which quote "the newspapers that appeared at the time of the Liberation of Paris, in August 1944 . . . those days of childish heroism, when the body was steaming with bravura and boldness." The headlines are printed in block capitals: " 'PARIS ALIVE!' 'PARISIANS ALL IN THE STREETS!' 'THE AMERICAN ARMY IS ON THE MARCH IN PARIS' 'STREET FIGHTING CONTINUES' 'THE BOCHES HAVE SURRENDERED' 'TO THE BARRICADES!' 'DEATH TO THE TRAITORS' " (11). The "steaming" body is thrust onto a historical stage where treason is on everyone's mind. Actual headlines from newspapers of the period are nearly identical to Genet's, with "treason" and "traitor" appearing as often as "victory" or "resistance." The front page of the August 24, 1944, *France Libre* praises "THOSE OF THE LIBERATION, THOSE OF VENGEANCE . . . those who refuse treason."[6] The front page of *Front National* on the same day proclaims: "The lesson of the barricades—the confidence in our people, in all our people except the traitors—has always been the principle of our grand movement, the National Front for the liberation and the independence of France."[7] Praise of the Resistance is constantly founded on condemnation of traitors and insists there can be no confusion between the two. (At this point "traitor" seems to appear more frequently in the French press than "collaborator.") The nation was redefined as all those who had fought; traitors and collaborators were not properly "French."

Long before the Liberation, or even the war, Genet had been writing fiction predicated on an idiosyncratic ethical code in which treason and betrayal were major virtues. The motley crew of criminals and pimps that populate Genet's other works are traitors to the French nation and to one another. Genet, a self-declared illegitimate son of a prostitute, abandoned and placed in a home by Assistance Publique and heading for a life of crime by age fourteen, constantly claimed that rejection by his family, his country, and its institutions led to a lifelong estrangement from France's religious, political, social, and moral codes.[8] Genet takes treason to new lows in *Funeral Rites*, where traitors are not petty criminals but German collaborators and specifically the Militia.[9] The social profile of the Militia corresponded to that of the criminal population that Genet exalted in his earlier novels. "Recruited mainly from among hoodlums, since they had to brave the contempt of public opinion," the militiamen "were considered to be worse than whores, worse than thieves and scavengers, sorcerers, homosexuals, worse than a man who, inadvertently or out of choice, ate human flesh. They were not only hated, but loathed" (*Funeral Rites*, 77–78). The militiamen, then, perfectly fit the Genetian traitor profile, as well as the narrator's—a scavenger of Jean D.'s soul, a sorcerer, a homosexual, and a self-proclaimed "cannibal." "I was happy to see France terrorized by children in arms," Genet writes, "but even more so because they were crooks and little rats" (78).

This fortuitous appearance of a nationally despised traitor is highlighted in a pivotal scene in *Funeral Rites*. In the days following the Liberation, exhausted from Jean D.'s funeral, the narrator retreats to a movie theater. As usual, a newsreel is shown before the feature. The audience around the narrator laughs and applauds as a young militiaman appears on the screen beside a French soldier who victoriously carries the defeated militiaman's rifle. The narrator, sickened by the crowd, remarks that "neither the world's laughter nor the inelegance of caricaturists will keep me from recognizing the sorry grandeur" of the traitors. Genet joins Vercors in his critique of propagandistic caricature, and he too complicates those caricatures through an erotic identification with the enemy. But whereas Vercors responds to reductive caricature by creating a more nuanced Nazi (von Ebrennac), the narrator in *Funeral Rites* wholeheartedly embraces the militiaman in all his foulness. "My hatred of the militiaman was so intense, so beautiful, that it was equivalent to the strongest love. No doubt it was he who had killed Jean" (54). Miserable over Jean's death, the narrator decides that "the best trick" he can play on "destiny" is "to invest" the militiaman with desire and even love (45–55). The narrator christens him "Riton," who then becomes a character in the novel. The narrator's alienation from French patriotism is transmuted into a powerful identification with the object of its abhorrence. He speculates that Riton must feel "an evil joy, the joy of being joyous and handsome in a desperate situation which he had evilly got himself into, out of hatred for France (which he rightly confused with Society). . . . I have the soul of Riton. It is natural for the piracy, the ultra-mad banditry of Hitler's adventure, to arouse hatred in decent people but deep admiration and sympathy in me" (116). Genet finds his cherished virtue usurped by France/bourgeois "Society," and proceeds to paint a flagrantly, gloriously treasonous universe that will puncture the patriotic hypocrisy of the "decent people." For Genet, the most potent way to do this is to literalize the form of treason that perhaps produced the most anxiety: sexual treason.

It is important that Genet set *Funeral Rites* during the Liberation, a period of intense national crisis about political identity.[10] As Lynn Higgins writes in *New Novel, New Wave, New Politics*, "with the departure of the Germans . . . there was no longer a clear sense of who the enemy might be or from where violence might come. The distinction between collaborators and resisters was no longer a usable one. Especially among the majority, which was neither" (48). In order to reassert the collective national identity—a nation of loyal antifascists—in this period of chaos, France chose a number of scapegoats, among them the women who had slept with the enemy. In August and September 1944, women accused of having had sexual relations with Nazi soldiers were rounded up and publicly humiliated. Usually, their heads were shaved—thus, they were known as *les tondues* or "the shaved"—and were then paraded through the towns, often stripped, their faces and chests sometimes painted with swastikas. Although there is no agreement on the number of *tondues* there were, Corran Laurens suggests this method of vigilante justice was "massive in its repetition" ("'La femme au turban,'" 156). The punishment of the *tondues* (whom I will discuss in more detail in chapter 6) served to solidify a postwar sense of nationalism and to mark a distinction between loyal French citizens and traitors. Genet shapes his treasonous encounters in *Funeral Rites* around this most abhorred "horizontal collaboration," as consorting sexually with German soldiers is often called. The narrator is clear that his erotic project in *Funeral Rites* is driven by "thoughts" that are "forbidden" (68).

In this atmosphere, then, Genet's narrator goes to Jean D.'s house after his funeral, and there he meets Erik, a young Nazi soldier who, the narrator is convinced, is the lover of Jean's mother. That ostensible treason is not remarked upon, but it is the gateway for a much more elaborate fantasy of sexual treason. The narrator eyes the handsome soldier, imagines Erik wrapped in a Nazi flag, and "attempt[s] to retrace the course of his life" via a curious route: his uniform. "I got into his uniform, boots, and skin. . . . I wormed my way into his past, gently and hesitantly at first, feeling my way, when the iron toe-plates of one of my shoes accidentally struck the curb. My calf vibrated, then my whole body. I raised my head and took my hands out of my pockets. I put on the German boots" (36). Having "entered" Erik through the fetishistic elements of the uniform, the narrator assumes the Nazi's persona and voice, which reproduce the rhetorical tropes of fascist ideology. He imagines "a singing of harps," "a swan flapp[ing] its wings on a lake" (36)—preindustrial, even kitsch, images of a return to a glorified state of nature—and the assurance of birthright and historical destiny. "The day would see the reign of God. . . . I was eighteen, a young Nazi on duty in the park" (36). These are the "tomorrow belongs to me" sentiments of Hitler Youth songs.

This is only the first of many cases where *Funeral Rites* abruptly switches among different first-person and third-person voices espousing opposing political positions. In the middle of a paragraph, for example, the voice may change from that of a Communist Resistance fighter to a member of the SS. The first-person expressions of Nazi subjectivity have alarmed some critics, many of whom argue that only by complicity with Nazism can one write in such a voice.[11] Throughout *Funeral Rites*, the narrator is self-conscious about this style of narration, which he calls "sorcery" and "magical," and links it to the project of exhuming Jean D. in order to "contain" both Jean and his killers. After speaking through and as Erik, the narrator imagines a scene from the Nazi's past. A younger Erik is on duty in a park, alone and weary, when a massive stranger, "the Berlin Executioner," approaches him. They have a nervous conversation, half cruising one another, during which the Executioner notices Erik's "trembling," his "timorous flutter," and decides to push him around. Suddenly Erik is "sure of [his] power over the brute," and a game of subtle manipulation begins. Genet highlights the shifts of power between the characters. When the Executioner asks Erik if he is scared, Erik flirtatiously admits, "I wanted to be mean and I said yes." The Berlin Executioner then abruptly changes from a character of crushing bulk to a sad, lonely, rather domesticated man under Erik's erotic power. Erik is "thrilled" as the Executioner pushes him up against a tree, where they intertwine in an embrace that is alternatively controlled by the Executioner and by Erik. When the Executioner finally breaks away, having "discharged between Erik's golden thighs," the narrator states that "Erik loved the executioner" (71). One of the most striking features of this passage is its continual changes in tone, from violence to eroticism to love. This alternately hard-core and sentimental scene is as much about "tenderness" and "love" as it is about force. The Nazi context seems to fade in and out as the characters become strongly associated with violence and brutality, and then are imagined in another realm that is sadomasochistic but definitely sexual. Scenes that literalize the fear of sexual treason are complicated by the vacillations between the brutalities of Nazism and the imagined erotic charge of the SS.

The scene between Erik and the Berlin Executioner is sweet and pastoral compared to the subsequent meeting between Hitler and Jean D.'s older brother, Paulo. In substituting the historical persona of Hitler for the non-specific "Berlin Executioner," Genet substantially changes the tone of the scene, and the shifts between sadomasochistic eroticism and Nazi violence are more pronounced. Building on an already existing assumption about Hitler's sexual deviance, Genet imagines the Führer as an isolated figure, his loneliness the outcome of his castration by a "bullet that tore off both [his] balls in 1917." This, Hitler reports through the narrator's voice, "subjected me to the harsh discipline of the dry masturbator, but also to the sweet pleasures of pride" (127). Hardly a figure of strength or inherent power, Genet's Hitler—a self-described "puny, ridiculous little fellow"—takes his power from the men he amasses around him and exerts "upon the world a power extracted from the pure, sheer beauty of athletes and hoodlums" and from "the loveliest army in the world," (133) which he sends out to die. Alternatively, Hitler brings boys like Paulo to his "secret alcove" where he "love[s] and kill[s] his victims" (128).

As Hitler is transformed into an irascible gelding, Paulo, whose political role is ambiguous (the narrator speculates that he was with the Resistance like his brother but thinks he may have been a traitor),[12] embodies characteristics associated with the hard, cruel fascist. "Of all the little guys I like to stick in my books," Genet writes, Paulo is "the meanest." Paulo is empty, cold, and cruel, a "machine" of "inhuman severity" (51), "an instrument of torture, a pair of pincers, a serpentine dagger ready to function, functioning by its evil presence alone" (53). Unlike Hitler, whose carefully constructed public persona is shown to be a grotesque reaction-formation against his impotence, Paulo, in his "inviolable hardness" (133), acts out of instinctual sexual cruelty: "The essential part of Paulo the torture-machine was the penis. It had the perfection of clockwork, of a precision-tooled connecting rod. Its metal was solid, flawless . . . it was a hammer" (139). Like the monstrous monkey penis of the "doll-like" bandleader in Bataille's *Blue of Noon*, this ostensible Resistance fighter's member is more mechanical than human.

When brought before Hitler, Paulo is not intimidated, though he is "frightened" by Hitler's mustache: "Could it be that a simple mustache composed of black hair—and dyed perhaps—meant: cruelty, despotism, violence, rage, foam, asps, strangulation, death, forced marches, ostentation, prison, daggers?" (134). It occurs to Paulo that "this bimbo's just a little old guy of fifty, after all" (137). Hitler pushes Paulo onto his stomach on the bed; the scene that follows, in which Hitler thrusts into Paulo, at the end of which "the torture machine" has been subdued, is narrated by Hitler himself. "I grabbed his hand," Hitler remarks, "and squeezed it tenderly, that big, broad, thick hand became tiny, docile, and quiet and murmured, 'Thank you'" (137). In the same shift of power that occurred in Erik's scene with the Executioner, Hitler mollifies Paulo's viciousness. At the same time, the erotic contact allows Paulo to see Hitler through a new lens, and he narrates: "The mustache, the wrinkles, and the lock of hair suddenly took on human proportions, and by the grace of an unequalled generosity, the fabulous emblem of Satan's chosen people descended to inhabit that simple dwelling, the puny body of an old queen" (138). Hitler—"Madame"—is feminized and overwhelmed with guilt and paranoia while Paulo regains his mechanistic strength. Now submissive, Hitler pouts that Paulo "did not allow his naughty tool to lose any of its hardness, and I remained a poor fellow, a poor abandoned kid."

The dizzying shifts of power in these scenes are characteristic of sado-masochism in Genet's fiction. Here the author does explore erotic identifications with a fascist aesthetic of severity and cruelty, but Genet's relationship to this aesthetic is by no means straightforward, and the constant narrative slippage among different political voices further complicates the matter. The fixing of political advocacy in fantasy is a notoriously difficult affair. Jean Laplanche and Jean-Bertrand Pontalis have noted how elusive the subject can be within the structure of fantasy, which "is characterized by an absence of subjectivization."[13] The fantasy "is a scenario with multiple entries," in which the subject may appear as subject, object, or verb. In *The Practice of Love*, Teresa de Lauretis cautions against simplifying this idea to the point that the subject is said to be equally everywhere and nowhere in fantasy (141). She argues that in conscious fantasy (including fiction) or daydream "the scenario is basically in the first person, and the subject's place clear and invariable. The organization is stabilized by the secondary process, weighed by the ego: the subject, it is said, lives out his reverie." Indeed, in *Funeral Rites*, all the characters are mediated through the central narrator, "Jean Genet," whose voice expands to orchestrate, contain, and articulate the subjectivity of the Nazi Erik, the militiaman Riton, and so on. If the primary narrative subject in *Funeral Rites* is the narrator Jean Genet, what is his—and the author Jean Genet's—political position in that fantasy? I will propose a twofold means of approaching these scenes of eroticized fascism. The first draws on Wilhelm Reich's and Klaus Theweleit's sociopsychoanalytic formulations of sexuality and the fascist psyche. The second traces the historical correspondences between eroticism in *Funeral Rites* and the commentary on sexualized treason in contemporary Resistance journals.

The Troop Machine/The Torture Machine

Genet's descriptions of Paulo—"the torture-machine" with "the perfection of clockwork, of a precision-tooled connecting rod . . . solid, flawless"—resonate with Wilhelm Reich's description of the fascist psyche in his 1933 *Mass Psychological Structure of Fascism*. Reich asserts that fascist ideology develops in its subjects a "mechanical discipline" and "biological rigidity." This posture represses irrational impulses that would otherwise threaten the fascist soldier's rigid control, such as emotional vulnerability, voracious femininity, and, above all, the release of orgasmic pleasure. "The compulsion to control one's sexuality, to maintain sexual repression," Reich observes, "leads to the development of pathologic, emotionally tinged notions of honor and duty, bravery and self-control" (55). Klaus Theweleit's analysis of Freikorps writing in *Male Fantasies* also finds that the training of the fascist "soldier male" necessitates a "freezing up" of his psyche: "The person is split into an inner realm, concealing a 'numbing glowing, fluid ocean' and other dangers; and a restraining external shell, the muscle armor, which contains the inner realm the way a cauldron contains boiling soup" (1:242). The fascist body is formed into a "troop machine":

> The "new man" . . . born of the troop machine . . . is a man whose physique has been mechanized, his psyche eliminated—or in part displaced onto his body armor. . . . The soldier male responds to the successful damming in and chaoticizing of his desiring-production from the moment of his birth . . . by fantasizing himself as a figure of steel: a man of the new race. (1:164)

Both Reich and Theweleit assert that the fascist subject takes comfort in this rigid, prescribed structure because it holds emotional dangers at bay and gives the subject a set of clear boundaries within which to function. As in Nazi Germany, all "undesirable" elements that threaten the fascist vision of a unified nation and subject are cast out or eliminated (an inversion of Bataille's theory of fascist "heterogeneity").

Genet also implies that blocked sexuality plays an important role in Nazi character formation: Hitler's "castration had cut him off from human beings. His joys are not ours" (31). Similarly, the armored bodies of the SS and militiamen in *Funeral Rites* are constantly called "carapaces" or "shells": they are inhuman in their impenetrability. The young Nazi Erik, for instance,

> had joined the Hitler Youth in order to have weapons: a knife for show, and a revolver for pillage. . . . He developed his naturally hard muscles. . . . When he felt daring and wanted to shake the world, Erik had only to squeeze that unique neck of his with his large, thick hands to feel it was a firm column that supported the world, that held its being and head high, and rose above the world. (67)

Like the "body armor" of the Freikorps men, Erik's armored body, always striving for "hardness," is a rigid, phallic column that seems to act autonomously. "His life had to have the shape of his body," as if it were detached from, or acting in place of, his self. The emphasis on shape and restraining perimeters also foregrounds a psychic shell that completes the fascist illusion of the self as vacuum-sealed against outside assault. The hard bodies in *Funeral Rites*, encased in uniforms, boots, the "carapaces" (179) of guns and ammunition belts, luxuriate in this armor and feel "protected by the fabulous power of the Reich" (225). However, the subjects in these trappings also feel, at crucial moments in the narrative, confused and disoriented. Metaphors of rushing water and of drowning appear throughout *Funeral Rites* as the characters struggle for control. "Riton, lying on his back, was on Erik's shore. If he had a dizzy spell, he would fall into him and drown in the deep eddies that he sensed were rolling from the chest to the thighs" (148). Erik feels "protected" by his SS mantle, but he "felt he was composed of a skeleton as breakable and white as that cord. . . . If a shock occurred, if fear itself were lacking, he would crumble beneath the great weight of his head. . . . He was walking at the edge of the torrent and heard its roar" (110–11). Without the protection of the uniform, the SS mantle, the sea will overwhelm him and destroy his fragile body.

If the fascist soldier is fortified by his hard shell, then where is this "drowning," this "nausea," this *seasickness*, coming from? Theweleit notes a recurring image throughout the Freikorps literature: dammed-up water that bursts into an engulfing flood. Reich also speaks of the "damming up" of the libido by fascist ideology. As noted earlier in relation to Lawrence's leadership novels, the fascist flood within signals anxiety about the external forces that might "stimulate" that flood (Theweleit, 2:242). This rushing water and these bursting streams connote the orgasmic pleasure of ejaculation that threatens to dissolve the fascist soldier's body and ego boundaries. The thought of coming makes the fascist male sick with fear.

The contrast Theweleit finds in Freikorps rhetoric between fascist rigidity and the libidinal flood is especially striking in a scene in *Funeral Rites* in which the militiaman Riton, close to starvation, stalks a cat whose fur has a "softness and tenderness" that terrifies Riton, in spite of his carapace (86). Immediately, he feels a roaring body of water that makes him dizzy. Meanwhile, his allies, the German soldiers, see Riton as a vulnerable "animal with an extremely fragile body that emerges from a few holes in its protective shell" (88), not quite as well armored as they are. They decide not to let him shoot his rifle and instead appoint him ammunition carrier. He is "wrapped in bullets," "entwined from his belt to his neck in the mutely glittering coils that the Fritzes made him wear" (88). Even—or perhaps, most significantly—his penis is encased in a protective exoskeleton; it is "a kind of stone at the bottom of the sea, encrusted, among the algae, with tiny shellfish that made it even harder." The German ammunition allows him to withstand the raging sea, and his most vulnerable organ is recruited into the carapace.

Whereas sexual pleasure "bursts" the soldier male's shell, there is another kind of ejaculation in *Funeral Rites* that, though brought about by the same raging sea, does not threaten the soldier but rather fortifies him. When the

Nazi Erik gratuitously murders a child, "green waves" roll through him like "turbines . . . dynamos which emitted a terrible current." Erik feels his gun and thinks, "violence calms storms, the time has come," and the current turns into "a column of darkness or pure water" (106). The ejaculation of gunfire, unlike sexual ejaculation, strengthens the soldier. What makes the fascist soldier the perfect fascist instrument is the fact that he is kept in check for so long: fueled by the force of all the "dammed-up" psychic energy, when he is sprung, he will respond with incredible violence. "Guns," Theweleit writes, "have the capacity to do something of which the soldier is normally incapable: they can discharge and still remain *whole*" (2:179). This kind of violence exercised on another reinforces, rather than threatens, the subject's ego boundaries. The Nazi's grand public rituals, its rallies and parades, for example, functioned in the same way, Theweleit writes, as a "public staging of the forbidden . . . of flowing desire. Drives are given an outlet" (1:430). This discharge of sanctioned violence serves to maintain the fascist machinery, whereas orgasmic discharge threatens to dissolve its unity. The shame Erik feels in committing murder stems not from the act of taking a life but rather from allowing himself to get close to a body.

The sexualized fascist bodies in *Funeral Rites* are the antithesis of the "techno-body" that the Third Reich championed: the fascist fusion of the human body with the machine, a "man-machine symbiosis" in Herf's formulation (*Reactionary Modernism*, 79) exalted by German political reactionaries from Ernst Jünger on.[14] Like the machine, the techno-body is hard and dry (unless perhaps heroically bleeding). The fascist bodies in *Funeral Rites* are vulnerable and messy: they ooze and ejaculate and sweat. "Like all the other boys of the Reich," Genet writes, "Erik's face had retained something of the spatters of a royal sperm." Genet's corporeal, desiring fascist body undermines the mission and drive of the clean, hard techno-body.

Genet's narrative treatment of the sadomasochistic fantasy scenes in *Funeral Rites*, such as the scene between Erik and the Berlin Executioner, is very different from the way he discusses the historical "Hitlerian massacres" (11). The operation of recognition, with its shifting fields of power, characterizes the erotic dynamic between Erik and the Berlin Executioner. This stands in contrast to scenes of nonerotic violence in *Funeral Rites*, such as Riton's brutal murder of a child and a cat, in which the object is totally extinguished, and a scene in which Nazi soldiers rape Riton. On August 15, "Assumption Day" (230), when the boulevard was "decked out with two rows of French flags" along with British and U.S. ones, Riton "solemnly bade France farewell," realizing that "the flags were out for his treason." In contrast to the previous sadomasochistic courtships described as erotic adventures, Genet calls this a "rape," and Genet emphasizes the "hatred" of those watching, enjoying the "tortures" (238).

Sontag, in her attempts to discern why the SS would be the objects of eroticization, speculates that it is "because the SS was the ideal incarnation of fascism's overt assertion of the righteousness of violence, the right to have total power over others and to treat them as absolutely inferior" ("Fascinating Fascism," 99). The sadomasochistic fantasies of *Funeral Rites* suggest a different motivation. In Genet's erotic scenes, the fascist characters do not have "total power over others." Instead, according to the sadomasochistic dynamic, they both desire others and are subject to the desires of others. They respond and are responded to. This is a very different dynamic from the way violence is treated in the novel. *Funeral Rites*, then, seems to exemplify Theweleit's and Reich's formulations only up to a certain point. Genet represents the fascist psyche in the same terms but then complicates it by revealing how it disintegrates—and, moreover, by bringing about that disintegration in the service of pleasure. According to Reich and Theweleit, military "phallic" display is, ironically, an attempt to extinguish, not establish, sexuality: "The focus of repression in the fascist soldier is 'the desire to desire' . . . the core of all fascist propaganda is a battle against . . . enjoyment and pleasure" (2:7). Thus, Genet's eroticization of the fascist soldier body in *Funeral Rites* relies on and redeploys fascist aesthetics for ends quite antithetical to fascist ideology. Genet "disarms" his SS soldiers and militiamen by inscribing them in scenes of impending sexual pleasure, a most frightening position for the fascist subject.

La Femelle, Virility, and Cowardice

The fascist figures in *Funeral Rites* are terrified of softness and vulnerability; this tension is related to another underlying opposition, that between masculinity and femininity, which is especially evident in the character of Hitler in *Funeral Rites*. Although Genet pokes fun at Hitler, showing him as a sad, insecure "kid" in his tryst with Paulo, he is not precisely a comic figure. Unlike Charlie Chaplin's "Great Dictator," a clownish Hitler who performs a ballet, tossing the globe as if it were a beach ball, Genet's Hitler is increasingly desperate as he loses his ability to dominate and terrorize in the bedroom. Implying that these personal inadequacies led him to "unleash terrible acts on the world" (160), Genet portrays Hitler as all the more frightening for these irrational motivations. Throughout his scene with Paulo, Hitler is feminized. At one point, he is even compared to Joan of Arc.

"Before the war," Genet writes, "cartoonists caricatured Hitler as a Maid with clownish features and a movie comedian's mustache. 'He hears voices,' said the captions. . . . Did the cartoonists feel that Hitler was Joan of Arc?" Genet worries that there may be more truth to this story than caricature. "Hitler will perish by fire if he has identified with Germany, as his enemies recognize. He has a bleeding wound at the same level as Joan's on her prisoner's robe" (158). The startling conflation of the menstruating French saint with a castrated Hitler operates on a number of levels. First, it is the caricatures that initiate the comparison. As for Vercors, Genet self-consciously filters the image of Hitler through popular representations. These prewar cartoons, like so much of the early foreign press on Germany, tragically misjudged Hitler. But why the comparison to Joan of Arc? The patron saint hardly benefits from the analogy; it seems like something Genet himself would dream up to offend his French readers. Earlier in *Funeral Rites*, Joan of Arc—Jeanne d'Arc in the French—is compared to the more obvious double contained in her name, Jean D. "During the funeral ceremony, the priest said a few words, including the following: 'He died on the field of honor.' . . . He . . . showed him as a hero of the just cause against evil, like the purehearted knight confronting the beast" (98). Both Jean D. and Joan of Arc fought and died for patriotic political causes. That "purity" "impresses" the narrator Genet but causes him to side even more with the Ritons of the world: "The more Jean's soul inhabits me—the more Jean himself inhabits me—the fonder I shall be of cowards, traitors, and petty no-goods" (98–99). By becoming the voice of patriotism and morality during the Occupation, the Resistance was on the side of self-righteousness, which Genet associated with bourgeois law and order. Genet's merging of Hitler with Joan of Arc makes use of the media's prewar comparison and holds it accountable for its own historical error. Hitler's "voices" are the babble of patriotic fervor—and its madness. In the Nazi barracks, Riton, who has betrayed his country by joining the Militia, also hears voices and thinks, "I'm like Joan of Arc" (93). Riton sees his own fate as similar to Joan's—she was killed for heresy, and he will be executed for treason. In an irony of which Genet must have been aware, the figure of Joan of Arc was enlisted by Vichy propagandists, who drew parallels between her and *Le Maréchal* Pétain: "For the Germans," writes Patrick Marsh in "*Jeanne d'Arc* during the German Occupation," Joan of Arc "was seen as the heroine of the struggle against the English; for the French . . . she was seen as the heroine of the struggle against the invader" (139). In 1943, German propaganda in France published a poster extolling Joan of Arc for her resistance to the English. On this poster, Joan proclaims: "I would rather sell my soul to God than be in the hands of the English,"[15] implying that the true war to be fought was against Britain rather than Germany. Genet brings out the painful historical twist by which the chief collaborator, Pétain, was aligned with the most sacred symbol of French patriotism.

The question of Hitler's cross-gendering is more complex. In "Qu'est-ce qu'un collaborateur?" Jean-Paul Sartre suggests that "the fascist is empty (of Frenchness) . . . weak . . . 'feminized'" and linked to "passivity."[16] For Genet, however, such "softness" makes Hitler an ally against the usual patriotic militarism. The physical "wounds" of the Maid of Orleans (the gush of menstrual blood) and Hitler's castration mark them as vulnerable in ways unacceptable to the fascist idealization of bodies that are impermeable and therefore "manly." Genet demonstrates the urgency with which the fascist soldier attempts to drive out all signs of weakness: while "buggering Riton," Erik thinks about what "caused him to beat and torture." It is "so as to be surer of his freedom and his own strength and then take revenge for having been weak" (250). Thus, femininity is aligned against fascism in *Funeral Rites*, as it subverts Nazism from within. The fact that Genet equates menstruation with castration indicates his idiosyncratic conception of femininity.[17] Femininity and masculinity are not gender-based concepts for Genet but are rather associated with positions of weakness and strength. "Femininity" is Genet's signature for certain culturally constructed features he associates with homosexuality. Hitler's abhorred "femininity" stands in for a homophobia particularly evident during the Occupation, represented not only by the notoriously homophobic Nazi policies but also by the more subtly pernicious homophobia of the political left in France.

Les Lettres françaises, the communist journal popular in the occupied zone, and for which many of Genet's friends, including Sartre, wrote, presents a context within which the sexual and gender dispositions of the fascist characters in *Funeral Rites* powerfully resonate. In *Literature and the French Resistance*, Margaret Atack finds that "the main target of *Les Lettres françaises* is the literary and cultural expression of the edifice of collaboration. . . . There are several constants in these deliberately polemical analyses," including "cowardice" and "homosexual fascination with the virile German victors" (42–44). And Philip Watts notes that for writers such as Paul Eluard, "hate and sexual deviance are . . . privileged terms for denouncing the Nazis and their collaborators" (*Allegories*, 112). Not only did *Les Lettres françaises* target two themes in which Genet was particularly invested—treason and homosexuality—but it also brought them together in a constellation that Genet replicates in *Funeral Rites*. An article in the November 1943 issue takes as its target the collaborationist writer Jacques Chardonne, who worked under

Drieu la Rochelle at *La Nouvelle Revue Française*.[18] Chardonne's Nazi sympathies were well established, and the article's insistence that Vichy supporters should be confronted with the policies in *Mein Kampf* is convincing. However, one strange passage focuses on Chardonne's sexuality in relation to the Nazis. Just as "a female athlete on a racetrack" who seemed to "change into a man," Chardonne desired to "give voice to the feminine that lurks within him." The occasion that made that possible was "the defeat of France: soldiers and refugees jumbled on the roads, the swastika on our edifices, our words annexed by the enemy, and our people tortured and executed." The occupation inspired Chardonne to convert to "Hitlerism," and to embrace a masochistic femininity. He "celebrates the beauty of the young conquerors" and gives himself "like a woman after a slap in the face."[19]

Amidst legitimate observations about National Socialism and the violence of its Occupation policies, this account of Chardonne's sexual attraction to Nazism repeats the conflation of feminine passivity and treason. It makes use of a sexological theory of homosexuality—the woman trapped inside the man's body—and proposes that fascist politics may be similarly dormant within a French body. By becoming a masochistic feminine collaborator, Chardonne could ostensibly achieve the ecstasy he sought. Hence, "totalitarianism and homosexuality belong together."

It was not only the patriotic French Resistance that figured collaboration as a sexual pact and homosexuals and women as scapegoats: the Vichy premier Pétain described his "National Revolution" (in collaboration with Germany) as "a strongly human and virile reaction to a feminized republic, a republic of women and homosexuals."[20] And the collaborator Robert Brasillach wrote, in an article published on February 19, 1943, "Like it or not, we [Germans and French] have lived together; French(men) of some reflection during these few years will have more or less slept with Germany, and the memory of it will remain sweet to them."[21] The anxiety that Nazis may become libidinal objects for both collaborators and Resistance fighters appears as a concern in writings of the French Occupation and Liberation. However, homosexual "horizontal collaboration" does not seem to have been punished in the *épuration* (purging) period, whereas women were targets of revenge.

Corran Laurens considers the shearing an "attempted symbolic reversal of women's emergent power, and an exorcism of the image of threatened masculinity from public memory."[22] The anxiety of sexual contact with the enemy was exacerbated by a general crisis of masculinity brought about by France's military defeat and enforced occupation. The disparaging use of the term *la femelle*—it is generally used only for animals—in *Les Lettres françaises* to strengthen the charges against collaborators such as Chardonne, demonstrates the same symptomatic fears, except that the worry about women is displaced onto homosexuals. Genet literalizes these anxieties about homoerotic and feminine treason. The *femelle* is embraced against the disapproving and self-righteous voice of patriotism in *Les Lettres françaises*. Genet's desires were deemed "perverse" by those who were ostensibly most concerned with liberation and freedom; spitefully, he makes his desire still more defiantly deviant and elaborately treasonous.

The sexual treason Genet imagines in *Funeral Rites* would become an important issue some twenty years later in the *mode rétro*.[23] This interest during the 1970s in revisiting the less heroic elements of France's involvement in the Occupation included Marcel Ophuls's *The Sorrow and the Pity* and Robert O. Paxton's *Vichy France*, which questioned the reigning Gaullist myths of France's heroism in the face of the German Occupation. The history that emerged suggests that most French citizens were not bold barricade fighters; rather, a substantial proportion of the population did not actively resist.[24] The *épuration* period was also revisited, including the brutal treatment of women suspected to have consorted with the enemy. (In *The Sorrow and the Pity* Ophuls interviews Denis Rake, a British secret agent in occupied France who confesses that he had an affair with a German officer.) *Funeral Rites* reflects many of these complicated histories of the Occupation and Liberation, but its prescient commentary came too early—and was too aggressively provocative—to be accepted as respectable testimony.

Fantasies of Evil

Finally, after the political dimensions of *Funeral Rites* are explored, the reader is still left with the question of Genet's erotic aesthetic. When the narrator of *Funeral Rites* "puts on the German boots," this is no ironic postmodern put-on (as Sontag describes Robert Morris's self-portrait of the artist as naked macho soldier in a metal helmet and draped in bullets). In Genet's novel, the narrator's clear libidinal attachment to those boots cannot be dismissed. The erotic aesthetic of *Funeral Rites* elaborates upon a perverse reading of propaganda in which the muscled, brutish enemy is also an object of desire. Genet's treatment of the fascist soldiers sets forth a number of erotic tropes that remain iconic.

The bodies in *Funeral Rites* are almost always concealed by and revealed through their uniforms. Uniforms are a crucial part of Genet's erotic treatment of the prohibited body, whether the Chicago policeman or the fascist soldier. "Power," Genet once remarked, "protects itself by means of theatricality."[25] Military uniforms, the principal trappings of national, institutional power, are theatrical in that they simultaneously display and restrain the male body. In *Funeral Rites*, the Nazi Erik's body is all "the more mysterious for being alive beneath that funereal cloth which also concealed a paraphernalia (such as is no doubt hidden behind a black curtain in special houses) of straps, belts, steel buckles, teamster's whips, boots, which the sound of leather had conjured up, thighs whose strength derived from a fascination with death" (148). This body is erotic precisely for the prohibitions it represents, for the tension between its connotations of death and the body pulsingly "alive beneath" the uniform. Throughout the novel, Genet deploys what Atack calls the major "economical markers" of Germany in French Resistance literature—the "uniform, especially the boots" (*Literature and the French Resistance*, 77). Like Reik's description of a masochist's "uniform ritual," the narrator of *Funeral Rites* forges an erotics of restraint and prohibition.

Genet's reading of the fascist body concentrates on the taut boundaries and rigid postures that hold sexual impulses in check, the places where hardness disguises softness, where the seams of the uniform are strained: the bulge in the skintight regulation pants and the insignia stretched over the hard biceps. (As the cliché of women loving men in uniforms affirms, this is not an exclusively gay male aesthetic. The female artist G. B. Jones, for example, transposes this aesthetic into lesbian fantasy in her drawings of female prison guards in labia-hugging uniforms facing off with female deliquents.)[26] Kenneth Anger's brawling bikers in *Scorpio Rising*, Tom of Finland's policemen,[27] and Paul Cadmus's sailors also convey this erotic charge. Cadmus's 1934 painting *Fleet's In* depicts U.S. soldiers in a drunk and disorderly state, cavorting with prostitutes but showing notable sexual interest in each other's bodies, which swell beneath their uniforms. When this piece appeared at the Corcoran Gallery, it was pulled from the show, and Cadmus received an anonymous letter threatening him and calling him "You damn traitor." Cadmus's "crime" was that he violated codes of military masculinity—its restraint, repression, and heterosexuality.

Genet's love of the cultural outsider and his paradoxical eroticization of Nazism have been highly influential among postmodern artists. His graphic sexual passages and detailed description of the erotic charge of political paraphernalia translate well into the visual realm. The work of the contemporary artist John O'Reilly usefully illustrates how Genet's juxtapositions function, by inserting images of fascist figures into incongruous scenes and fusing historically and politically diverse contexts into an erotic fantasy image. In a

Polaroid collage series entitled *Occupied Territory and Dance of Death*, O'Reilly replicates Genet's scenario of Occupation, placing sexualized Nazi images in a classical French landscape. In *Brinner* (1995), he places an anonymous amateur's photograph of the head of a Nazi soldier (taken from a collection of photographs of Nazis on holiday) on a body from a gay porn magazine and sets the figure in the pastoral French landscapes of Jean-Baptiste-Camille Corot's *Baccante with Tambourine* (1860). O'Reilly explains that he "picked Corot to stand for French art and let the brutality intrude on it. The Nude is to suggest Everyman. The helmet suggests the brutality that goes with the body. The brutality of the hard brick against the softness of the background is also intended."[28] Reproducing the opposition in *Funeral Rites* between hardness and softness, O'Reilly's collages produce a fascist body that is susceptible to desire. In the process, O'Reilly brings into play the psychic mechanisms of desire that Genet unmasks in *Funeral Rites*: the eroticization of the politically repudiated object based on the very strictness of the Nazi's "shell" and the brutality of his oppressive politics. The beauty and figurative availability of the nude male body from the porn magazines is juxtaposed with the Nazi paraphernalia—the helmet, and so on—which is designed, as Reich and Theweleit suggest, to prevent just such erotic interpretations.

John O'Reilly, *Brinner* (1995). Courtesy of Howard Yezerski Gallery, Boston; Julie Saul Gallery, New York

In *Funeral Rites*, the fascist body (like the "macho straight male body" that, as D. A. Miller notes in *Bringing out Roland Barthes*, is "a body wholly given over to utility" [31]) is rendered erotic, despite its armored constitution, and given over to pleasurable expenditure. Genet's carnal criminals—prisoners of sex and perhaps love—undermine both the French left's construction of its heterosexual, properly aligned desires and the Nazi cult of heterosexual masculinity. Perhaps what is ultimately most impressive about *Funeral Rites* is how Genet manages to provoke the left's fear of sexual treason and fascist fears of exposure and vulnerability while realizing private fantasies. The novel sustains its antifascist historical frame while articulating the most elaborately "treasonous" sexual fantasies. Thus, even as some parts of the novel allow politically recuperative readings, Genet thwarts that certitude in his elaborately choreographed, calculatedly inflammatory, scenes of forbidden eroticism. Nazism is, for Genet, simultaneously "appalling" and "charged with a magnetism that would panic us for a long time."[29]

The sexual demographics of the authors I have examined thus far dispel the notion that eroticized fascism is exclusively "a gay thing." As the chronological and national range of these fictions demonstrates, eroticized fascism appears wherever fascism is associated with a sexual deviancy that surpass its political and historical properties. The next chapter will turn to a rival cliché: the heterosexual women's masochistic attraction to fascism. This, too, is a fantasy that crosses national boundaries and is, I will argue, particularly relevant to the international project of feminism.

Chapter 6

"Every woman adores a Fascist":
Marguerite Duras, Sylvia Plath,
and Feminist Visions of Fascism

> Fascism is the first thing in the relationship between a
> man and a woman.
>
> —Ingeborg Bachmann

> Hitler couldn't have made it without the women. And
> Shirer had said in his memoirs that at the Nuremberg ral-
> lies, the women went into a trance when Hitler spoke. . . .
> The women's faces were upturned and blissful, ecstasy lit
> up their eyes. . . . The women adored Hitler. They were
> in love with him.
>
> —Emily Prager, *Eve's Tattoo*

In 1997, the collection of erotic and romantic epistles sent by German
women to their Führer, which had been found among the ruins of Hitler's
chancellery, was assembled by the Jewish Theater of New York into a series of interlocking monologues and performed as *Love Letters to Adolf
Hitler*.[1] The letters begin with such salutations as "My darling sugar-sweet
Adolf" and "Dear Adi." One woman gushes, "I could kiss you a thousand
times and still not be satisfied. My love for you is endless, so tender, so hot
and so complete."[2] Another woman fervently choreographs a night with
Hitler in the absence of any response from her interlocutor: "I am making
you keys to my front door and to my room," she states, and proceeds to
outline a series of instructions for finding the house and circumventing the
maid. "My parents (they could be your in-laws) say you can come any
time," she concludes, "so we can spend the night together at my parents'
house."[3] The level of detail in these reveries shows a startlingly undis-
turbed delusion of intimacy with Hitler that was apparently shared by more
than a few German women. Although most reviewers of the play agreed
that its effect is not pro-Nazi, protesters picketed the 1997 production, and

its director received death threats. An eroticized Hitler was perceived as disrespectful to the memory of the Holocaust, despite the fact that the play was staged by a theater group committed to preserving that memory. Several critics contended that the play was "implicitly anti-feminist."[4] Helmut Ulshöfer, the Frankfurt historian who collaborated on the editing of the letters, responded to criticisms of the play: "It's hard to explain how people could write letters like these to someone responsible for so much terror and suffering. . . . Part of it has to do with the relationship between women and power that has always existed, and the erotic aspect of that relationship."[5] The notion that the erotically infused daydreams confided to Hitler in epistles are a threat to feminism insofar as they seem to reinforce a stereotypical dynamic "between women and power" raises the question of how feminism defines the relationship between politics and desire. In this chapter I argue that contemporary feminism is deeply invested in an analogy between fascism and patriarchy. Nonfeminist theoretical formulations of fascist psychology frequently posit an originary, constitutional female masochism, and contemporary feminists have protested this. However, the idealized formulation that replaces pathological masochism, a "feminist" sexuality that fully reflects the ideological goals of feminism and hence does not harbor fantasies of submission or domination, presents its own set of problems. Just as democratic and liberal discourse in general has powerful investments in sexual respectability and in defining proper and deviant desire, feminism has its own version of this discourse of regulation, in which fascism is a central term.

As I have been arguing throughout this book, fascism was, from its earliest appearance, imagined—in propagandistic, psychoanalytic, historical, and literary discourses—as a political regime with a particularly sexual dynamic. The fascist scenario of power is typically presented either as homosexual attraction or as a gendered sadomasochistic encounter between a male fascist and a subservient female (or the collectively feminized "masses"). For Wilhelm Reich, "the sexual effect of a uniform, the erotically provocative effect of rhythmically executed goose-stepping, the exhibitionistic nature of militaristic procedures, have been more practically comprehended by a salesgirl or an average secretary than by our most erudite politicians" (*Mass Psychological Structure*, 33). Reich's characterization of fascism as a form of politics with a libidinal dynamic that is especially evident to women (and working-class women in particular) remained influential among scholars, who joined the "erudite politicians" in attempting to fathom the sociological dynamics of dictatorships. Throughout the 1950s and 1960s, the scenario of the fascist leader and his mesmerized female followers continued in theoretical formulations of fascism. When, in *Dialectic of Enlightenment*, Max Horkheimer and Theodor W. Adorno sought an analogy for describing totalitarianism, they echoed Reich's assumption that women are constitutionally susceptible to the tyrant's libidinal allure:

> Just as women adore the unmoved paranoiac, so nations genuflect before totalitarian Fascism. . . . They follow a man who looks through them, who take[s] them not as individuals but as material for any purpose. . . . The penetrating and distant gaze, the hypnotic and the disinterested look, are of the same type; in both cases the subject is extinguished. Because such gazes lack reflection those who do not think are electrified by them. (191)

Horkheimer and Adorno attribute to women less perceptiveness regarding the allure of fascism (and less intelligence) than Reich does. They imply that the state of thralldom that fascism produces in women is involuntary and masochistic; women—and the masses—are drawn to a man who does not grant them recognition. Certainly, Horkheimer and Adorno's conclusions are open to a feminist critique, but they also seem to be corroborated by *Love Letters to Adolf Hitler*. The German women writing to their Führer presupposed an intimate relationship with a man from whom they would never receive a reply. Some of the letters imagine making personal contact with Hitler at one of his massive rallies, at which he could only have "looked through" the faces in the crowd. But what is important about such theoretical formulations is that they are not applied just to fascist subjects. For Reich, "sexually frustrated" women in general—women in capitalist societies, not just women under fascism—are drawn to men and institutions that require their submission and the effacement of their autonomy. This broadening of gendered characteristics sets up "fascism" as a central term in postwar and postmodern feminist analyses. However, though we might expect the critical strategy against such theories to be specificity—that is, making distinctions between women in fascist cultures and women in nonfascist cultures and delineating the very different institutional forces that shape the lives of each—in fact, there is a strong interest within feminism to do just the opposite and to instead argue the profound parallels between fascism and nonfascist patriarchy.

The important and influential 1984 anthology *When Biology Became Destiny: Women in Weimar and Nazi Germany*, edited by Renate Bridenthal, Atina Grossman, and Marion Kaplan, begins with a note that places the book's essays on German history in relation to contemporary debates between U.S. feminists and the New Right about women's social welfare and, particularly, their reproductive rights. "Seeking a 'usable past,'" the editors write, "we looked back to German history where those issues were dramatically, unequivocally, and in the end horrifically decided" (xi). While cautioning against "facile or potentially misleading comparisons" (xii) between contemporary U.S. history and Nazi Germany, the editors frame their anthology "as a contribution to the debate on how feminists and the left—and leftist feminists in particular—could respond to the New Right's assault" on women's rights (xi).

This comparison between Nazi Germany and contemporary democratic culture underpins a great deal of the feminist discourse on fascism. Since the rise of fascism, feminists have perceived structural, ideological parallels between German National Socialism and Italy under Mussolini and their own national patriarchies. Simone de Beauvoir's *The Second Sex* (1949), for example, presents Nazism as a cautionary tale for women in democratic countries, pointing out that the *Kinder, Küche, Kirche* culture of Nazism arose at the precise historical moment that would most "systematically hinde[r] the progress of feminism" (141). Twenty years later, Kate Millett's *Sexual Politics* (1970) describes fascist ideology as "the most deliberate attempt ever made to revive and solidify extreme patriarchal conditions" (159) by dissolving existing women's groups, turning back the clock on women's participation in higher education and the workplace, banning abortion, preventing the distribution of contraceptives, and reinstating separate spheres for men and women. Another important feminist text published in 1970, Germaine Greer's *The Female Eunuch*, introduces the theories of "Nazi anthropologists" on its very first page to illustrate the specious ends to which biology is used to justify generalizations about gender and sexuality. In some feminist texts, the comparison of Nazi ideology and nonfascist patriarchy is carried much further. Betty Friedan's *Feminine Mystique* (1963) includes a chapter called "Progressive Dehumanization: The Comfortable Concentration Camp," which rather surprisingly compares Nazi oppression and contemporary U.S. patriarchy. Friedan argues that the passivity observed in suburban teenage girls and housewives is induced by a destruction of identity comparable to conditions in Nazi concentration camps (305). Although Friedan's analogy may seem extreme or irresponsible, versions of the fascism/patriarchy analogy appear in a range of feminist discourses, from Virginia Woolf's early writings on fascism to consciousness-raising texts like Friedan's to new historicist studies and recent feminist work informed by queer theory.[6]

What is gained by this analogy, and what is lost? Feminism gains an urgent historical precedent that shows gender- and sex-based oppression to be deadly. The historical imbalances between Nazism and democratic patriarchy are self-evident and do not need to be reiterated here. However, what is less evident is how the analogy erases questions about women's desire, complicity, and consent under both fascism and patriarchy. For example, Adrienne Rich, in *Of Woman Born* (1976), links the fascism/patriarchy analogy directly to "fascinating fascism":

> In the mid-1970s, a reaction [to feminism] has made itself felt in the form of what Susan Sontag has perceived as an eroticization of Nazism, a cult of fascist aesthetics. It is no accident, I think, that this fascination with the regalia of stormtroopers has arisen along with a pervasively changing consciousness and a new self-definition on the part of women. Nazism had a clear and unmistakable political formula for women and where they belonged. (65)

This reading has a compellingly neat sense of causality, but it slips all too quickly from "eroticization" and "fascination" to fascism's "political formula," losing the very terms that initiated the observation: desire and fantasy. Here "sexual politics," a concept that allowed feminists in the 1970s to perceive intimate links between the personal and the political, has the effect of effacing desire by translating it into political formulas. The specification of a particular consciousness and set of preferences as feminist is a foundational strategy for an argument that endorses some forms of sexuality as feminist and disapproves of others.[7] Although women also produced fictions of eroticized fascism, as this chapter will show, Rich assumes that this fascination is not shared by women with feminist convictions. This assumption is common in both feminist discussions of fascism and in feminist discourses on sexuality in general. The antipornography argument, for example, which was central to U.S. and British feminist discourse in the 1980s and 1990s, illustrates the way that fascism and sexual fantasy are positioned within one influential feminist discourse. Andrea Dworkin's *Pornography* (1979) enlists Nazism to argue that erotic fantasy and politics are both grounded in reality-based desires and wishes. Comparing the sexual politics of fascism with those of U.S. patriarchy, Dworkin posits the combination of sadism and racism in Nazism as a model that illustrates most dramatically how contemporary pornography oppresses women (142–47).

I do not mean to overstate the idea that feminism "represses" fantasy or to present a monolithic "feminism"; in fact, the most articulate resistances to the antipornography position have also been produced by feminists. Rather, I want to point out the strand of feminism that resembles those regulative democratic, liberal politics that, I have been arguing, construct a sexually deviant fascism in relation to a sexually normative, idealized politics. Just as the idea of the unconscious and nondemocratic desire played an important role in the early definition of German authoritarianism, the feminist analogy between fascism and patriarchy is organized around a particularly narrow notion of desire. Juliet Mitchell's *Psychoanalysis and Feminism* (1974) argues that "desire, phantasy, the unconscious or even unconsciousness are absent from the social realism of, amongst others, Reichian and feminist critiques" (9). Although true of many feminist formulations of sexuality and fantasy around 1974, this is by no means true of all feminist writing of the time: in the 1970s, Nancy Friday's and Shere Hite's works and Erica Jong's *Fear of Flying*, for example, presented radical but distinctively feminist reconsiderations of women's sexual fantasy.[8] Mitchell's point is even less valid today, with theorists such as Teresa de Lauretis, Laura Kipnis, Jacqueline Rose, and Sandra Lee Bartky reevaluating the relationship between feminism and fantasy. Nevertheless, the idea that anything less than total resistance to patriarchy is a feminist failure does strongly persist.

The feminist polemics of Dworkin, Friedan, and Rich are curiously comparable to eroticized fictions of fascism in that they also entail conflations, slippages, and erasures. Crucial historical imbalances are effaced in the feminist analogy (for example, the average 1950s home in the United States is described as a "comfortable concentration camp"), just as dimensions of fascism are distorted in eroticized fictions. But whereas eroticized fictions of fascism foreground their own investments in these distortions through representations of desire and fantasy, feminists who posit an analogy between fascism and patriarchy usually present the distortions as realistic, historically grounded parallels. This difference is most striking in the way the feminist alignment of U.S. patriarchy with fascism relies on a monolithically oppressive and nonerotic model of patriarchy. Desire is resolutely erased. This is especially true of the feminist writings that constituted the so-called sex wars of the 1980s, in which the political and social dangers of contemporary pornography and sadomasochism were often argued through comparisons to Nazism,[9] and in which slippages between the genocide of fascism and the infinitely more ambiguous "punishments" in sadomasochistic fantasy were endemic. The distinction Bataille, Genet, and the other authors discussed in this book make between erotic, consensual sadomasochism and fascist "sadism" is overwritten in these accounts. The motivation for such a collapse of registers is perhaps understandable if one believes deeply that any power imbalance is ethically corrupt. However, many levels of historical specificity must be ignored to make this comparison, which also relies on an indifference to scale. Erotic sadomasochism and nonfascist patriarchy both allow participants a degree of agency that fascism typically obliterated in its victims.

For Horkheimer and Adorno, the "fascist present" is a moment "in which the hidden side of things comes to light" (*Dialectic of Enlightenment*, 231)— and particularly the "hidden side" of sexuality. Just as many modernist writers figure fascism as democracy's "dark side," where "undemocratic" desires are aroused, much feminist discourse constructs its sexual politics against fascism. In this chapter, I argue that Marguerite Duras and Sylvia Plath trouble this construction. For Duras and Plath, fascism is symbolically male but is not a purely oppositional, onerous force in relation to women; rather, it involves complex libidinal relations. The point is not to establish Duras's and Plath's involvement in organized feminist movements or to show their "feminist" or "antifeminist" beliefs. Rather, I will examine their fiction as it demonstrates a struggle with the relationship between sexual desire or fantasy and politics, a relationship that underpins the feminist fascism/patriarchy analogy but is not usually acknowledged.

The respective contexts in which Duras and Plath wrote—postwar and postmodern France and the United States in the 1950s—permit different degrees of representational freedom. For Duras, eroticized Nazism raises the phantom of women's erotic treason. However, the political pressure on such a position in postwar France, when Duras wrote *Hiroshima mon amour*, and the still fraught relationship France had with its past in the 1980s, when *La douleur* appeared, produced a narrative that is not completely articulated but that must enact its own repression. Erotic relationships with the enemy are not just fantasies to Duras but are rendered real and visible when they are actively, publicly punished in the purge following the Liberation. Duras's texts are, as Lynn A. Higgins has suggested (borrowing Linda Hutcheon's term), "historiographic metafictions" that are concerned with how the past is known and constructed in the present (*New Novel, New Wave*, 3). Duras obsessively reworks the ethical question of wartime erotic collaboration. Plath writes with a very different relationship to the past and with more distance from the war. Nazism is an iconic event for Plath, a storehouse of images of evil, rather than the intimate political and national experience it is for Duras. Although Plath was criticized for presumptuous or glib metaphors of Nazism and the Holocaust, this distance, I will suggest, permits her to go further than Duras in her exploration of women's erotic complicity with patriarchy, intensifying interrogation of the terms of the feminist patriarchy/fascism analogy. Just as, in the previous chapters, I suggested that many modernist writers perceived fascism as expressing repressed fantasies of the democratic subject, I will now propose that the image of the subjugated woman embracing the fascist beast is a recurring, if disavowed, fantasy of feminism.

Early Formulations of Feminism and Fascism: Katherine Burdekin and Virginia Woolf

Katherine Burdekin's *Swastika Night* was published in Britain in 1937, under the pseudonym "Murray Constantine." Appearing twelve years before George Orwell's *1984*, *Swastika Night* was not only one of the earliest science fiction novels to take as its subject the increasingly powerful European fascist dictatorships. It was also one of the first feminist critiques of fascism, pointing out the violence and masculine domination of Nazi culture.[10] Set in Germany in the "seventh century of Hitlerian millennium," Burdekin's dystopia is dominated by the Japanese and Nazi empires. Jews have been completely exterminated. The novel opens in the "Holy Hitler chapel," a building in the shape of a swastika. A yearly ceremony, the "Quickening of the Blood," is in progress. A Holy Knight encourages his congregation to "believe in pride, in courage, in violence, in brutality, in blood-shed, in ruthlessness, and all other soldierly and heroic virtues." He leads his flock in a sober recitative specifying the ascending social hierarchy of the culture: worm (at the bottom), woman, man, foreign Hitlerian, Nazi, Knight, and finally "Der Fuehrer" (7). This society is founded on men's disgust and scorn for women. Male citizens are taught that women are morally and intellectually only slightly more advanced than worms, and that the way the "Hitlerian" race is perpetuated is through rape (13). Along with racial and religious discrimination and nationalism, this feudal order of male supremacy is propped up by women's subordination and sexual violence.

Swastika Night introduces many of the issues that Virginia Woolf takes up in her treatise against fascism published the following year, *Three Guineas*. The pretext for *Three Guineas* is a question that was addressed to Woolf: "How in your opinion are we to prevent war?" (3). Woolf is surprised: war has always been an affair among and for men. "Since when before has an educated man asked a woman how in her opinion war can be prevented?" The question reminds Woolf of H. G. Wells's assertion that "there has been no perceptible woman's movement to resist the practical obliteration of their freedom by Fascists or Nazis" (43). Woolf responds that if this is so, it is because British women are already subject to a form of totalitarianism—

patriarchy—that hinders their ability to fight fascism abroad. Both British patriarchs and fascist dictators, Woolf observes, insist that women's activities be limited to home and family; both deny women basic rights and any degree of self-realization. Aren't Nazi dictators and British patriarchs "the same thing"? (53), Woolf asks. In both systems, women are subjugated and men wield all sociopolitical power. Woolf bolsters her structural comparisons between fascism and patriarchy with an inquiry into the motivations behind men's domination of women.

> What are the powerful and subconscious motives that are raising the hackles on your [men's] side of the table? Is the old savage who has killed a bison asking the other old savage to admire his prowess? Is the tired professional man demanding sympathy and resenting competition? Is the patriarch calling for the siren? Is dominance craving for submission? And, most persistent and difficult of all the questions that our silence covers, what possible satisfaction can dominance give to the dominator? (129)

As if reworking Hegel's master-slave dialectic, Woolf stipulates a complex series of motives in which the patriarch—the "dominator"—may in fact be dependent on the "siren," and in which dominance may even be symptomatic of a "craving for submission." The patriarch or tyrant is subject to insecurities and compensations stemming from "subconscious" motives that are vigorously repressed, lest they disturb the patriarchal social order.[11] In an illuminating footnote, Woolf presents as "evidence of the complex nature of satisfaction of dominance" an article in the *Daily Herald* from August 1, 1936, regarding a wife's complaint to Bristol Police Court that her husband makes her call him "Sir," "clean his boots, fetch his razor when he shaves, and speak up promptly when he asks [her] questions" (181). The same edition of the *Herald* reported that Sir E. F. Fletcher "urged the House of Commons to stand up to dictators." For Woolf, these articles together "would seem to show that the common consciousness which includes husband, wife, and House of Commons is feeling at one and the same moment the desire to dominate, the need to comply in order to keep peace, and the necessity of dominating the desire for dominance—a psychological conflict which serves to explain much that appears inconsistent and turbulent in contemporary opinion" (181–82). It is not clear if this double consciousness—domination and complicity—is present in men and women alike or whether the terms are gendered (that is, whether men desire to dominate and women to submit in order to keep the peace) and interlocking pieces of a total social consciousness. However, given the psychic ambiguities Woolf perceives at play in masculine domination, one would expect a similar analysis of women's relationship to domination. In fact, as *Three Guineas* unfolds, Woolf does not, evidently, perceive the wife as "craving" either submission or domination. The "need to comply" is a perfunctory means of keeping peace rather than a source of libidinal gratification.

From this picture of domestic British patriarchy, Woolf moves on to Francisco Franco's dictatorship, describing the photographs of "dead bodies and ruined houses that the Spanish Government sends [the British press] almost weekly" (141).[12] Then, like a camera moving in for a close-up, Woolf lights on another, more corporeal, image:

> Another picture has imposed itself upon the foreground. It is the figure of a man; some say, others deny, that he is Man himself, the quintessence of virility, the perfect type of which all the others are imperfect adumbrations. He is a man certainly. His eyes are glazed; his eyes glare. His body, which is braced in an unnatural position, is tightly cased in a uniform. Upon the breast of that uniform are sewn several medals and other mystic symbols. His hand is upon a sword. He is called in German and Italian Führer or Duce; in our own language Tyrant or Dictator. And behind him lie ruined houses and dead bodies—men, women, and children. But we have not laid that picture before you in order to excite once more the sterile emotion of hate. On the contrary it is in order to release other emotions such as the human figure, even thus crudely in a coloured photograph, arouses in us who are human beings. For it suggests a connection and for us a very important connection. It suggests that the public and the private worlds are inseparably connected. . . . It suggests that we cannot dissociate ourselves from that figure but are ourselves that figure. (142)

Woolf's description of the dictator in the flesh repeats the ubiquitous tropes of fascist masculinity, including the stiff uniform, hardness, distance, virility, and cruelty. These are also the typical tropes of the enemy portrayed in propaganda, but Woolf explicitly distances her depiction from that medium, used to "excite . . . the sterile emotion of hate." Instead, she presents the picture of the dictator in order to "excite" or "arouse" "other emotions." Woolf's language suggests libidinal identifications; indeed, her description of the displayed fascist body includes the very terms that Jean Genet, Theodor Reik, Wilhelm Reich, and others read as simultaneously oppressive and potentially erotic. In images of eroticized fascism, it is precisely the fascist's tight control—he is "braced" and "encased"—and distance that render him seductive. This is not to suggest that every reader responds similarly to the same images, since libidinal readings of fascism such as Genet's are consciously framed as countercultural and idiosyncratic. Propaganda images do work "properly" on most readers—though they do regularly activate libidinal fantasies, as in Kipling's "Mary Postgate," for example—which are not recognized as such. For Woolf, the other "emotion" aroused by this dictator's body is identification, but a resolutely nonerotic identification: a recognition of "ourselves"—British patriarchy—in the dictator.

Woolf never names the other "emotion" excited by this figure: identification, as Woolf describes it, is not an emotion the way "hate" is. In *Mrs. Dalloway*, however, we glimpse alternative emotions aroused by a "tyrant" figure. The "embittered" pacifist Quaker, Miss Kilman, with her earnest devotion to righteous causes, reminds her rival, Clarissa Dalloway, of "one of those spectres who stand astride us and suck up half our life-blood, dominators and tyrants" (12). Anxious about Kilman's opinion of her class status and her relationship to her daughter, Clarissa feels "hatred" at the threat of "this brutal monster." Kilman, in turn, has "an overmastering desire to overcome" and unmask the upper-class Clarissa. She fantasizes about "subduing" Clarissa to "make her feel her mastery . . . humiliate her; bring her to her knees" (125). Women's "pleasure" in domination does appear in such fantasies, which deploy political and libidinal language. This could be attributable to a preference for, and cathexis of, a female rather than a male body; regardless, this atypically vivid and libidinally charged account of a pacifist's fantasy of domination suggests that the "tyrant" may arouse a number of ideological, psychic, and somatic conflicts that are not addressed in *Three Guineas*. Like Burdekin, Woolf limits her purview of fascism and patriarchy to dynamics in which women have no sexual identification with or libidinal desire for the patriarch/dictator.

This raises a problem that has persisted from the early days of the organized feminist movement to the present: the status of eroticism in a progressive movement for equality. At the end of the nineteenth century, many women's movement in Britain and the United States were also social purity movements. Seeking to reverse the old association of woman with Nature, of woman as therefore lacking (and needing) "masculine" civilization, many women's movements held up woman as the civilized sex and man as the libidinally driven "beast."[13] For many early feminists, sexual desire simply was not a feminist issue—or rather, it was an issue that could threaten to derail the more pressing concerns at hand, such as economic parity and suffrage. At this point, feminism had a great stake in proving its moral righteousness and social soundness, including its ability to rise above bodily desires and libidinal attachments. And at a time when birth control and abortion were not legally available and many venereal diseases could not be cured, sexual activity entailed heavy risks for women. However, the move to separate women from "mere physicality," to show their intellectual and moral dimensions, often led to an oversimplified picture of female desire. These oversimplifications continue in antipornography feminism in which women are understood as naturally nonviolent victims of ubiquitous male violence. As Jessica Benjamin points out, this necessarily "implies that violence, transgression, abomination . . . are alien to and absent from women. . . . And this conclusion is indeed problematic for feminists" (*Like Subjects, Love Objects*, 176–77). Reconverting women into the sexually pure Angel in the House was explicitly not Woolf's intention, but her blind spot to the more complex kinds of complicity binding women to patriarchy—a blind spot reinforced by the choice of fascism as a point of comparison to patriarchy—has persisted in many subsequent feminist formulations.

In retrospect, Woolf's act of equating women under British patriarchy to subjects under foreign dictators and her question—"Should we not help her to crush him in our own country before we ask her to help us to crush him abroad?" (53)—obviously grossly underestimate the violence of fascist activity. Still, the affinities between fascism and patriarchy that Woolf sets forth in *Three Guineas* proved crucial for subsequent feminist analyses. Even with Woolf's evasions of the matter of desire—and, I will argue, even *because* of it—the very bringing together of feminism and fascism proved fruitful for later feminist writers, including Duras and Plath. Both view fascism as a force that is politically oppressive but that also embodies those fantasies of domination and submission that are repudiated by progressive politics and particularly by feminism. If, in some instances, these images seem to confirm the theories of Reich, Horkheimer, and Adorno concerning the masochism of women, they also contradict the idea that women's real erotic desires favor balance, peace, and equality. These tenets are central to almost all forms of feminism and are also the basic tenets of nearly all democratic, liberal, and progressive political positions. But what do equality and nonviolence mean in the realm of eroticism and fantasy? Duras and Plath articulate rather than exorcise fantasies that contradict or seem to threaten a politics of sexual equality. In their works, the notion that "every woman adores a fascist" is both a political fallacy and a persistent fantasy.

"I Kissed My Enemy": Duras

Throughout her novels, Marguerite Duras dramatizes what she has called "impossible" love: love between people of different classes, races, and nations;

between siblings, between young and old, heterosexual and homosexual, and mad and sane. Female desire is always at the center of her tales, and for this reason she has been embraced as a voice of feminist poetics. In her stories of self-destructive and unsatisfied desire, as Leslie Hill observes in *Marguerite Duras: Apocalyptic Desires*, "the most sexually desirable of other bodies is that very body with which, for reasons of cultural custom, social or personal circumstances, or even sexual orientation, no relationship is possible" (139). There is, however, one instance of "impossible love" that even Duras has difficulty writing about, and even more difficulty championing: an *amour fou* between a French girl and a Nazi soldier during the Occupation.

In *Hiroshima mon amour*, her 1958 script for the film by Alain Resnais, Duras writes about a Frenchwoman in her thirties who is in Hiroshima in 1957, playing the part of a Red Cross nurse in an "international" film about peace. She meets and has an affair with a Japanese architect. While they are in bed, the Japanese man asks, "What did Hiroshima mean for you, in France?" She replies that it signaled the end of the war and her departure from her home town of Nevers, a place where she was "mad with hate." As the film unfolds, her past in Nevers is told through images and through her elliptical comments to her Japanese lover. In 1944, living in Nevers, she had an affair with a German soldier. They met secretly and planned to go to Bavaria and marry, but he was shot before they could leave the country, on the night Nevers was liberated (66). A group of angry townspeople found the girl clutching his body; they seized her as a traitor and shaved her head in the town square. Her mother, fearing the townspeople would "do something more to her daughter" (95), then locked her in the cellar for months.

After the Liberation of France, local vigilante groups rounded up women who were suspected of having had sexual relations with Germans and brought them before public tribunals.[14] "There was apparently no national directive to shear heads," Corran Laurens notes, "but the practice was widespread. . . . As early as December 1943, a warning appeared in *L'Aurore* that women associating with Germans would be branded."[15] These acts were driven by the same spirit of mob revenge that Genet describes in the cinema scene in *Funeral Rites*. And, although the enveloping anger of post-Liberation swept up many people, most quickly disassociated themselves from these acts of revenge, only to have the memories exhumed twenty years later by the movement collectively known as the *mode rétro*. The treatment of the *tondues* emerges as one of the key themes of the *mode rétro*, since this dramatic and terrifying practice was one memory many French citizens wanted to forget and was typically erased from official versions of France's glorious Liberation. Ophuls's *Sorrow and the Pity*, for example, one of the most important contributions to the reevaluation of the war and the Liberation period by the *mode rétro*, shows scenes of nude *tondues* herded through town squares, walking a gauntlet of angry villagers screaming and prodding at them. In *Sisters in the Resistance*, Margaret Collins Weitz suggests that among all the acts of revenge in the *épuration*, the treatment of the *tondues* was exceptional: "What is striking in all accounts of the 'cleansing' is the intensity of the vengeance unleashed against women who consorted with the enemy" (176). The fact that the female body is the chosen site for punishing treason is consistent with historical and psychoanalytic accounts of fascism that see it as a male force to which women are especially drawn.[16] Women were supposed to be most susceptible—sexually so—to fascism, and their sexual treason posed a threat to the social order that was different from male political treason. Political traitors could be jailed or executed. Sexual treason—or "horizontal collaboration," as it is sometimes called—presented a different problem: irrational and corporeal, it was answered in kind with punishments of dubious legality. In making her protagonist a *tondue*, Duras stirs up feelings and memories about this nationally detested and repudiated figure of treasonous female desire.

As a Resistance fighter and former member of the Communist Party who was critical of the French Left's ideological rigidity, Duras examines the wartime myths of both the right and the left.[17] Having joined the French Communist Party (PCF) in 1944, at the height of her Resistance involvement, Duras became disillusioned with the Party's division after the Liberation, especially on the question of the Soviet Union. Duras was distressed by the Party's internal repression of dissent and spoke out against it. She resigned in January 1950 and was officially expelled the following month. This fall away from formal political alliances and rejection of the left's dogmatism played a crucial role in Duras's political outlook.[18] In telling the story of a love affair between a *tondue* and a Nazi, Duras breached perhaps the strongest cultural prohibition in postwar France. However, her treatment of the affair in *Hiroshima mon amour* involves narrative tactics of evasion, postponement, and displacement that are unusual even for Duras, whose narratives are famous for their elliptical, elusive style, signalling the level of authorial resistance to the subject posed within Duras's own narrative.

Within the book published as *Hiroshima mon amour*, there are multiple layers of text and several different renderings of the same narrative. There is a main script, the "Scenario," which Resnais's film follows almost word for word, and which is supplemented by Duras's directorial notes. There is also a synopsis Duras wrote after the film was shot, which tells the story in broad thematic terms and adds interpretive detail. Finally, there is an extensive collection of appendices which, as Duras notes in her preface, "were not included in the original scenario (July, 1958)," but "were annotated before the shooting in France (December, 1958)": "('Pretend you were annotating not a future film, but a finished film,' Resnais told me.) They therefore represent a work apart from the script. . . . In the script itself only passing reference is made to them" (7). Each of these appendices plays an important role in the story of the Frenchwoman: the script alone tells only half the story, while the appendices supplement, clarify and, in some cases, contradict the main narrative.

The woman's past emerges in stops and starts throughout the narrative set in Hiroshima. Scenes of her with the Japanese man are spliced together with scenes of her with her German lover, indicating the increasing encroachment of the woman's past on the present. Cathy Caruth's *Unclaimed Experience*, Sharon Willis's *Marguerite Duras: Writing on the Body*, and other works have argued that the narrative gaps, elisions, and epistemological uncertainties of *Hiroshima mon amour* reflect the Frenchwoman's traumatic memories. Lynne A. Higgins agues that the "general 'inability' to tell coherent stories"—which Caruth and Willis link to Freud's definition of the hysteric's discourse—is a constant feature of the *nouveau roman*, as are the "asocial behavior and ahistorical attitudes" in the "absence of any clear perspective, on the part of either the characters or the stories, toward social and historical reality" (*New Novel, New Wave*, 21). Rather than look at how the woman's past in Nevers is repeated and recuperated with the man in Hiroshima, I will focus on how certain parts of that story cannot be recuperated and are instead placed entirely outside the main narrative. Both traumatic and transgressive, these phenomena function too specifically and idiosyncratically within the narrative to be attributed to generic New Wave strategies.

Duras's explanation that the appendices represent "a work apart from the script" is intriguing in light of the stories they contain. By definition the appendix is a subsidiary text that is not essential to the completeness of the primary text. Duras's title for one section of the appendix, "NOCTURNAL NOTATIONS," indicates the tone of these texts, a shadowy darkness behind the main script, composed, as it were, from the Nevers cellar. The appendices in *Hiroshima mon amour*, most of which center on the girl's affair in Nevers and her punishment in the cellar, are a site onto which Duras displaces crucial dimensions of the love story that she chooses not to include in the main script. Some appendices emphasize details of the main script or shift narrative perspective. The girl's punishment, for example, is told quite differently in the appendices and in the main script. In Resnais's film, there is a shot of the woman as a girl sitting with her face smeared with blood, her eyes closed, and her hair sheared. She is surrounded by women, one of whom holds a pair of scissors. A man in a white shirt and tie stands behind her. In an appendix, Duras elaborates on the details of this scene:

They shaved her head.

They do it almost absent-mindedly. She had to be shaved. Let's do it. We have plenty of other things to do somewhere else. But we're doing our duty. . . .

They are shaving someone's head somewhere in France. Here it's the druggist's daughter. The wind bears the strains of the "Marseillaise" to the crowd and encourages the exercise of a hasty, ridiculous justice. They haven't time enough to be intelligent. . . .

After she has been shaved, the girl still waits. She's at their disposal. The city was made to suffer. This compensates. Helps work up an appetite. The girl has to leave. It's ugly, maybe disgusting. (98–99)

In the screenplay, the avengers are figured only through the damage they inflict on the heroine. But in this appendix, Duras sketches the psychology of the vigilante group from both a first- and a third-person point of view, switching the narrative voice from the distanced and judgmental third-person "they" to the identificatory first person ("Let's do it"), a precarious balance of identification and disapprobation. Duras's appendices bring out the irony of this "hasty, ridiculous justice" set against the official song of French freedom (just as in Genet's *Funeral Rites*, the militiaman Riton is knocked out and raped while the "Marseillaise" is heard through the window). Behind the posture of patriotism and justice, Duras implies, is gratuitous, hypocritical, and misdirected violence.

Other appendices add crucial information that may alter our understanding of the main script. For example, the reader learns only in an appendix—to be precise, in a footnote to the appendix (thus in a doubly displaced text)—that the Frenchwoman's mother spent the Occupation in the south of France because she "was Jewish [or separated from her husband]" (103, brackets in the original). The suggested detail that the Frenchwoman may be Jewish intensifies the significance of her affair with a Nazi. Still, there is a note of doubt in the footnote, which marks Duras's hesitancy to develop the full political implications of the affair. The appendices in *Hiroshima mon amour* reveal Duras's narrative hesitations and censorships of the main narrative. They also contain an intensified account of France's traumatic history—the treatment of the *tondues*, which was excised from official accounts of the Liberation.

In one of the most significant appendices, "Nevers. (As a reminder) / [The Frenchwoman] herself tells of her life at Nevers," is the fullest and only linear account of the Frenchwoman's experiences in Nevers. In its clarity and distinct chronological progression, this text stands out from the others gathered under the title *Hiroshima mon amour.* It suggests a nostalgic desire to narrate in a more traditional style. It also suggests the repetition compulsion, with its attempt to restage and correct the trauma. But the appendix does more than this: it reveals residual anxiety produced by telling the story of the eroticized Nazi in the main script. The Frenchwoman begins with a commonplace observation made by civilians during wartime: "The only men in the city were German. I was seventeen years old. The war was interminable. My youth was interminable." She hints at what is to follow: "My mind was already confused by different standards of morality" (104). She recalls meeting the German soldier (she calls him "the enemy" until their secret "marriage," and, even then, gives him no proper name) in her father's pharmacy: "I bandaged his hand as I had been taught, filled with hate. The enemy thanked me. . . . And yet, that evening, I felt especially fed up with the war" (104).

One evening, when she is playing the piano for her father, the French girl sees the German outside her window in the darkness, listening. "The enemy raises his head toward me and smiles slightly. I feel as though I were witnessing a crime. I close the shutters as upon some loathsome scene" (92). This sequence recalls Vercors's *The Silence of the Sea*, with its suggestion that an exceptional German, von Ebrennac, is more sensitive than the average *boche*. But, having shut out the *boche*, the girl in *Hiroshima* experiences a shift in her feeling toward the enemy:

> I knew that for the first time in my life a man had listened to me play the piano.
>
> The man came back the next day. Then I saw his face. How could I keep from looking at him again? . . .
>
> I began to dream of an enemy, at night, during the day. And in my dreams morality and immorality were so intertwined that soon I couldn't tell one from the other. (105–6)

The German follows her silently around Nevers, and finally they meet in the woods and thereafter arrange to meet secretly. In the screenplay, Duras calls for "a shot of love at Nevers. Bicycles racing. The forest, etc. . . . Rivers. Quays. Poplar trees in the wind, etc. The quay deserted. The garden" (48). Accordingly, Resnais's film shows bucolic scenes of the young woman riding her bike in the beautiful forests of Nevers, pedaling down pathways deep in the woods. "We kissed behind the ramparts," the woman recalls. "Deathly afraid, but utterly happy, I kissed my enemy. . . . It was inside the ramparts of the city that I became his wife" (88). A subsequent heading of a note in the appendix takes up her euphemism and announces, "THE MARRIAGE AT NEVERS" (92). Swept away like Emma Bovary in a romanticized vision of her furtive affair, the French girl idealizes a "marriage" that transcends provincial Nevers, but this illusion is quickly crushed. Speaking in Hiroshima to her Japanese lover, the Frenchwoman herself seems to scoff at her youthful fantasies of "marriage" to the soldier. She belittles herself as the "Silly little girl. / Who dies of love at Nevers. / Little girl with shaven head, I bequeath you to oblivion. / Three-penny story" (80), reading her own story as puerile and cheap.

In her commentaries, Duras is ambivalent about whether this affair should be read as pathetic or noble. She considers the scene of the crime, the city of Nevers, to be a symbol of France. It is "bounded on one side by the Loire river" ("the best-known, the most beautiful in France" [89]) and is bordered "on the other by the ramparts. . . . Nevers closed in on itself. . . . At Nevers, more than anywhere else they keep a close watch over love. . . . Love is unpardonable there. At Nevers, love is the great sin" (90). Duras proposes that the girl's treason pales beside the self-righteousness of parochial France, where love and desire are vigorously policed. In her synopsis, Duras comments on the *tondues:* "To shave a girl's head because she has loved—really loved—an official enemy of her country, is the ultimate of horror and stupidity" (12). This treason is different from the treason of Genet's *Funeral Rites.* More akin to *The Silence of the Sea*, this is a love born not of rebellion but of attraction in spite of politics. It is the love of unexpected virtue in the exceptional German. "I excluded this enemy from all others," Duras's Frenchwoman muses in the appendix (106). Significantly, the German soldier in *Hiroshima mon amour* is never called a "Nazi" in the script, nor is there a swastika on his uniform in Resnais's film. In order to make him believably human, Duras removes the most obvious symbols signaling his "Naziness," in direct opposition to propagandistic and more mainstream representations of Nazis, which were pure symbol, the stereotype of the evil *boche.* In Duras's narrative treatment, the "Naziness" of the German is not directly eroticized; although the ways the German manages to overcome his political affiliations are the basis of the romantic plot, they too are not precisely eroticized.

Instead, the *tondue's* punishment and her masochism are treated in a highly sexual manner by Duras.

Far removed from the romantic scenes of the Loire and the Nevers quays, the scenes of the period the French girl spent locked in the cellar are starkly terrifying; they are also infused with the erotic dynamics delicately veiled by the Frenchwoman's own account of her affair with the German soldier. In the main script, the affair is depicted almost exclusively in the flashbacks of the girl riding her bike to meet her lover in the forests away from the town. The absent sexual relationship with the Nazi seems to be displaced onto the Japanese man in the present (the opening shots show the intertwined bodies of the Frenchwoman and the Japanese man). But in the appendices, which purport to tell the whole story of the affair, the Nazi is again remarkably absent. That is, his body as an object of desire is missing: he is only an object of desire when he is dead. Duras writes in an appendix that the French girl dreams of her dead lover when she is in the cellar and "wants him so badly she can't bear it any longer. . . Her mouth is moist. Her pose is that of a lustful woman, immodest to the point of vulgarity . . . disgusting" (96). She "scrapes her hands like an idiot" against the rough concrete walls "and then sucks her blood. Grimaces and begins again. One day, on a quay, she learned to love blood. Like an animal, a bitch" (95). Only an "animal" could love a man who was her enemy. Only a "bitch" would sleep with him. Even the damp cellar walls "full of saltpeter" (59) are an aphrodisiac to her: "[She] eats the walls. She also kisses them. She is in a universe of walls. A man's memory is in these walls" (96). "Lustful," "disgusting," and "bitch": Duras's descriptions exceed Resnais's images, which instead project sympathetic abjection and desperation.

It is unclear whether the Nevers affair is a silly "three-penny story" or an impossible love that (boldly or stupidly) defies convention. If we read it as triumphant vengeance on the small-minded Nevers hypocrites, we still have to account for the fact that it is only after the affair, when the girl is punished, that Duras allows its sexual dimensions to emerge—and even then, only in an appendix. This is a love that has to "go underground" in several senses. Duras exiles the sexual relationship to a subterranean appendix of the main script, and then sexualizes the punishment rather than the affair itself. The treasonous sexual passion can only, it seems, be expressed in this masochistic (pathologized), retroactive, and objectless form. (Although the eroticism of the scenes in Hiroshima might be read as a reflection of the affair in Nevers, this too is a displacement.) Duras's appendices begin the work of the *mode rétro*—unearthing and exposing repressed parts of history— but they do not bring their findings up into the main narrative. The *tondue* is theoretically a perfect example of a challenge to socially approved behavior and conventions and seems to embody Duras's determined dismantling of the idea that desire and politics are coextensive and harmonious. In practice, however, the *tondue's* story is too ethically inflammatory to occupy a comfortably central place in either the Frenchwoman's consciousness or in Duras's own narrative.

One other instance of eroticized fascism appears in Duras's work—in her memoir, *The War* (*La douleur*)—but this also requires a narrative evasion. Published much later than *Hiroshima*, in 1985, *The War* is a compendium of Duras's experiences as a Resistance fighter during the Occupation. In the first part she names herself as the protagonist; in the second part, the cast of characters from the previous part remains, with the exception of Duras. In her place, a female protagonist called "Thérèse" appears. In "Albert of the Capitals," Thérèse and her Resistance group gather to deal with an informer. She is especially cruel in her interrogation and in her order that he be tortured. Other members of her Resistance group suggest she has gone too far, and that the information she is seeking—the color of forged identification cards—is not worth the savage beating she is inflicting on the man. In these harrowing scenes of escalating torture, Thérèse's behavior is startlingly brutal.

In another episode, "Ter of the Militia," the Resistance group, including Thérèse, is transporting a captured militiaman to a new location. He, "Ter," is twenty-three and handsome:

> You can see the muscles in his long young forearms. He has a narrow waist and his leather belt is drawn tight. . . . A blue silk shirt. Suede shoes. His belt's made of raw pigskin. If it wasn't for the silk, the suede, and the belt you might take him for a member of the group. . . . He hasn't a thought in his head, only desires; he's got a body made for pleasure, riotous living, fighting, girls. (150)

The differences between Duras's sensuous description of the fascist body, "a body made for pleasure," and Woolf's description of the fascist body in *Three Guineas*, previously cited, are remarkable. Both bodies are marked by tautness ("his body, which is braced in an unnatural position, is tightly cased in a uniform" [Woolf]; "his leather belt is drawn tight" [Duras]) and distance. But where Woolf's dictator is a static and foreboding symbol of oppression, Duras's Nazi collaborator is also suffused with a libidinal allure for her narrator, over and against his repulsive politics. Thérèse is attracted to Ter and fascinated by his dumb good nature and animalistic sexuality. He is also her double, as the similarity of their names makes evident.

Thérèse's tendency toward sadism and her erotic interest in a militiaman set her apart from the myth of the noble Resistance fighter—and from the persona "Marguerite Duras" in the earlier part of *La douleur*. However, in her introduction to the second part of *La douleur*, Duras collapses the distance between character and author: *"Thérèse is me. The person who tortures the informer is me. So also is the one who feels like making love to Ter, the member of the Militia. Me. I give you the torturer along with the rest of the texts. Learn to read them properly: they are sacred"* (115). Addressing the sadism of the politically righteous—even those devoted to "freedom"—Duras does away with Woolf's bifurcation of male aggression and female submission, and with the imagined boundaries between the mind of the brutal fascist and that of the virtuous socialist freedom fighter.[19] Significantly, it is only with the alibi of the third person that Duras can voice these critiques and the sexual appeal of the enemy. Just as the erotic treason of *Hiroshima mon amour* is buried in the appendices, in *La douleur* a consideration of the sexual appeal of the enemy requires the smoke screen of the third-person voice, "Thérèse." As the libido "betrays" Resistance principles, a reconfigured picture of the relationship between fantasy and history emerges, a picture in which even those characters most socially committed to justice have a fantasy life based on the very system of oppression they fight politically.

Plath: "Appalled by Secret Want"

Sylvia Plath's 1962 poem "Daddy" (published in her collection *Ariel*) is probably the most infamous literary example of sexualized fascist imagery. Her snarling declaration that "every woman adores a Fascist / The boot in the face, the brute / Brute heart of a brute like you" (50) is as much a part of the Plath mythology as her gas-oven suicide, which mirrored the Holocaust imagery in her poems. Although references to fascism and the Holocaust appear in only a handful of her poems, they loom large in Plath criticism and are particularly problematic for feminist critics. Whereas Duras's poetics of indeterminacy and rhetorical reversals have generally drawn critics' attention away from her depictions of Nazism, Plath's fiercely concrete words and explosive images have been a lightning rod for the "unanimous impulse to moralize" about her work. Where Duras's writing treats extreme but plausible scenarios, Plath's poems are more clearly cast as fantasy—almost dreamscapes of Nazism. Duras's Nazis are unusual, but they are treated realistically; Plath's Nazis, and their victims, are more distorted and fantasmatic and often materialize through metaphors. These different narrative treatments reflect the two authors' very different relationships to Nazism. Like those of Vercors, Bataille, Bellmer, and Genet, Duras's images of fascism were influenced by her own experiences of fascism and by the accounts of Nazism circulating in France at the time. But just as the speaker of "Daddy" lives in the shadow of her dead "fascist" father, Plath had a mediated relation to the imagery of World War II. In fact, it was no less powerful for this re-move, which rather seems to make the events more open to fantasmatic dis-tortion. As James E. Young remarks in " 'I May Be a Bit of a Jew': The Holo-caust Confessions of Sylvia Plath," the fact that the Holocaust "was not known first-hand by Plath makes it all the more typological, all the more de-pendent on the forms and figures of the media by which Plath has come to these events" (140). This distance from Nazism seems to have freed Plath from the restrictions Duras places on her writing. Just as Communism was the bête noire for the United States during the Cold War, Nazism has a cen-tral place in Plath's poetic lexicon as a case of absolute historical terror. Plath uses Nazi genocide to imagine the most provocative libidinal dramas. Just as Duras takes up the German soldier to challenge the polarizing myths of France's political left and its rigid understanding of desire, Plath deploys im-ages of World War II to push to its limits an exploration of the relationship between politics and fantasy. Plath returns to the link between fascist and pa-triarchal oppression forged by early feminist writers such as Burdekin and Woolf, but then infuses both terms of the analogy with sadomasochistic erotics. Fascism signifies a series of opposites for Plath: subjugation and op-pression, control and freedom, destruction and creation, sadism and masochism, hate and love. These pairs are generally polarized by gender: Daddy and his daughter, who sees herself as a Jew; Herr Doktor and Lady Lazarus. However, like Thérèse, Duras's autobiographical persona in *La douleur*, Plath's female speakers identify with both the Jewish victim (though not all victims of the Holocaust were Jewish by any means, they are gener-ally so in Plath's work) and the Nazi torturer.

In her book, *The Haunting of Sylvia Plath*, Jacqueline Rose brilliantly dis-cusses Plath's relationship to fantasy and sexuality. While Rose reads Plath's Nazi images primarily in terms of the Holocaust and second-generation Holocaust survivor fantasies, I will focus on Plath's work as a continuation of the responses to fascism forged earlier in the century. Also, whereas Rose suggests that Plath's case reveals a particular relationship women have to fan-tasy, I read Plath's work as continuous with the authors discussed in previous chapters whose representations of fascism are not limited to a particular gen-der or sexual orientation but are rather part of a larger response to their cul-ture's strategic constructions of fascism.

Like Duras's work, Plath's poetry expresses a suspicion of ideologies of sexual normativity and of America's strategic political scapegoating.

> Why do we electrocute men for murdering an individual and then pin a purple heart on them for mass slaughter of someone arbitrarily labeled "enemy"? Weren't the Russians Communists when they helped us slap down the Germans? And now. What would we do with the Russian nation if we bombed it to bits. . . . How could we control them under our "democratic" system, we, who even now are losing that precious commodity, freedom of speech?[20]

Plath's critiques of the United States in the Cold War era, of militarism, anti-Communism, propaganda, the Rosenberg executions, Nagasaki, Hiroshima, and the limitations imposed on the women of her era, put her in a position similar to authors such as Lawrence, Genet, and Vercors, who were also critical of many elements of nationalism and contemporary democratic politics. Whereas Duras questions the hypocrisies of Resistance politics, Plath explores democracy and pacifism, which for her is a position of unacknowledged impulses of aggression and masochism. Like Duras, Lawrence, Genet, and others, Plath is interested in libidinal investments in politics and particularly in disavowed desires.

The poem "Daddy" brings together both terms (fascism and patriarchy) of Woolf's *Three Guineas* analogy. However, in "Daddy" the speaker's relationship to both terms is highly ambivalent, with equal measures of hatred and erotic desire, the very factor that Woolf carefully excludes from her treatise. Beneath the speaker's bitter hatred for the "Panzer-man," whom she needs to destroy—"Daddy, I have had to kill you" (*Ariel*, 6)—is a strong libidinal connection between the two. Direct addresses to the dead man—"you" (and *du*), "your," and "Daddy"—occur twenty-nine times, compared to the speaker's thirty "I" 's, a ratio demonstrating Daddy's enormous psychic importance to the speaker. Even though Daddy is gone, the narrator has internalized him and his paternal law:[21] she has "lived like a foot / For thirty years, poor and white, / Barely daring to breathe or Achoo" (3–5). She has been reduced to groveling at the feet of the tyrant father. She "used to pray to recover" him; she "never could talk to" him (24): "The tongue stuck in my jaw. / / It stuck in a barb wire snare. / Ich, ich, ich, ich" (25–27). The speaker's fear of her father has made her seek out another language uncontaminated by his barbwire German: now she talks "like a Jew. / I think I may well be a Jew" (34–35). In "Little Fugue," a precursor to "Daddy" (published in Plath's *Collected Poems*), the father's language is an aristocratic Prussian Fraktur, the

Gothic script of early German, spindly and spiky like barbwire: "I see your voice / Black and leafy, as in my childhood / / A yew hedge of orders / Gothic and barbarous, pure German / Dead men cry from it" (188, 23–27). The speaker is snagged on these barbs of Daddy's language, but this captivity is also a captivation, and an erotic captivation at that.

The desire to re-create the father in memory (in "The Colossus," as a re-construction of Daddy's pieces) leads, in "Daddy," to a self-destructive repe-tition compulsion: "I made a model of you, / A man in black with a Meinkampf look / / And a love of the rack and the screw. / And I said I do, I do" (64–67). But this sexualized love of the "screw," the masochistic desire to slavishly serve the father's memory, is disrupted when the goal of the rep-etition compulsion seems to be achieved: "So daddy, I'm finally through" (68). The speaker's desire in the second stanza ("I have had to kill you. / You died before I had time") appears to be resolved in the penultimate stanza— "If I've killed one man, I've killed two" (71). Unable to kill her father, she has killed the man resembling "Daddy," whom she selected to prolong her tor-ture ("The vampire who said he was you," 72–74). The last three stanzas mark the speaker's final rejection. She rips "the black telephone . . . off at the root, / The voices just can't worm through" (69–70), effectively ending the unintelligible communication with Daddy. Despite the exaltation of driving a stake through Daddy's "fat black heart" (77), the final line—"Daddy, daddy, you bastard, I'm through"—is still so full of rage and so full of *Daddy* that neither his death nor the speaker's freedom is certain. Instead of a movement from exhumation to burial,[22] "Daddy" moves from the speaker's passive masochism to her active sadism, but both positions doggedly refer to Daddy.

This articulation of desire in relation to the fascist / patriarch has opened the way for the most damning criticism of Plath, which focuses on her ap-propriation of Holocaust imagery. Leon Wieseltier's 1976 article in *New York Review of Books*, "In a Universe of Ghosts," blames Plath for leading the way in the parade of "death camp chic" (20) with her poems "Daddy" and "Lady Lazarus." (In the latter, the speaker describes her skin as "bright as a Nazi lampshade," her "face a featureless, fine / Jew linen"). But it is significant that Plath tends to construct similes rather than metaphors to express the figura-tive relation between Nazism and the speaker's personal history: her skin is not a Nazi lampshade but rather "bright *as* a Nazi lampshade"; the engine in "Daddy" is "chuffing" her off "*like* a Jew." Plath once remarked of "Daddy" that the speaker's "father was . . . a Nazi and her mother very possibly partly Jewish,"[23] sustaining the same ambiguity Duras introduces in *Hiroshima mon amour* with the suggestion that the mother of the heroine *may* be Jewish. This psychic distance from her poem's speaker—she "may be a bit of a

Jew"—signals that Plath is working with history through fantasy and the fanciful and grotesque distortions of that mediation. "Remember the illogic of the fantasy," Plath reminds herself in her diaries.[24] Plath is interested in the libidinal power structure of fascism, and she goes much further toward exploring it than Duras. In a desperate letter in which she contemplates suicide, Plath writes, "I can begin to see the compulsion for admitting original sin, for adoring Hitler, for taking opium. I have long wanted to read and explore the theories of philosophy, psychology, national, religious and primitive consciousness . . ." (*Journals*, 56). Again, Plath's distance from Nazism allows her to see it in relation to abstract theories, while Duras can move only so far away from the original referent. Here and throughout Plath's poems, Nazism has the same particular relationship to the "primitive unconscious" and to repressed aggressive desires as it did for early propagandists and theorists of fascism. Plath links this primitive, irrational fascism to her female speakers' libidinal compulsions.

Plath's speakers stand out in sharp relief against the Cold War rhetoric of the United States in the 1950s, smug with postwar prosperity, extolling democracy's triumph over fascism and crowing its ethical imperative to do battle with the next monster, Communism. Plath opposes the happy homemaker smiling beside a shiny refrigerator or a reliable washing machine to the frustrated, self-destructive female artist. Plath's poems about the conflicts of trying to be a creative intellectual woman while fulfilling the duties of motherhood and marriage link fascism and patriarchy together in a manner reminiscent of *Three Guineas*. Plath's female speakers inhabit a world of violence and brutality colored by vicious sexuality. Dissatisfied with their culture, which shuts out opportunities for them, these women savor and theatricalize their abjection and revenge. They replace romantic myths of love with a carnal imbalance of powers where the torturer and his victim ("Daddy," "Rabbit Catcher," "Jailer") are bound together by hate, resentment, and lust. The relationship between Plath's speakers and their fascist "Daddies" is reminiscent of Reich's claim that "Hitler conquers power with his negation of statistics and by making use of the dregs of sexual misery" (*Mass Psychological Structure*, 103). Daddy's love and the security of marriage was a compensation for limited horizons, but all the repressed desires for social power and sexual liberation are aroused by the female speakers' long-delayed rebellions against "Daddy."

Although the connection Plath develops between patriarchy and Nazism is a well-established feminist trope, the picture Plath paints of female desire—driven by masochism and suicidal self-destruction—is not what most of us would recognize as feminist. The line "every woman adores a Fascist" is not as ironic as most progressive feminist readings of Plath suggest. Her poems parade stereotypes of innate female masochism, such as the speaker's "love of the rack and the screw" in "Daddy" and the archetypal Medea in "Aftermath" (*Collected Poems*, 114) walking through a burnt-out house like a "housewife . . . cheated of the pyre and rack" (31). Cherishing martyrdom and seeking it out as the role they play best, these women do seem to revel, as Richard Howard writes of the *Ariel* poems, in "utter surrender (like the pride of O, naked and chained)."[25] But Réage's O is never self-conscious or angry, as Plath's speakers invariably are. Nor are Plath's women simply throwing themselves at the feet of "a man who looks through them, who takes them not as individuals but as material for any purpose."[26] The masochistic martyrs in *Ariel* and *The Colossus* are whirling dervishes of revenge: they are Medea herself, rising above the landscape of dirty dishes and smelly diapers to rage, burn, and murder men.[27] They are neither passive nor admirable but rather active and terrifying. If Plath's language is one of female victimization, it is not a language we are accustomed to hearing, for it always contains its double: a lashing, vindictive triumph. Nowhere is this clearer than in "Daddy." Even as the speaker rebels against the oppressive patriarchal father, the speaker of "Daddy" recapitulates the violence of the Nazi father. Her anger is reactive, and she does not succeed in freeing herself from him. Her punishment of "Daddy" shows she identifies with his Nazi cruelty rather than overcoming it. At the end of the poem, she is still addressing him; she is still caught within the dialectic of Daddy. While this is not a hopeful model of change, Plath suggests that it is a reflection of the psychic conflicts of women under patriarchy: their desire for control and authority, which has no other model than patriarchal power.[28]

Female masochism is a commonly recognized psychological construct, but female aggression is another matter. Plath repeatedly links female fury and violence to sexual expression and fascism.[29] In her poetry, she attempts to work out her feeling, as she put it, that she could not "gratify [herself] promiscuously and retain the respect and support of society . . . and because I am not a man: ergo: one root of envy for male freedom."[30] Plath did not address this conflict directly in manifestoes or political essays but rather in poetry, in which metaphors of Nazism represent her psychic conflicts with patriarchal structures, and where the dynamics of oppression are presented from the perspective of both the subjugated and the dominator. "Rabbit Catcher," for example, explores the difficulty of negotiating power and the "sexualising and aestheticising of power" (Rose, 137) that was often Plath's way of approaching the problem. The language in this poem is as extravagantly sadomasochistic as Baudelaire's "L'Héautontimorouménos" ("I am the knife and the wound it deals / I am the slap and the cheek / I am the wheel and the broken limbs / hangman and victim both!") (*Les Fleurs*, 79–80) and also as full of reversals and ironies, which, as I have argued throughout, are characteristic of sadomasochistic erotics. Beginning with the circular assignation of agency in the first stanza— the speaker is gagged by her "own blown hair"—the speaker's identification of the relationship as "force" is offset by her aesthetic and emotional investment in the "torture." The center of the poem is the psychic knot between the speaker and the unnamed "Rabbit Catcher," the "tight wires" and "pegs too deep to uproot" that hold them fast. The images—"the malignity of the gorse," the "black spikes"—hearken back to "Daddy," with his malignant roots and spiky Fraktur voice. The same language that signals "force," restraint, and violence also produces a seductive erotic aesthetic.

Plath's early poem "Pursuit" tells of a woman's panic at desire: "Appalled by secret want, I rush / From such assault of radiance. / Entering the tower of my fears, / I shut my doors on that dark guilt, / I bolt the door, each door I bolt. / Blood quickens, gonging in my ears" (*Collected Poems*, 23). In *Bitter Fame*, Anne Stevenson reads this poem biographically; written in the early stages of Plath's relationship with Ted Hughes, these lines expressed "not so much lust as her own libidinous double, the deep self full of violence and furor she was suppressing under poised and capable appearance" (78). The "libidinous double" is ever-present in Plath's poems of sexualized power struggles. "In Plaster" shows the sadistic and masochistic impulses wed in one woman's body and dueling each other for supremacy. The speaker's cast becomes her double: "There are two of me now: / This new absolutely white person and the old yellow one" (*Collected Poems*, 158). Impatient with the double, the speaker strikes out, but "she held still, like a true pacifist." The speaker sneers at the pacifist who "takes it," even "lapped it up," and whose "slave mentality" (like "the love of the rack and the screw" in "Daddy") exacerbates the speaker's cruelty (12–21). The love-seeking pacifist and the cruel double are dependent on each other and even coextensive. Throughout Plath's poems, the liberal or pacifist and the fascist are doubles of each other: for Plath, dominance is not monolithic. In "The Jailer" the speaker is the captive but again exerts power. Although the speaker has been "drugged and raped / Seven hours knocked out of my right mind," she is the "lever" of her captor's "wet dreams" (*Collected Poems*, 226). Despite her subjugation, the speaker knows, as does the double of "In Plaster," that she has influence over her jailer. "What would the dark / Do without fevers to eat? / What would the light / Do without eyes to knife, / what would he / Do, do, do without me?" (226). Again, this is the sadomasochistic dynamic of recognition and interdependence that Lawrence, Genet, Bataille, and others oppose to the strictly hierarchical violence of fascism. As in *Three Guineas*, dominance here is "craving for submission," and "the patriarch" is "calling for the siren" (3). However, for Plath, submission also has a great interest in domination.

The difference between Woolf's and Plath's models of female psychology under fascism and patriarchy is illustrated by their respective identifications with Greek heroines. In *Three Guineas*, Woolf points to Sophocles's *Antigone* as proof that women can and have rebelled against the Father's unethical laws (142). When women in the past wanted independence from their fathers, Woolf writes, "they wanted, like Antigone, not to break the laws but to find the law" (138). In Sophocles's play, Creon, the new king of Thebes after Oedipus's tragic fall, forbids that Polyneices, the son of Oedipus, should be buried. Creon's niece, Antigone (daughter of Oedipus), insists that her brother Polyneices have a proper burial, for otherwise his spirit cannot rest. For Woolf, Antigone is a model of visionary female bravery who is able to rise above her situation and perceive that "there are two kinds of law, the written and the unwritten" (184). The patriarch Creon's edict violates the more sacred human laws and needs to be challenged. Plath also turns to Attic Greek drama for her model of female insurrection, but she chooses Aeschylus's Electra, a daughter whose relationship to her tyrannical father—Agamemnon, who sacrificed his other daughter, Iphigenia, to the winds—is entirely different from Antigone's. After Agamemnon is killed, Electra's mother, Clytemnestra, and her lover, Aegisthus, abuse Electra because of her loyalty to her father's memory. The chorus of Mycenaean women warns Electra to temper her rebellion against her mother, but she persists until her exiled brother returns and kills Clytemnestra and Aegisthus. Electra continues to love her deeply flawed father long after he is dead.

Whereas Woolf reads *Antigone* thematically, in the service of polemic, Plath's reading of *Electra* takes into account unconscious and ambivalent psychic responses. In an introduction to "Daddy" prepared for the BBC, Plath explained that

> the poem is spoken by a girl with an Electra complex. Her father died while she thought he was God. Her case is complicated by the fact that her father was also a Nazi and her mother very possibly part Jewish. In the daughter the two strains marry and paralyze each other—she has to act out the awful little allegory once over before she is free of it.[31]

In the case of both Duras and Plath, it is the female speaker's mother who "may be" Jewish and who connects the speaker to a position of victim that she both savors and repudiates. In her attraction to the fascist male/father, Plath's daughter is both betraying her mother and repeating her mother's possible fate as a Jew married to a Nazi. But murderous Mother Clytemnestra and Mother Medea (who deceives her father and kills her brother to aid her lover Jason, only to be abandoned by him and driven to slay their children in a jealous rage) are hardly passive victims. The daughter's transformation of the mother into a victim in "Daddy," then, may be an act of wish fulfillment (giving a cruel mother a fate in which she is acted upon just as cruelly) or a sign of the daughter's own jealous rage.

The "Electra complex," as scripted by Sophocles, entails devotion to the father and hatred of the mother. Plath, with her interest in psychoanalysis, seized on it as the thematic counterpart of the Oedipus complex. In "Daddy," the pull of patriarchy is so strong that even when the daughter has resolved to kill her father, she is still half in love with him. The speaker's love for the Panzer-man is not as evident as her hate: the fact that Plath still speaks of it as an "Electra complex" indicates the extent to which she is revising both Freud and Sophocles. In *The Music of What Happens*, Helen Vendler notes this change by which the good daughter ("the sacrificial victim of the bee poems," who "speaks in a style of obedient, paralyzed sentences, in a dead-toned drama" [280]), is gradually transformed into the speakers of "Lady Lazarus" and "Daddy," whose "style turns to slashing caricature of Freudian self-knowledge" (231). Plath's Electra is Antigone's "libidinous double." She contains within her Antigone's rebellion but cannot shake her eroticized love-hate relation to her father. (The fact that Hitler's own father, Alois, was an avid beekeeper who preferred cultivating his hives to spending time with his family adds another dimension to the speaker's relationship to male figures in the "bee poems.")[32]

In "Electra on Azalea Path" (1959), an early version of "Daddy," Plath ironically comments on her appropriation of this Greek myth. The speaker, fashioning herself as Electra, addresses her dead father: "O pardon the one who knocks for pardon at / Your gate, father—your hound-bitch, daughter, friend. / It was my love that did us both to death" (*Collected Poems*, 117). She assumes that her incestuous love caused his death and her disasters; as in "Daddy," the daughter's love for her father is bound up with guilt, death, and resentment. Plath's Electra reads her history through Sophocles's narrative, recalling Agamemnon's sacrifice and Clytemnestra's fury: "*The day your slack sail drank my sister's breath / The flat sea purpled like that evil cloth / My mother unrolled at your last homecoming*" (*Collected Poems*, 117, emphasis in the original). But Plath's Electra also jeers at her recourse to myth as a device to elevate her own story into mythological proportions: "I borrow the stilts of an old tragedy." Plath calls attention to her literary devices and the artifice of placing one's life within such a framework. Her references to Freudian psychoanalysis, reducing people and familial dynamics into schematized types, function similarly. Plath's simultaneous reiteration of and departure from two dominant fictions of power and desire (psychoanalytic, feminist)—one is either Electra, in love with and respectful of patriarchal/fascist power, or Antigone, scornful of it—shows the conflicted emotions within one woman. Plath's transformation of the Oedipal father into the fascist father encapsulates how an individual is imbued, by virtue of his place in the family, with the mythic phallic power—the "Law of the Father."

For Plath, "Daddy" is an object of erotic fantasy, and not just for women who write love letters to Hitler. Ironically, it is the rebellious daughter (the potential feminist) who tries to free herself from "Daddy" for whom he looms largest in fantasy. Even though institutions change and women gain ground in their struggle to gain independence from "Daddy," Plath suggests that he stubbornly persists in the realm of fantasy. This point is difficult to reconcile with a feminist vision for social change: Are we condemned to be haunted by the tyrannical "Daddy" even as he is renounced in political life? Domination and submission are the two repudiated poles of feminist and democratic values: both surface in Plath's poems as the substance of eroticized fantasy, linked to fascism. For Plath, we are bound to our libidinal investments in the tyrannical "Daddy" all the more in that he is politically rejected and constructed as the polar opposite of the good, democratic, feminist daughter.

Duras and Plath suggest that it is not just fantasies of submission that most progressive politics foreclose: the masochistic impulses of Plath's speakers are rivaled by fantasies of domination. In *Femininity and Domination*, Sandra Lee Bartky writes of the old and continuing feminist conflict "between our formal commitment to justice and equality on the one hand—a commitment that the women's movement is determined to force the larger society to honor—and the profoundly authoritarian character of our various systems of social relationships on the other" (62). Even as feminism works actively against women's submission, it also generates, as Bartky's own terminology suggests, the impulse to "force" one's politics in a way that repeats the "authoritarian character" of patriarchy. The line "every woman adores a Fascist," then, can be read in two different ways: every woman fantasizes about submission, and every woman fantasizes about domination as an active agent. But this is not just a problem for feminism, nor would I agree with Jacqueline Rose's suggestion that "the wager" of Plath's work is "whether the woman might not have a special relationship to fantasy . . . that it is a woman who is most likely to articulate the power—perverse, recalcitrant, persistent—of fantasy as such" (*Haunting of Sylvia Plath*, 238–39). In the previous chapters I have proposed that the social endorsement of some desires and sexualities and the condemnation of others do not just exert force over women. Nor should feminism be singled out as a particularly repressive politics. Rather, feminism is only one variant of liberal and democratic politics, with the same disavowal of those libidinal impulses that run counter to its ideology. Just as Lawrence and Genet could be said to suggest that "every man adores a Fascist," with the same two possible readings—a desire for submission and for dominance—feminism occupies the place of liberalism on the political spectrum in relation to Nazism, forbidding and therefore giving rise to fantasies with an "authoritarian" character. Despite the post-1960s questioning of the assumption of an authoritative position, of the subject-supposed-to-know, the desire for social and political power in its present forms—the desire to possess it and to be its subject—persists. Whether these impulses, unconscious or deliberate, are considered fundamental human "urges" and "drives" or culturally constructed desires that could theoretically be changed, the problem eroticized fascism poses for feminism, liberalism, and democracy in general is that even (and especially) under political systems designed to eliminate the desire to exercise power or subjugate oneself to it, these impulses themselves show no sign of abating.

William Reich argues that, "*sexually awakened women, affirmed and recognized as such, would mean the complete collapse of the authoritarian ideology*" (*Mass Psychological Structure*, 107, emphasis in the original). Duras and Plath propose that, on the contrary, a woman who is "sexually awakened" may still harbor fantasies of submission and domination with a distinctly authoritarian character, and that such fantasies are aroused precisely in a climate of ostensible sexual liberation. Fascism's position within feminist discourse—the dystopic nightmare, the ultimate embodiment of patriarchy—is perfectly placed to become the material of fantasy. Duras, with her treasonous masochistic *tondue* and her sadistic alter ego, Thérèse, and Plath, with her Daddy's girl, Electra, insist that domination and submission retain a powerfully erotic allure, which the liberal discourses of both democracy and liberal feminism have failed to address. Perhaps with a less defensive recognition of how fantasy transforms and contradicts political commitment and makes manifest the points at which political agendas disavow libidinal impulses, feminism can relinquish fascism as its paradigm of patriarchal oppression and instead look more directly at the psychic conflicts closer to home.

Conclusion
"This Cellar of the Present"

I have argued in the previous chapters that eroticized fictions of fascism illuminate the central importance democratic discourse assigns to fascist sexual deviance. But how does this essentially modern, nationalistic construction of democracy figure in the late-twentieth and early-twenty-first centuries? Even without the immediate threat of fascism (though neofascism is a growing concern), and in an increasingly transnational world, images of eroticized fascism are just as common as they were in the first half of the twentieth century. Although postmodern culture is well aware of its own clichés of eroticized fascism and has an acute consciousness of the dissonance between these images and fascist genocide, there is virtually no recognition of how these clichés came to be or how they continue a very old discussion.

As I mentioned earlier, there was a particular concentration of images of eroticized fascism in the United States and Europe in the 1970s. Interestingly, this was also the period of the historical *mode rétro* in France, with its return to a painful national past. In a 1974 interview, the members of the editorial staff at *Cahiers du Cinema* asked Michel Foucault, "How is it that films like Louis Malle's *Lacombe Lucien* or *The Night Porter* can be made today? Why do they meet with such a fantastic response? . . . After Marcel Ophuls's film *The Sorrow and the Pity* [one of the classic projects of the *mode rétro*] the floodgates have been opened. Something hitherto completely repressed or forbidden has flooded out. Why?" (*Foucault Live*, 89–90). Foucault responds that "this comes from the fact that the history of the war, and what took place around it, has never really been written except in completely official accounts" (90). Although Foucault seems to connect works such as *The Night Porter* to the *mode rétro*, elsewhere he clearly distinguishes the "shoddy" fantasies of Nazism in pornography, for example, from work such as Ophuls's. Similarly, Henry Rousso, in his discussion of the *mode rétro* in *The Vichy Syndrome*, mentions the "series of pornographic films, inaugurated (unwittingly)" by Liliana Cavani's *The Night Porter*, including Mark Stern's *Elsa Fraulein SS* (1977) and José Benazéraf's *Bordel SS* (1978); but Rousso calls them "Opportunists," guilty of exploiting or sensationalizing Nazism (235). Anton Kaes makes a similar point in *From Hitler to Heimat: The Return of History as Film*, claiming that, in the "Nazi porn" films of the 1970s, "the Third Reich itself was often reduced . . . to a semiotic phenomenon: SS uniforms, swastikas, shaved napes, black leather belts and boots, intimidating corridors and marble stairs have become mere signs unmistakably signaling 'fascism'" (22). If Dalí was the modernist opportunist, these filmmakers would seem to be his postmodern equivalents.

The most important commentators on "fascinating fascism"—Sontag, Foucault, and Saul Friedländer—all make the same distinction that Rousso does between high and low culture, with the former doing serious cultural work and the latter dabbling in the playpen of exploitation. Although they all allude to pornography with fascist imagery as the most disturbing form of "fascinating fascism," none actually discusses any of this material. *The Night Porter*—hardly pornographic—is the most sexually explicit text these critics discuss in any detail. If pornography is the most troubling contemporary exploration of eroticized fascism, it seems worthwhile to examine it. Indeed, in 1939, George Orwell thought it important enough to discuss the puzzling appearance of Nazi imagery in U.S. pornography.

> When hatred of Hitler became a major emotion in America, it was interesting to see how promptly "anti-Fascism" was adapted to pornographic purposes by the editors of the "Yank Mags". . . . There is the frankest appeal to sadism, scenes in which the Nazis tie bombs to women's backs and fling them off heights to watch them blown to pieces in mid-air, others in which they tie naked girls together by their hair and prod them with knives to make them dance, etc. etc.[1]

I have suggested that the conflation of political sentiment and "pornographic" titillation began much earlier than World War II, with World War I propaganda that invested the enemy with libidinous appetites. But the stakes of fascist imagery would seem to have changed radically after the Holocaust. Since the 1970s, eroticized fascism often appears in visual and literary genres that are low on the cultural scale, such as pornography and horror, in "sexploitation" B movies from the 1970s such as *SS Girls* and *Ilsa: She-Wolf of the SS*, and in deliberately outrageous material such as the independent filmmaker Bruce La Bruce's *Skin Flick* (1999), a self-conscious feature about the sexual exploits of a group of neo-Nazis, which caused controversy when it played in international gay film festivals. These extreme and often macabre works set forth in sharp contrast the contradictions of postwar images of eroticized fascism. For that reason, I will briefly look at the kind of pornographic images that critics claim to be most symptomatic of "fascinating fascism" but which they nevertheless delicately step around.

To return to Orwell's observation, propaganda and pornography share generic affinities. Both cultivate inflammatory fantasies. The difference is that propaganda enlists those fantasies toward a particular political end, whereas the end point of pornography is pleasure (but pleasure is not without political implications). Pornography is, of all the fantasy genres, perhaps the most oblivious to the reality principle, setting forth desire and its contradictions with relish. In *Bound and Gagged*, Laura Kipnis suggests that "pornography is the royal road to the cultural psyche," laying bare the culture's anxieties and desires (162). Pornography puts on display appetites that are, either because of their intensity or because of their content, not represented elsewhere, and it capitalizes on the resulting frisson.[2] (The same is true of horror, and many post-1970 fictions of eroticized fascism combine the two forms.) It is not surprising, then, that images of eroticized fascism, which from their genesis were linked to a widespread discourse about the unconscious, surface so frequently in pornography. (I use the term "pornography" here in its most standard sense. Although some of the texts I have examined could be said to be "pornographic"—for example, *Funeral Rites* or *La croix gamahuchée*—they are nevertheless traditionally classified as literature or fine art.)

The pornographic (and nonpornographic) postmodern figurings of fascism I will consider here share the same characteristics as modern fictions of eroticized fascism: prohibition, fetishism, and sadomasochism. Moreover, they are predicated on antifascism. Two pulp pornographic novels from the Kinsey Institute Collection, *Captured Virgins of Nazi Terror* and *Nazi Sadist* (which represent both heterosexual and gay pornography) demonstrate this. Both are part of sadomasochistic series about war ("War Horrors" and "Combat Books," respectively). Both are antifascist. *Captured Virgins of Nazi Terror* focuses on a Jewish woman, Anna, who is imprisoned in a concentration camp.[3] The novel portrays her sympathetically, if pruriently, as simultaneously a damsel in distress and a masochistic "Justine" type: "Sex provided her only escape . . . but the craving for revenge burned in her inner core!" (4). She is forced to marry "the sadistic Otto Reichmann," a Nazi commander whose "sadism" and "perversion" is emphasized in nearly every sentence: Reichmann was "really a quite dashing man, in his own perverted way. The perverseness of his being was reflected in his face. . . . He put all of his perverted lust into practice, in the name of German fascists" (15). *Nazi Sadist* is similarly repetitive, with the signifiers "sexual-sadistic" fascism endlessly reiterated (the first words of the book are "The sadistic German Baron"). The narrative voice of *Captured Virgins* sides with Anna against the Nazis; similarly, *Nazi Sadist* follows its hero, a U.S. soldier named "Rocky Busto," as he is tortured by the baron and another Nazi sadist, "Cockheimer." Both novels conclude with Nazi defeat and punishment. True to fetishistic logic, these narratives oscillate between an insistence on Nazi cruelty and an excited engagement with it.

The same anti-Nazism structures the horror of B movies such as the cult film *Ilsa: She-Wolf of the S.S.* (1974), directed by Don Edmunds. *Ilsa* (one of a series of *Ilsa* movies set in various exotic locales, including Arabia) takes place in a German concentration camp where prisoners are used for medical experiments rendered in horrifyingly grisly detail. *Ilsa* is more horror than porn, but it reproduces exactly the dynamics Orwell described in 1939. Presiding over the almost unwatchable scenes of torture is Ilsa, a snarling, statuesque blonde wearing a tight Nazi uniform and wielding a whip. The sadistic female Nazi is an almost exclusively postwar image. The stock stereotypes of female Nazis, described by Claudia Koonz in *Mothers in the Fatherland* as "either the passive-docile or the heartless-brutish model . . . vapid Eva Brauns or cruel Irma Grieses" (12), seem to have been created by the press after the war. Irma Griese, a prison guard who sexually exploited and tortured prisoners, was highlighted in postwar reportage, which, as Jane Marcus argues in "Laughing at Leviticus," "singled out individual women as symbols of Nazi sadism and cruelty" (249). I read this phenomenon as a gendered extension of the earlier trope of fascist male sadism, since female violence and sexual violence are even more culturally aberrant than male sadism.[4]

In *Ilsa*, prisoners call this female guard "the Black Widow" since she kills the male prisoners who service her sexually. At the end of the film, the Allies enter the camp. As the prisoners are liberated, the buildings raided, and the Nazi personnel rounded up, soldiers march in to shoot Ilsa. As the bullet strikes her, she shatters, in slow motion, like a doll, a suggestion that she was never quite human. Like the uncanny dolls of Bataille and Bellmer, which oscillate between erotic objects and harbingers of death, Ilsa's shattered body perpetuates the tropes of propaganda—the monstrous, inhuman enemy—and the distortion of such propaganda in fantasy. The Nazis inevitably lose in these texts but only after they have been co-opted into the world of erotic fantasy and have served their purpose as prohibited objects that structure transgressive desire.

Even as such films and books trade on the thrill of prohibition and bad taste, they continue to make the distinctions that were fundamental to earlier fictions of eroticized fascism. The realism of the sets and uniforms and the references to real Nazi personalities establish the historical framework inside which erotic fantasy then distorts Nazism. *Ilsa*, for example, is preceded by a disclaimer that rolls across the screen:

> The film you are about to see is based upon documented fact. The atrocities shown were conducted as "medical experiments" in special concentration camps throughout Hitler's Third Reich. Although these crimes against humanity are historically accurate, the characters depicted are composites of notorious Nazi personalities; and the events portrayed have been condensed into one locality for dramatic purposes. Because of its shocking subject matter, this film is restricted to adult audiences only. We dedicate this film with the hope that these heinous crimes will never occur again.

Certainly there is some disingenuousness in this claim, since the film, having declared the politically canny refrain "never again," proceeds to reiterate the "heinous crimes" with a prurient aim. Still, this disclaimer is only a more clumsy version of the sequence that opens Lena Wertmüller's acclaimed film *Seven Beauties*, a black humor tale of a prisoner in a concentration camp who uses sex to outwit a beefy female guard. It begins with a sequence of newsreel footage splicing together images of Hitler, Mussolini, and military decimation. Shifting between acknowledgment and disavowal, these texts maintain that they know fascism's murderous history, but still they imagine fascism as erotic or sexualized. As Annette Insdorf writes of *Seven Beauties* in *Indelible Shadows*, it "tests audience thresholds of laughter and horror" (74) by refusing "the complacency of a fixed moral structure. It doesn't tell us what to think; it doesn't offer answers" (77). These films take their viewers through the fetishistic oscillations of horror and titillation.

My point is not that films like *Ilsa* and pulp pornographic novels are equivalent to more sophisticated and thoughtful works like Wertmüller's or Cavani's or Visconti's but that they also perpetuate the tropes and strategies set forth in the fictions of the 1930s and 1940s. This is not necessarily done out of any deliberate referencing of a narrative tradition. Rather, the association of fascism with deviant sexuality and perversity is so well established, so widely assumed, that it surfaces in nearly every genre and has become a cliché in already very cliché-laden genres, as well as in more self-conscious and introspective genres.[5]

Some postmodern fictions do work with the formulas of fetishism, sado-masochism, and antifascism more thoughtfully. Liliana Cavani's *The Night Porter* is perhaps the most widely discussed and intelligently realized articulation of eroticized fascism in film. A metafiction that explores territory similar to that considered by the *mode rétro*, Cavani's film centers on a masochistic relationship between Lucia, a concentration camp survivor (played by Charlotte Rampling) who meets up with her ex-Nazi lover, Max, in postwar Austria. During the war, Max, the camp photographer, "rescued" her, first taking photographs of her along with a group of naked prisoners, then pulling her out of the camp and doing her favors, expecting sex in return. Now, years after the war, Max is living in a hotel under an assumed identity, and Lucia happens to arrive at the same hotel. At first, she avoids him, and he fears that making contact with her will lead to his capture. But they are drawn to each other in a tormented reunion. Scenes of the two making love in Lucia's hotel room are interspersed with flashbacks of her in the camp, starving, naked, and suffering, her head shaved. In one highly stylized flashback, in which the lighting and composition of shots suggest a dream or fantasy, Lucia sings cabaret-style for the SS officers, topless and wearing long leather gloves, suspenders, and a Nazi cap (see introduction). Echoes of Marlene Dietrich are undercut by the emaciation of Lucia's body and the character's real lack of agency, despite the ruse of the act, which Kaja Silverman calls a "voluntary exhibition" that displays Lucia's "pleasure in her own pain and victimization" ("Masochism and Subjectivity," 6). Max's presentation of a box, inside which is the severed head of a Nazi guard Lucia hates, reinforces this skewed construction of agency. In the present, Max is part of a network of ex-Nazis who have set up a judicial system in which they stage what they call "trials" and symbolically acquit one other of their war crimes, thus erasing their histories. Max keeps putting off his "trial," and when he finds Lucia, he tries to hide her so that the ex-Nazis will not discover her. Lucia and Max try to avoid the Nazi inquisitors by hiding in the hotel room. They run out of food and starve. Long shots show them lying on the floor, barely breathing. The world finally encroaches and the film ends in utter abjection.

Cavani circles back to the earlier psychological discourse around fascism and the unconscious and to the association of fascism with sadomasochism. The constant switching back and forth between shots of the concentration camp and shots of the hotel room shows the same shift between historical referents of fascism and erotic fantasy as the texts of eroticized fascism I discussed earlier. The emphasis on enclosure in the present—the fact that the characters must lock themselves in a room to be together, to shut out the world—emphasizes the mechanism by which fantasy both takes up and distorts or "brackets" history. Cavani remarks, on the making of *The Night Porter* :

> Fascism is not only an event of yesterday. It is with us still, here and elsewhere. As dreams do, my film brings back to the surface a repressed "history"; today this past is still deep within us. . . . What interested me was to explore this cellar of the present, to inquire into the human subconscious; it was to offer up that which troubles me in order to trouble others so that all of us can live wakefully.[6]

When Cavani puts history in quotation marks, she signals her interest in how fascism has become part of the cultural imaginary in ways that contradict history as we understand it. Just as, for Duras, the "repressed 'history' " of libidinal fantasies about Nazism must remain partially in the "cellar," Cavani uses metaphors of surface and depth to describe fascism as something "with us still" in fantasy. With *The Night Porter,* Cavani attempts to exhume these fantasies and bring them "back to the surface" and into consciousness. The fact that Cavani chooses a story of sadomasochistic eroticism as the vehicle for such an exploration, and that she associates fascism with the repressed and the "subconscious," suggests that her work follows a narrative of politics and desire forged some sixty years earlier.

What exactly about fascism is "with us still"? In *Reflections of Nazism* (1982), Saul Friedländer, considering how Nazism took hold and what it means to postmodern culture, proposes that "more than ideological categories, it is a matter of rediscovering the durability of these deep-seated images, the structure of these phantasms common to both right and left":

> Neither liberalism nor Marxism responds to man's archaic fear of the transgression of some limits of knowledge and power (you shall not eat the fruit). . . . Linked as it is to a great extent to the rise of modernity, does this vision still run through our imagination, does it remain a temptation for today and for tomorrow? We know that the dream of total power is always present, though dammed up, repressed by the Law. (136)

Friedländer's assumption of an unavoidable and dangerous desire for omnipotence that is "close to everyone's heart" reprises the fundamental premise of World War I antiauthoritarianism. Fascism offers libidinal gratification and solicits pleasures that are otherwise denied by liberalism and Marxism. The libido theorists' suggestion that liberal and socialist politics can transcend totalitarian dreams of "total power" have dropped out of sight.

Cavani casts these "dreams" in fiction, arguing that it is better to "live wakefully" than to repress. Repression can of course take public and political forms. The impulse to censor politically and socially undesirable fantasies is based on a fear that fantasies may become reality. But will censorship of violent fantasies make them disappear? In *Evil Sisters: The Threat of Female Sexuality and the Cult of Manhood*, Bram Dijsktra proposes that "we need to change the nature and the quality of our fantasies before we can change the quality (as opposed to the fetishized desire-structures) of our social environment." Dijsktra calls for an "exorcising" of "the vampires of misogyny and race-hatred from our infinitely variable imagination" (7). This is surely preferable to censorship, but if we all sit down and try to will ourselves into new, politically advantageous fantasies, they are no longer fantasies but consciously constructed personal improvement programs. Jessica Benjamin suggests that "the point cannot be to 'get rid of' dangerous fantasies; rather, it must be to contain and transform them" through enactment in the psychoanalytic encounter between therapist and patient (*Like Subjects, Love Objects*, 204). Although this is still a rehabilitative approach to fantasy, it at least acknowledges the nature of the imagination.

Daphne Merkin's autobiographical essay "Dreaming of Hitler: A Memoir of Self-Hatred" (1997) suggests a different understanding of fantasy. Following the epigraph, "A thinking woman sleeps with monsters," Merkin describes a recurring dream she had as a young girl: a romantic scene in which she convinces Hitler to change his mind about his Final Solution. They have a "gentle argument, of the sort two lovers might engage in," as she explains to Hitler that his real quarrel isn't with the Jews but with his brutal father, Alois. "At one point during our conversation Hitler even stroked my hair—the hair of a Jewess, I remember thinking deep within the dream" (347). Merkin connects her dream to her recollections of growing up in Manhattan, the daughter of "German Jews, of authoritarian inclinations" (348). She remembers seeing the tattoo of her cousin who survived the camps: "There must have been something titillating, even pornographic, about those blue digits tattooed on white flesh—a violent confusion of the usual, rigidly maintained categories of childhood. . . . This numbered human arm was a glimpse of something wholly adult: human behavior that partook of the bestial" (355). The "pornographic" charge of this mark of atrocious violence registers as "titillating" because it signifies "bestial" human behavior so contrary to ethical decency. Merkin captures the complex asymmetry between fantasy and politics with impressive clarity: "Just as there is no sign that the world has grown more fond of the Jews," she writes, "so there is no sign that I will ever be free of a certain fascination with the darker impulses at work in myself and others" (363). Merkin articulates fascism's murderous racism at the same time that she acknowledges the distorted fantasies given rise to by fascism's unimaginably grotesque horrors.

Debates about the political and social implications of sexual fantasy raise a fundamental question that has been implicit throughout this book: Why is sexuality privileged as the key to fascism and one of its most significant reflections? In the discourse of deviant fascism, sexuality is an index of truth, an essential indicator of ideology. The wartime propaganda climate is gone, but the associations remain. Even as the concept of "nation" is shifting, nationalism remains founded on what Benedict Anderson has called an "imaginary community" of sameness that, all too often, is predicated on racism, ethnic and religious prejudice, and sexual bias. But is sexuality really such an accurate reflection of political ideology? Should sexual fantasy be held to the same standards as political behavior? The fictions I have examined suggest that the politically forbidden and repudiated is just as likely to be the substance of erotic fantasy as the chosen political object. The fact that sexual deviation is so often emphasized in accounts of fascism indicates an anxiety about sexuality and a need to regulate it, an anxiety so strong that sexual behavior is posited as a primary determinant of some of the most terrifying political movements in history. Sexually deviant fascism secures sexual normativity and democracy. But isn't one of these values more pressing than the other? Is it really advantageous to make sexual "abnormality" equivalent to genocide?

Fantasies can powerfully illuminate the substructures of our politics and the repression and accommodations that accompany our interpolation into the political order. Images of sexualized fascism derive their meaning precisely from the distance mainstream culture puts between itself and deviation, a distance represented as the distance between democracy and fascism. The contemporary focus on fantasy and sexual deviance as the primary root of violence is a smoke screen for more difficult and complicated political and social problems. Similarly, the focus on sexual deviation as the cause of fascism is a way to more completely sever fascism from democracy, down to the most basic, intimate psychic structures of desire. What stands out, beneath the political commentary, is the notion that sexuality in contemporary Western culture remains deeply confounding. The social and political meanings of sexuality can, as a result, be manipulated as a means of political regulation in ways we may not fully recognize. As images of eroticized fascism continue to circulate in culture, they are reminders that the act of casting an abnormal or deviant fascist "id" against a democratic "ego," correct in its aims, pleasures, and object, is an old arrangement that, though designed to separate fascism from democracy, necessarily implicates one in the other. Whether the project of democracy in the twenty-first century will continue to rely on this nearly century-old formula, or whether it is ready to relinquish it, remains to be seen.

Notes

Introduction: "Fascinating Fascism"

1. Ruth La Ferla, "The Latest Look: Unforgiving," *New York Times*, Sunday, 12 November 2000, sec. 9, pp. 1–4. "Fascism—I hate to say it, but it's sexy," writes one editor. "It expresses the idea of taking and then relinquishing control." Fashion Institute of Technology professor Valerie Steele remarks that "fascist chic" asserts "the image of the outcast, the rebel against the dangerous world. That's what makes it different from a straight-up fascist aesthetic."
2. These books draw their evidence from numerous studies and articles, both scholarly and sensational, dating from the 1930s to the present, all of which presuppose that the Third Reich had a particularly sexual and perversely erotic structure. Historical sources include William L. Shirer's *The Rise and Fall of the Third Reich* (Greenwich: Crest, 1962); Alan Bullock's *Hitler: A Study in Tyranny* (London: Harper, 1952); Joachim E. Fest's *The Face of the Third Reich* (New York: Da Capo Press, 1999); Walter Langer's *The Mind of Adolf Hitler: The Secret Wartime Report* (New York: Meridian, 1985); Glenn B. Infield's *Hitler's Secret Life* (New York: Stein & Day, 1979) (which includes chapters on "The Führer's Strange Habits," "Operation Seduction," and "Sex Under the Swastika"); and Robert G. L. Waite's *The Psychopathic God Adolf Hitler* (New York: Basic, 1977), a "psychohistory" that dwells on "The Case of the Missing Testicle" and on Hitler's love affairs. Even much earlier analyses remark on Hitler's sexual psychology: Stephen H. Roberts's *The House That Hitler Built* (New York: Harper, 1938) asserts that Hitler was "warped" by his mother (3) and speculates, "I am not certain that [Hitler] would not actually like being tortured; he would love playing the martyr" (8). There are some historians who insist on Hitler's sexual normality; Robert Payne's *The Life and Death of Adolf Hitler* (New York: Praeger, 1973), for example, states that Hitler was "a man with normal sexual appetites" (225) and challenges Geli Raubal's complaints about her uncle's sexual demands.
3. Bernhard Schlink's *The Reader* was published in German in 1995 and in English in 1997 (trans. Carol Brown Janeway [New York: Vintage, 1997]). Peter Watson's thriller *The Nazi's Wife* (Garden City, N.Y.: Doubleday, 1985) and Daphne Merkin's *Dreaming of Hitler: Passions and Provocations* (New York: Crown, 1997) also explore erotic fantasies about Nazism.
4. On punk's appropriation of Nazi iconography, see Greil Marcus, *Lipstick Traces: A Secret History of the Twentieth Century* (Cambridge, Mass.: Harvard University Press, 1989); and Jon Savage, *England's Dreaming: Sex Pistols and Punk Rock* (London: Faber and Faber, 1991), which identifies British punk as a response to both the context of Britain's Nazi collaborators and the political climate of the mid-1970s. For a discussion of fascism and queer culture, see Juan A. Suárez's *Bike Boys, Drag Queens, and Superstars* (Bloomington: Indiana University Press, 1996); and Matias Viegener, " 'The Only Haircut That Makes Sense Anymore': Queer Subculture and Gay Resistance," in *Queer*

Looks: Perspectives on Lesbian and Gay Film and Video, ed. Martha Gever, John Greyson, and Pratibha Parmar (New York: Routledge, 1993), 116–33.

5. Michel Foucault, "Film and Popular Memory," in *Foucault Live*, trans. John Johnston (New York: Semiotext(e), 1989), 97–98. Originally published in *Cahiers du Cinéma*, nos. 251–52 (July–August 1974).

6. Christopher Isherwood, *Down There on a Visit* (New York: Avon, 1959), 61.

7. In a 1972 article ("On the So-called Fascism of Some Modernist Writers," *Southern Review* 5, 3 [September 1972]: 225–30), K. K. Ruthven argues that "now that fascism has replaced sex as the matrix of unforgivable behaviour, evidence of political deviation shocks people as much as sexual deviancy used to do" (229). I argue that the two matrixes—the political and the sexual—are actually interlocking elements of the discourse of modern democratic nationalism.

8. For a description of the "close collaboration" among the Allies on their propaganda programs, see Robert Cole, *Britain and the War of Words in Neutral Europe, 1939–45: The Art of the Possible* (London: Macmillan, 1990), 53.

9. Leonida Répaci's *Il deserto del sesso* is "built," Alberto Traldi writes, "on a scarcely believable dichotomy of sexually normal anti-Fascists and sexually aberrant Fascists who live in Nazi-Occupied Milan during World War II" (197). Traldi's *Fascism and Fiction: A Survey of Italian Fiction on Fascism* (Metuchen, N.J.: Scarecrow, 1987), from which the previous passage was cited, catalogues sexualized images of Mussolini in Italian fascist and antifascist literature.

10. See Stanley G. Payne, *A History of Fascism: 1914–1915* (Madison: University of Wisconsin Press, 1995); Walter Laqueur, *Fascism: A Reader's Guide: Analyses, Interpretations, Bibliography* (Berkeley: University of California Press, 1976); and Roger Griffin, *Fascism* (Oxford: Oxford University Press, 1995) and *International Fascism: Theories, Causes and the New Consensus* (London: Oxford University Press, 1998).

11. See Lionel Trilling's argument about the academic domestication of modernism's most negative, violent tendencies in *The Liberal Imagination* (Garden City, N.Y.: Doubleday, 1953).

12. For a more detailed analysis of Sacher-Masoch's work as a response to social issues, see my article "'With This Ring I Thee Own': Masochism and Social Reform in *Ulysses*," in *Genders 25: Sex Positives? The Cultural Politics of Dissident Sexualities*, ed. Thomas Foster, Carol Siegel, and Ellen Berry (New York: New York University Press, 1997), 225–64.

Chapter 1: Fascism and Sadomasochism

1. Sigmund Freud, "Reflections upon War and Death," in *Character and Culture*, ed. Philip Rieff (New York: Collier, 1963), 113.

2. Jessica Benjamin points out that "the violent character that sexuality assumes in fantasy is not simply the unconscious content coming to light, the opening of Pandora's box, as early psychoanalytic discussions seemed to imply. . . . Psychoanalysts formerly took literally the idea that the lifting of repression revealed an unconscious wish. . . . This supposition reflected a simple inversion of the notion that people want what they consciously express, that reality lies on the surface of consciousness. It collapsed the distinction between the symbolic meaning expressed by such a wish and its literal enactment, between the symbolic and the concrete" (*Like Subjects, Love Objects: Essays on Recognition and Sexual Difference* [New Haven: Yale University Press, 1995], 179). Nevertheless, the idea of the unconscious as an entity of outlaw desires was strong in the modern period, as the writings of D. H. Lawrence and others confirm.

3. George Orwell, "England Your England," in *A Collection of Essays* (New York: Harcourt Brace Jovanovich, 1981), 259.

4. Fredric Jameson's assertion that Wyndham Lewis's depiction of Prussianism is an exception to a general understanding of Prussianism as connoting the "repressive superego" (89) is complicated by the frequent representation of Prussia as the id in a wide range of texts from World War I. *Fables of Aggression: Wyndham Lewis, the Modernist as Fascist* (Berkeley: University of California Press, 1979).

5. See, for example, M. L. Sanders and Philip M. Taylor on "Prussian militarism" (*British Propaganda during the First World War, 1914–1918* [London: Macmillan, 1982], 140) and Klaus Theweleit's discussion of "The Body Reconstructed in the Military Academy" (143) and "Prussian Socialism" (174) in *Male Fantasies*, vol. 2: *Male Bodies: Psychoanalyzing the White Terror*, trans. Erica Carter, Chris Turner, and Stephen Conway (Minneapolis: University of Minnesota Press, 1989).

6. See chapter 9 ("The Wake of 1870") in Daniel Pick, *War Machine: The Rationalisation of Slaughter in the Modern Age* (New Haven: Yale University Press, 1993).

7. J. H. Morgan, quoted in John Horne and Alan Kramer, "German 'Atrocities' and Franco-German Opinion, 1914: The Evidence of German Soldiers' Diaries," *Journal of Modern History* 66 (March 1994): 12–13.

8. Nicoletta F. Gullace ("Sexual Violence and Family Honor: British Propaganda and International Law during the First World War," *American Historical Review* 102, 3 [June 1997]: 714–47) discusses gendered sexual violence in British World War I propaganda. Ruth Harris ("The 'Child of the Barbarian': Rape, Race and Nationalism in France during the First World War," *Past & Present* 141 [1993]: 170–206) discusses French World War I propaganda. While each offers a different interpretation of the political significance of images of sexual violence, the images themselves are remarkably similar.

9. "By a strange perversion of values," Trevor Wilson remarks in *The Myriad Faces of War: Britain and the Great War, 1914–1918* (Cambridge: Polity Press, 1988), the real atrocities "paled into insignificance once tales became current of raped women and mutilated children. In some quarters of the USA even the American dead of the Lusitania could not match the supposed Belgian victims of sexual outrage" (190).

10. Demonized Germans were often presented in the guise of humor. The *Daily Express* published S. Strube's and W. F. Blood's *The Kaiser's Kalendar for 1915, or The Dizzy Dream of Demented Willie* (London, 1915). Each month features an illustration of the foolish Kaiser—with waxed mustache, dachshund, sausages, and iron crosses—accompanied by a list of significant dates in British history. For example, October shows the Kaiser sitting in the middle of a decimated landscape playing a lute with the caption, "I play the 'loot' over the ruins of the bank of England." A more serious note on the first page of the book reads, "The Daily Express warns purchasers not to send these calendars to troops at the front, as the Germans have been known to inflict punishment on prisoners on whom they have found caricatures of the Kaiser." Not only are the Germans brutes, but they have no sense of humor.

11. See Horne and Kramer and, for a contemporary British view of German propaganda, W. G. Knop's *Beware of the English! German Propaganda Exposes England* (London: Hamish Hamilton, 1939). While Knop's compilation of German propaganda is obviously a piece of propaganda itself, it demonstrates that German anti-British propaganda emphasized British hypocrisy over deviance. German propagandists mainly used tropes of sexual deviance for antisemitic and racialized slanders.

12. For an early postwar account of the primary atrocity stories, see Arthur Ponsonby, *Falsehood in War-Time: Containing an Assortment of Lies Circulated throughout the Nations during the Great War* (London: George Allen & Unwin, 1928). Both Paul Fussell (*The Great War and Modern Memory* [New York: Oxford University Press, 1975]) and Cate Haste (*Keep the Home Fires Burning* [London: Allen Lane, 1977]) suggest that many of the atrocity stories were wildly exaggerated, a position that

has been modified in Wilson, *The Myriad Faces of War*, and Horne and Kramer, "German 'Atrocities.' "

13. George Orwell, "Inside the Whale," in *The Collected Essays, Journalism and Letters of George Orwell*, ed. Sonia Orwell and Ian Angus (New York: Harcourt Brace Jovanovich, 1968), 1:517–18.

14. W. H. Auden, "Romantic or Free?" *Smith Alumnae Quarterly* 31 (August 1940): 357. The actual statement by Carl Jung to which Auden seems to be referring is from a BBC radio talk show in which Jung remarked: "In Hitler, every German should have seen his own shadow, his own worst danger" ("The Fight with the Shadow," *The Listener* [1946]; repr. in *Essays on Contemporary Events* [London: Ark Paperbacks, 1988], 6). My thanks to Steven F. Walker for locating this reference for me.

15. See Horne and Kramer, "German 'Atrocities' "; Sanders and Taylor, *British Propaganda*, 143; and Gullace, "Sexual Violence and Family Honor."

16. World War I poster reproduced in Harris, "The 'Child of the Barbarian,' " 171.

17. World War I cartoon reproduced in Gullace, "Sexual Violence and Family Honor," 744.

18. Rudyard Kipling, *Morning Post*, 22 June 1915, quoted in Phillip Knightley, *The First Casualty: From Crimea to Vietnam* [London: HBJ, 1975], 84). Kipling's son was killed in the war in 1915.

19. E. G. Glover's *War, Sadism and Pacificism* (London: Allen & Unwin, 1935) argues that a certain degree of sadism is involved in all wartime positions, including pacifism and militarism. Glover urges pacifists, soldiers, and policy makers alike to consider the ways they project their own sadism on their enemy. Glover goes so far as to propose what he calls "a new sixth commandment" to those who want to avoid war: "Know thine own (unconscious) sadism" (46).

20. The possibly apocryphal anecdote is reported in Robert Graves's *Good-bye To All That* (New York: Doubleday, 1929), chap. 23. The quip is also sometimes rendered as, "I should try to interpose my body."

21. In *Reproductions of Banality: Fascism, Literature, and French Intellectual Life* (Minneapolis: University of Minnesota Press, 1986), Alice Yaeger Kaplan reverses this argument, claiming that fascism fashions itself as "a new woman, a new mother" (11).

22. Herbert Marcuse, quoted in Martin Jay, *The Dialectical Imagination: A History of the Frankfurt School and the Institute of Social Research, 1923–1950* (Berkeley: University of California Press, 1973), 59. Reich makes a similar argument about how revolutionaries should oppose "pathological pleasure" with their own "positive sex-economy" (*Mass Psychology of Fascism*, 141).

23. Jean Améry's description of Nazi torture contradicts Theweleit's claim in *Male Fantasies*, which he bases on one man's testimony, asserting that SS camp commanders masturbated during floggings. Theweleit writes that these "descriptions are not 'typical'—but that is hardly the issue" (1:300). In fact, it is very much the issue. This discussion in *Male Fantasies* appears when Theweleit is addressing the question of fascism and homosexuality. Sadomasochism for Theweleit is real violence meted out on the bodies of concentration camp victims. I have been arguing that a distinction must be made between erotic sadomasochism and violence, which may or may not be sexualized, and Améry's testimony bears out this distinction. For Améry, the Nazi torturer props himself up, realizes himself, at the expense of the victim's humanity. The goal of "sovereignty" is achieved by "nullifying" and "negating" the other.

24. In "The Question of Fascist Erotics" (*Faultline: Interdisciplinary Approaches to German Studies* 1 [1992]), Marcia Klotz argues that the sexualized violence of fascist writers such as Ernest Jünger is properly characterized as sadism: "The soldier's right to kill or maim the enemy's body does not depend on any logic of consent; it is institutionally legitimized by the nation-state" (77). This is consistent with the definition of fascist violence as a lack of recognition and consent, as opposed to eroticism.

Chapter 2: The Libidinal Politics of D. H. Lawrence's "Leadership Novels"

1. See John R. Harrison, *The Reactionaries: A Study of the Anti-democratic Intelligentsia* (New York: Schocken, 1966); William York Tindall, *D. H. Lawrence & Susan His Cow* (New York: Columbia University Press, 1939); and K. K. Ruthven, "On the So-called Fascism of Some Modernist Writers," *Southern Review* 5, 3 (September 1972): 225–30. For more nuanced later treatments, see Peter Scheckner, *Class, Politics, and the Individual* (Rutherford: Fairleigh Dickinson University Press, 1985); Barbara Mensch, *D. H. Lawrence and the Authoritarian Personality* (New York: St. Martin's, 1991); Scott Sanders, *D. H. Lawrence: The World of the Major Novels* (London: Vision, 1973); and Lee Horsley, *Fictions of Power in English Literature: 1900–1950* (London: Longman, 1995).

2. In "A Letter from Germany" (in *Phoenix: The Posthumous Papers of D. H. Lawrence*, ed. Edward D. McDonald [London: Penguin, 1978]), thought to have been written around 1924, and published in 1938, Lawrence is sharply attuned to the approach of National Socialism. Noting Germany's defeat in World War I, skyrocketing inflation, and unemployment, he writes that he feels a "latent sense of danger" (109). He observes that "something has happened to the human soul, beyond all help"; "the old, bristling, savage spirit has set in. . . . The hope in peace and production is broken. . . . [Germany is] returning again to the fascination of the destructive East, that produced Attila" (111). Here, instead of opposing propaganda, Lawrence uses its terms: the "Germ-Hun."

3. The thorny problem of the relationship between authoritarianism and fascism has produced many varied theories. Fascist regimes are authoritarian, but not all authoritarian movements and regimes are fascist. Stanley Payne theorizes the difference as principally one of degree. "The fascists were in general more interested in changing class and status relationships in society" than the radical and conservative authoritarian right, which aimed more toward preserving the status quo (*A History*, 18). Payne suggests that "the authoritarian right" is "more moderate and generally more conservative on every issue than were the fascists" and "emphasized direct conservative and legal continuity" whereas fascist movements sought a radical break and transformation (*A History of Fascism, 1914–1915* [Madison: University of Wisconsin Press, 1995], 18–19).

4. Cornelia Nixon, *Lawrence's Leadership Politics and the Turn against Women* (Berkeley: University of California Press, 1986), 10. In *D. H. Lawrence's Nightmare: The Writer and His Circle in the Years of the Great War* (New York: Basic, 1978), Paul Delany identifies Lawrence's homosexual panic as a turning point in 1915. Upon finishing *The Rainbow*, Lawrence paid a crucial visit to Bertrand Russell in Cambridge, where he met John Maynard Keynes and Duncan Grant and discovered their homosexuality, sending him into a depression. Lawrence's hysterical letters from this period, in which he dreams of black beetles, are indicative of his deep conflicts. According to Cornelia Nixon, it was this confrontation with homosexuality that prompted Lawrence to "begin to formulate a political scheme that would channel his apparent desire for bonding with other men and render it acceptable to himself as a force for rebuilding the world once the war had destroyed the old political order. And he began to denounce women, blaming them, and their self-conscious sexuality in particular, for the state of the world" (15).

5. Sigmund Freud, "On Narcissism: An Introduction" (1914), in *General Psychological Theory*, ed. Philip Rieff (New York: Collier, 1963), 72.

6. In his essay "Blessed Are the Powerful," Lawrence specifies that "a will-to-power seems to work out as bullying. And bullying is something despicable and detestable. Tyranny, too, which seems to us the apotheosis of power, is detestable" (*Phoenix II*:

Uncollected, Unpublished, and Other Prose Works by D. H. Lawrence, ed. Warren Roberts and Harry T. Moore [New York: Viking, 1968], 437). Lawrence's understanding of Nietzsche, from whom he takes the term *Wille zur Macht*, calls for some explanation. At the end of *Aaron's Rod*, the politically strident Lilly opines, "We've got to accept the power motive, accept in deep responsibility. . . . The will-to-power—but not in Nietzsche's sense. Not intellectual power. Not mental power. Not conscious will-power. Not even wisdom. But dark, living, fructifying power" (288). The definitions of the "will to power" Nietzsche offers are not so different from Lawrence's. Nietzsche is also disgusted with contemporary rationality and the repression of instinct, and he makes many of the same distinctions that Lawrence does between a lowest common denominator will—the weak, cringing, guilty will of Christianity—and the will cultivated by strong, spontaneous individuals for whom "life is will to power." Both Nietzsche and Lawrence call for individual autonomy against the mediocrity of the majority: for Nietzsche, this is a pure instinct that makes a lion throw down a lamb and for Lawrence, it is a primal libidinal response that overrides the intellect. See Eleanor H. Green, "The *Wille zur Macht* and D. H. Lawrence," *Massachusetts Studies in English* 5, 2 (1975): 25–30, for a fuller discussion of Lawrence's understanding of Nietzsche.

7. D. H. Lawrence, "Tickets, Please," in *The Complete Short Stories*, 3 vols. (New York: Penguin, 1981), 2:1.

8. Ibid., 2:102.

9. Editorial notes from D. H. Lawrence, *Aaron's Rod*, ed. Mara Kalnis (Cambridge: Cambridge University Press, 1988), 313.

10. George Bernard Shaw, letters reprinted in *Bernard Shaw and Fascism* (n.p.: Favil, n.d.).

11. Jeffrey Meyers has pointed out the flaws in Lawrence's picture of Australia. The country was in fact politically stable and not in the same revolutionary state as Italy, contrary to what Lawrence suggests. Australian fascism, the New Guard, postdated the setting of *Kangaroo* by some ten years.

12. In *Crowds and Power* (trans. Carol Stewart [Harmondsworth: Penguin, 1973]), Elias Canetti describes the crowd as "rhythmic or throbbing" in a movement similar to the ocean; given British's imperial naval history, Canetti argues, this metaphor is particular to the British figuring of crowds (35).

13. In *Libidinal Currents: Sexuality and the Shaping of Modernism* (Chicago: University of Chicago Press, 1998), Joseph Boone finds a similar trope of the flood, employed to describe female sexual awakening, in Lawrence's *Virgin and the Gipsy*.

14. D. H. Lawrence, "Herman Melville's *Moby Dick*," in *Selected Literary Criticism*, ed. Anthony Beal (London: Heinemann, 1973), 391.

15. See George L. Mosse, *The Image of Man: The Creation of Modern Masculinity* (New York: Oxford University Press, 1996), for analysis of how the German Jewish man was often portrayed as feminized, in opposition to the "masculine" fascist.

16. See Lee Horsley's lively reading of *The Plumed Serpent* (in *Fictions of Power in English Literature: 1900–1950* [London: Longman, 1995]) in relation to popular British women's fiction.

Chapter 3: The Surreal Swastikas of Georges Bataille and Hans Bellmer

1. See Jose Pierre, ed., *Investigating Sex: Surrealist Research 1928–1932*, trans. Malcolm Imrie (New York: Verso, 1992).

2. This is Dalí's account of the meeting as given in Salvador Dalí, *The Unspeakable Confessions of Salvador Dalí as told to André Parinaud*, trans. Harold J. Salemson (New York: William Morrow, 1976), 126. Paul Eluard apparently warned Dalí's wife, Gala, of "the

almost insurmountable difficulties which this Hitlerian-paranoiac attitude of Dalí, if it persists, will entail. *He absolutely must* find another delirious subject. . . . This eulogy of Hitler . . . is unacceptable and will bring about the ruin of Surrealism" (quoted ibid., 135).

3. Salvador Dalí, quoted in Pierre Ajame, *La double vie de Salvador Dalí* (Paris: Éditions Ramsay, 1984), 126–31.

4. See Ian Gibson's careful consideration of Dalí's politics in *The Shameful Life of Salvador Dalí* (London: Faber and Faber, 1997). Dalí's politics were primarily opportunistic, and so even what would seem to be a clear statement of political conviction is always open to question. There is a significant difference in the ways Dalí portrayed Hitler and Franco. In Dalí's 1944 novel *Hidden Faces* (trans. Haakon Chevalier [New York: William Morrow, 1974]), for example, the perspective is not that of someone who is "turned on" by the Führer but someone terrified of the events that have unfolded. The same is true of Dalí's 1973 painting of *Hitler Masturbating*, in which Hitler is defeated and alone.

5. André Breton, *Manifestoes of Surrealism*, trans. Richard Seaver and Helen R. Lane (Ann Arbor: University of Michigan Press, 1969), 181. Hereafter cited in the text.

6. Gibson, *Shameful Life of Salvador Dalí*, 267–70.

7. Anthony Stephens, "Georges Bataille's Diagnosis of Fascism and Some Second Opinions," in *The Attractions of Fascism: Social Psychology and Aesthetics of the 'Triumph of the Right,'* ed. John Milfull (New York: Berg, 1990), 82.

8. Salvador Dalí's "Honneur à l'objet!" was originally published in *Cahiers d'art* 1–2 (1936): 53–56. It is reprinted in *Oui*, vol. 2: *L'Archangélisme scientifique* (Paris: Denoël/Gonthier, 1971), 79–84. Page numbers given in the text refer to this version. All translations are mine.

9. In Barcelona Troppmann dreams that he is in Leningrad, in a cathedral-like structure that contains a museum full of monuments to the revolution. Murals of the French Revolution have been hastily drawn by an artist whose work was interrupted. Oppressive, deadly, and unclean, the place is described in the same terms as Lazare; alongside images of Lenin are feminized inscriptions of "Lenova!"

10. Sigmund Freud, "The Uncanny," in *The Standard Edition of the Complete Psychological Works*, trans. James Strachey (London: Hogarth, 1953), 17:220.

11. Ibid., 226.

12. As a result, politicized claims have been made that the "perverse" fantasies in Bellmer's work express a rebellion against the Oedipal father, the Law of the Father (see Janine Chasseguet-Smirgel, *Creativity and Perversion* [New York: Norton, 1984]), or the fascist dictator Father. Foster argues that Bellmer "contests" fascism "from within its own construction of masculine subjectivity—contests it with that which this subjectivity represses and/or abjects" (*Compulsive Beauty* [Cambridge: MIT Press, 1995], 118). For Foster, the dolls are a reflection of fascism's glorification of "masculinity": "the fear of the feminine within may also be the fear of this diffusive or destructive drive within. And this in turn may be where the Bellmer dolls participate most deeply in the fascist imaginary, only to expose it most effectively" (122).

13. Hans Bellmer, quoted in Peter Webb and Robert Short, *Hans Bellmer* (London: Quartet, 1985), 26.

14. Webb and Short propose that Bellmer's friendship with the famous dollmaker Lotte Printzel was a significant influence. Printzel told Bellmer about the life-sized doll Oscar Kokoschka had made and took everywhere with him as a fetishistic compensation for his disappointing love life with human beings.

15. Webb and Short, *Hans Bellmer*, 30.

16. Foster reiterates this claim, asserting that sadism "is fundamental to Surrealism, perhaps evident in its very mandate, in painting, collage, and assemblages alike to destroy the object as such" (*Compulsive Beauty*, 13).

17. D. W. Winnicott writes that "this change (from object-relating to object-usage) means that the subject destroys the object . . . placing it outside the area of the subject's omnipotent control. . . . 'You have value for me because of your survival of my destruction of you.' Here fantasy begins for the individual. The subject can now use the object that has survived" ("The Use of an Object," in *Psycho-Analytic Explorations*, ed. Clare Winnicott [London: Karnac, 1989], 222). Benjamin suggests this is a paradigm for later adult relations ("the ongoing oscillations between omnipotence and recognition throughout life" [*Like Subjects, Love Objects* (New Haven: Yale University Press, 1995), 91]) and that this aggression becomes pathological only when the subject is incapable of recognizing the other's individuality and autonomy.

18. When this book was going to press, Sue Taylor's *Hans Bellmer: The Anatomy of Anxiety* (Cambridge: MIT Press, 2001) appeared. Taylor argues similarly that Bellmer's work is informed by a feminine identification.

19. Bellmer, quoted in Webb and Short, *Hans Bellmer*, 122.

Chapter 4: Beauty and the *Boche*

1. See Alain Vircondelet, *Duras: A Biography*, trans. Thomas Buckley (Normal, Ill.: Dalkey Archive Press, 1994), on the publishing policies of Vichy.

2. In *The People's Anger: Justice and Revenge in Post-Liberation France* (London: Hutchinson, 1986), Herbert R. Lottman suggests that the novella was not printed in Britain but on a small press in France (281). See also S. Beynon John, "The Ambiguous Invader: Images of the German in Some French Fiction about the Occupation of 1940–44," *Journal of European Studies* 16 (1986): 187–200, for the history of *Le silence de la mer*. John points out that Vercors completed the story in late summer 1941 with the intention of publishing it in a clandestine review, *La Pensée Libre*, but that its appearance was delayed when the Gestapo raided the journal's offices.

3. Vercors, *The Silence of the Sea*, trans. Cyril Connolly (New York: Macmillan, 1944), 3 and 7. Unless otherwise indicated, all subsequent passages in English are taken from this edition.

4. In his introduction to Vercors's *Le silence de la mer* (New York: Pantheon, 1951), Henri Peyre points out that von Ebrennac never engages "the favorite topic of Nazi propaganda, that France has become soft through concentrating too much on the arts and on literature" (20).

5. Vercors, *A dire vrai: Entretiens de Vercors avec Gilles Plazy* (Paris: Éditions François Bourin, 1991), 32.

6. In *Vercors, "Le Silence de la Mer" et Autres Récits: A Critical Introduction to the Wartime Writing* (Glasgow: University of Glasgow, 1991), William Kidd reads Vercors's strategy favorably, as an attempt to "unmask collaborationism, not by portraying a direct confrontation between the occupying forces and French Resistance fighters, still few in number in 1941, but by making a cultured and civilized German officer the dupe of his own propaganda" (18).

7. Philip Watts argues that Sartre's writing on literary conformity and the postwar purge has been regularly cast, by writers such as Marguerite Duras and Jacques Derrida, "as the foil and the representative of a totalizing thought" that Sartre's work does not bear out (*Allegories of the Purge: How Literature Responded to the Postwar Trials of Writers and Intellectuals in France* [Stanford: Stanford University Press, 1998], 203). While I find Watts's readings of the "splits and ruptures" in Sartre's texts convincing, it is clear that writers persistently set themselves up against a Sartrean orthodoxy—correct or not. It is that perception of the orthodoxy of the left, embodied by Sartre, that I am interested in here.

8. Peyre, in Vercors, *Le silence de la mer*, 16.

9. Vercors, *A dire vrai*, 69. Unless otherwise indicated, all translations are mine.

10. Pierre Daix, "Entretien avec Pierre Daix" in *Les Lettres françaises*, 6 April 1961.

11. Kidd, one of the more evenhanded readers of Vercors, recognizes the possible double meanings in this "work whose capacity to mythicise the Occupation simultaneously articulates and undercuts its didactic (anti-German) message" (*"Le silence de la mer,"* 18). However, Kidd does not consider the implications of the fact that the reversal turns on a romance between a Nazi and a Frenchwoman.

12. Peter Opie and Iona Opie, *The Classic Fairy Tales* (New York: Oxford University Press, 1980), 179–95.

13. Ibid., 181.

14. Bruno Bettelheim reads the Beast as representing sexuality itself, of which the child is afraid but comes to view differently through the forces of socialization. This seems incompatible with Bettelheim's insistence on the strict division of good and bad characters in fairy tales.

15. Jean-Paul Sartre, quoted in Alice Yaeger Kaplan, *Reproductions of Banality: Fascism, Literature, and French Intellectual Life* (Minneapolis: University of Minnesota Press, 1986), 15. In addition to Kaplan, see Andrea Gisela Snell, "'Die Franzosen' and 'Les Allemands': Cultural Clichés in the Making (1650–1850)" (Ph.D. diss., Yale University, 1982).

16. Vercors, *A dire vrai*, 31.

17. *Catalogue général de la Librairie Française*, index to vol. 26, 1913–1915 (Paris: D. Jordell, 1920).

18. In her memoir, *Testament of Youth* (London: Fontana, 1978), Vera Brittain recalls "studying with mixed feelings the competitive journalistic outbursts over the shooting of Nurse Cavell" (203). *Through German Spectacles* (1915), the *Daily Express* compilation of German press clips, also tells the story of Miss Cavell: "Had the [German] rulers not been insane they would have seen that the secret murder of Miss Cavell was the blunder of madmen, as well as the crime of assassins drunk with blood. . . . Kaiser made it worse by trying to justify it" (74).

19. Quoted in Annie Renonciat, *Livre mon ami: Lectures enfantines 1914–54. Catalogue établi et rédigé par Annie Renonciat* (Paris: Mairie de Paris, 1991), 11.

20. Vercors, who considered himself as much an illustrator as an artist by trade, was familiar with such political caricatures. Vercors's *L'apogée (1862–1932)*, *"Moi Aristide Briand, Essai d'autoportrait"* (vol. 1 of *Cent ans d'histoire de France* [Paris: Plon, 1982]) is a so-called autobiography of the political and "psychological enigma" Aristide Briand (8), whose most controversial belief was that it was important to pursue a peaceful Franco-German alliance before declaring war, a view with which Vercors sympathized and which von Ebrennac reprises as a romantic ideal in *The Silence of the Sea*. In Vercors's sympathetic account of Briand's life, a caricature (not by Vercors) depicts Briand dozing on a bench with a beefy Teutonic woman in Brünnhilde braids and a pickelhaube (260). The political alliance between Germany and France is figured as a courtship, and Briand has been caught napping. Any moment now, the cartoon hints, the German maid will burst into her *boche* persona, tearing the French nation to pieces as gleefully as von Ebrennac's fiancée ripped the legs off mosquitoes.

21. Reprinted in *Designing Modernity: The Arts of Reform and Persuasion, 1885–1945*, ed. Wendy Kaplan (New York: Thames and Hudson, 1995), 342. My thanks to Camille Cauti for drawing my attention to this image.

22. Pauline Réage, quoted in Régine Deforges, *Confessions of O. Conversations with Pauline Réage*, trans. Sabine d'Estrée (New York: Viking, 1979), 73.

23. Ibid., 130.

24. Ibid., 119.

25. Louis de Bernières's *Corelli's Mandolin* (New York: Vintage International, 1995) recapitulates many of the structures and themes of *The Silence of the Sea*. Set on Cephallonia, a small Greek island, which is abandoned by the Allies and subsequently taken

over by Mussolini and then Hitler, de Bernières's novel centers on a trio of characters in the same configuration as *The Silence of the Sea*. Dr. Iannis and his daughter, Pelagia, are forced to take an Italian officer, Captain Antonio Corelli, into their home. Dr. Iannis browbeats Corelli, making fun of his ignorance of Greek life whenever possible; he is "inwardly delighted with the successful inauguration of his novel project for resistance" (171). Pelagia tries to maintain some semblance of resistance but is charmed by Corelli's beautiful playing of the mandolin and his courtesy, and they soon fall in love. De Bernières's fascist officer is, like von Ebrennac, an exception to propagandistic versions of the brutal, uncivilized enemy.

Chapter 5: Horizontal Treason

1. In *Genet: A Biography* (New York: Alfred A. Knopf, 1993), Edmund White points out that the French title is argot for "funeral blow-jobs" (248).
2. See Bertram M. Gordon's account of the history of the Milice in *Collaborationism in France during the Second World War* (Ithaca: Cornell University Press, 1980).
3. Jean-Jacques Gautier, *Le Figaro*, 4 March 1949, quoted in *The Theater of Jean Genet: A Casebook*, ed. Richard N. Coe (New York: Grove, 1970), 69.
4. François Mauriac, "The Case of Jean Genet," *Le Figaro Littéraire*, 26 March 1944, quoted in Coe, *Theater of Jean Genet*, 82.
5. This is the "Jean de Carnin" Cocteau and Sartre mention in their 1948 letter to the president of the French Republic, Vincent Auriol, asking him to grant Genet a pardon for the crime for which he had recently been sentenced.
6. "Hier et demain ce que nous sommes—hier, nous étions CEUX DE LA LIBÉRATION, CEUX DE VENGEANCE . . . ceux qui refusaient la trahison." *France Libre*, 24 August 1944, p. 1.
7. "La leçon des barricades—la confiance dans notre peuple, dans tout notre peuple hormis les traîtres—a toujours été le principe dirigeant de notre grand mouvement, Le Front National de lutte pour la libération et l'indépendance de la France." Pierre Viller, "La Leçon des barricades," *Front National*, 24 August 1944, p. 1.
8. To give a typical example of Genet's commitment to treason: when he was asked in 1964 about the recent assassination of President John F. Kennedy, he responded that he felt "solidarity" with Oswald. "Not that I have a particular hatred for President Kennedy—he doesn't interest me at all. But this lone man, who decided to oppose himself to a highly organized society in a world that condemns evil, oh yes, I am rather on his side. I sympathize with him in the same way I would sympathize with a great artist who is alone in the face of society, no more and no less. I am for every man alone" (*The Selected Writings of Jean Genet*, ed. Edmund White [Hopewell, N.J.: Ecco, 1993], 450).
   Genet's sometimes reckless and ideologically inconsistent antinationalism is demonstrated in "L'enfant criminel" (The Child Criminal), a text written for (and subsequently banned by) *La Radiodiffusion française* in 1949, which argues *against* the recent liberal reforms of correctional institutions for juvenile delinquents and compares them to concentration camps.
9. In *Collaborationism in France*, Gordon points out that the Milice was similar in spirit to the German Freikorps, formed after World War I to assure social "order" and to fight Communism: "Middle class and peasant in its social composition, the Freikorps attracted those who felt betrayed in 1918, just as many Miliciens felt betrayed by the Republic in 1940 and by Vichy in the subsequent years" (193).
10. Sartre notes that "when [the Nazis] were defeated, routed, humiliated, [Genet] began to love them." Genet often said that only the marginal status of the Black Panthers and the PLO, for example, permitted him to support them; as soon as they gained any

institutional power, he would have to withdraw his allegiance. Genet's interest in society's pariahs and "losers" is reminiscent of Proust's Baron Charlus, whose "life is a deliberate defeat." In the final volume of *Remembrance of Things Past*, Charlus's pro-Germanism is explained as a desire to side with the underdog.

11. For contrasting readings of this narrative feature of *Funeral Rites*, see John Leonard ("Portrait of the Artist as Narcissistic Hitler," *New York Times*, 19 June 1969), who calls the narrative voice "a consciousness capable of experiencing others only through manipulation and total control, employing and enjoying brutality, at once death-camp commandant and eager victim" (43). Leonard thus collapses the difference Genet clearly marks between erotic sadomasochism and Nazi executions. See also Leo Bersani (*A Future for Astyanax: Character and Desire in Literature* [Boston and Toronto: Little, Brown, 1969]), who finds in *Funeral Rites* "an esthetic and an ethic of the fragmented self" positioned against "the appeal of that unity of personality assumed by all humanistic psychologies" (310).

12. At the end of *Funeral Rites*, Genet's narrator remarks: "I could not keep from thinking that he was tied up with the Germans, and I included him among the militamen who, at the beginning of the insurrection, had joined the French Resistance. . . . Paulo seemed, under his dirt, to be fighting for freedom" (244).

13. Jean Laplanche and Jean-Bertrand Pontalis, quoted in *Formations of Fantasy*, ed. Victor Burgin, James Donald, and Cora Kaplan (New York: Routledge, 1986), 22.

14. "We have to transfer what lies inside us into the machine," Jünger writes in *Das Wäldchen* (quoted in Herf, *Reactionary Modernism: Technology, Culture, and Politics in Weimar and the Third Reich* [New York: Cambridge University Press, 1984], 79). See Herf's discussion of "the embrace of modern technology by German thinkers who rejected Enlightenment reason" and Hal Foster's "Armor Fou," *October* 56 (spring 1991): 65–97.

15. "J'aimerais mieux vendre l'âme à Dieu, que d'être en la main des Anglais." Cited in Dominique Rossignol, *Histoire de la propagande en France de 1940 à 1944: L'utopie Pétain* (Paris: Presses Universitaires de France, 1991), 74.

16. Jean-Paul Sartre, quoted in Alice Yaeger Kaplan, *Reproductions of Banality: Fascism, Literature, and French Intellectual Life* (Minneapolis: University of Minnesota Press, 1986), 14.

17. Hélène Cixous ("Laugh of the Medusa," in *New French Feminisms*, ed. Elaine Marks and Isabelle de Courtivron [Amherst: University of Massachusetts Press, 1980], 245–64) and Kate Millett (*Sexual Politics* [New York: Simon and Schuster, 1990]) both credit Genet with progressive and revolutionary portraits of femininity—a project, I would suggest, in which Genet demonstrates no real interest.

18. Atack points out that in his 1943 *Attachements*, Chardonne narrates a scenario with striking parallels to the plot of *The Silence of the Sea*. Germans arrive to occupy the house of a French veteran of Verdun, but unlike in Vercors's story, the owner of the house accepts the occupation and even offers the soldiers cognac (*Literature and the French Resistance: Cultural Politics and Narrative Forms* [Manchester: Manchester University Press, 1989], 66).

19. "Jacques Chardonne et *Mein Kampf*," *Les Lettres françaises* (11 November 1943): 2.

20. Marshal Philippe Pétain, quoted in Melanie Hawthorne and Richard J. Golsan, *Gender and Fascism in Modern France* (Hanover: University Press of New England, 1997), 85.

21. Robert Brasillach, quoted in Kaplan, *Reproductions of Banality*, 16.

22. Corran Laurens, " 'La femme au turban': Le femmes tondues," in *The Liberation of France: Image and Event*, ed. H. R. Kedward and Nancy Wood (Oxford: Berg, 1995), 177.

23. See Henry Rousso, *Vichy Syndrome: History and Meaning in France since 1944*, trans. Arthur Goldhammer (Cambridge: Harvard University Press, 1991); Alan Morris, *Collaboration and Resistance Reviewed: Writers and the Mode Rétro in Post-Gaullist France*

(New York: Berg, 1992); Steven Ungar, *Scandal and Aftereffect: Blanchot and France since 1930* (Minneapolis: University of Minnesota Press, 1995); Kedward and Wood, eds., *The Liberation of France*; and Lynn A. Higgins, *New Novel, New Wave, New Politics: Fiction and the Representation of History in Postwar France* (Lincoln: University of Nebraska Press, 1996).

24. Since the early 1980s, other historians have suggested that the truth was probably somewhere in between. Rousso proposes that Ophuls's film contributed to the creation of a "countermyth" that was actually subject to the same inaccuracies and distortions: "The image of a France united in resistance was supplanted (wrongly, we can now say in all serenity) by the image of a France equally united in cowardice" (*Vichy Syndrome*, 112).

25. Quoted in Hubert Fichte, "I Allow Myself to Revolt," in *Genet: A Collection of Critical Essays*, ed. Peter Brooks and Joseph Halpern (Englewood Cliffs, N.J.: Prentice Hall, 1979), 182.

26. Trial Balloon. *PartFantasy*. New York: Trial Balloon, 1992.

27. The Scandinavian artist Tom of Finland, best known for his illustrations of leathermen, admitted that the Nazi *feld-grau* uniforms epitomized his aesthetic ideal of masculinity. He explained that "the whole Nazi philosophy, the racism and all that, is hateful to me, but of course I drew them anyway—they had the sexiest uniforms! . . . Naturally—the designer of the Nazis' uniforms was gay!" (F. Valentine Hooven, *Tom of Finland: His Life and Times* [New York: St. Martin's, 1993], 30). The artist implies that the erotic charge he perceives in Nazi uniforms conforms to a preexisting aesthetic "type."

28. John O'Reilly, quoted in Francine Koslow Miller, "John O'Reilly's Miniature Polaroid Collages," *Print Collector's Newsletter* 26, 4 (September–October 1995): 126–29.

29. Jean Genet, *The Thief's Journal*, trans. Bernard Frechtman (New York: Grove, 1964), 189.

Chapter 6: "Every woman adores a Fascist"

1. The play was first performed by the Berliner Ensemble. See also "Love Notes to Hitler Are Basis for Play," *Boston Globe*, 27 October 1995, sec. 12, p. 5.

2. Quoted in Stephen Kinzer, "Love Letters to Hitler," *New York Times*, 25 May 1995, sec. A6.

3. Ibid.

4. Ibid.

5. Ibid.

6. See, for example, the place of Nazism in Eve Kosofsky Sedgwick's *Tendencies* (Durham: Duke University Press, 1993), 49; Biddy Martin's *Femininity Played Straight* (New York: Routledge, 1997), 21–25; and Judith Roof's *Come As You Are* (New York: Columbia University Press, 1996), xxix.

7. bell hooks, for example, remarked that the dedication she wrote for one of her books—"For you to whom I surrender—to you for whom I wait"—alarmed her editors, who suggested that the word "surrender" was incongruous with hooks's feminism. See Michel Marriott, "The Eye of the Storm," *New York Times*, 13 November 1997, final edition, sec. F.

8. See my discussion of Erica Jong's images of eroticized fascism in "'Every woman adores a Fascist': Feminist Visions of Fascism from *Three Guineas* to *Fear of Flying*" in *Women's Studies: An Interdisciplinary Journal* 29 (spring 2000): 37–69.

9. Irene Reti's *Remember the Fire: Lesbian Sadomasochism in a Post Nazi-Holocaust World* (Santa Cruz: HerBooks, 1986) is perhaps the most impassioned conflation of Nazism and sadomasochism. A number of essays in *Against Sadomasochism*, ed. Robin Ruth Linden (San Francisco: Frog in the Well, 1992), equate sadomasochistic erotics with

Nazism: see especially Linden's introduction and Susan Leigh Star's "Swastikas: The Street and the University."

10. In the afterword to Katherine Burdekin's *End of This Day's Business* (New York: Feminist Press, 1989), Daphne Patai speculates that *Swastika Night* may have been written in 1935 (177).

11. Woolf does qualify this as a socially constructed impulse. She suggests, however, that repression applies more to women than to men (see Virginia Woolf, *Three Guineas* [New York: Harcourt Brace Jovanovich, 1938], 105).

12. See Jane Marcus's discussion of the photographs and photographic imagery in *Three Guineas* (" 'No More Horses': Virginia Woolf on Art and Propaganda," *Women's Studies* 4 [1977]: 265–89) and Erin G. Carlston's reading of Woolf's appropriation and reversal of propaganda images in *Thinking Fascism: Sapphic Modernism and Fascist Modernity* (Stanford: Stanford University Press, 1998).

13. In her polemical writings for *The Suffragette*, for example, the British activist Christabel Pankhurst urges women to take the moral high ground of sexual abstinence. For a lively and compelling historical account of British feminist movements from the 1880s to World War I, see Lucy Bland, *Banishing the Beast: Sexuality and the Early Feminists* (New York: New Press, 1995). See also Judith Walkowitz's "Male Vice and Female Virtue," in *Powers of Desire: The Politics of Sexuality*, ed. Ann Snitow, Christine Stansell, and Sharon Thompson (New York: Monthly Review Press, 1983), 419–38.

14. See Corran Laurens, " 'La femme au turban': Les femmes tondues," in *The Liberation of France: Image and Event*, ed. H. R. Kedward and Nancy Wood (Oxford: Berg, 1995), 155, and Alain Brossat, *Les Tondues: Un carnaval moche* (Paris: Editions Manya, 1992).

15. Laurens, " 'La femme au turban,' " 155–56.

16. Laurens sees the treatment of the *tondues* as evidence of a more general demand to put women back in their place after "new-found independence and importance during the War—in economic life and in Resistance activity especially" (" 'La femme au turban,' " 177).

17. In 1943 Duras joined a Paris-based Resistance faction under the direction of François Mitterrand. According to Duras's biographer Alain Vircondelet (*Duras: A Biography*, trans. Thomas Buckley [Normal, Ill.: Dalkey Archive Press, 1994]), she made "her apartment on rue Saint-Benoît a secret rendezvous for members of the Resistance, a hideout for Jews, when directly above them lived Ramón Fernández, cultural adviser to Jacques Doriot's fascist Parti populaire français (PPF)."

18. In *Allegories of the Purge: How Literature Responded to the Postwar Trials of Writers and Intellectuals in France* (Stanford: Stanford University Press, 1998), Philip Watts suggests that Duras's treatment of Nazism—using "individualism to distance her characters from all forms of ideology"—is a "dangerous paradox" that effectively repeats the "bad faith" defense of the collaboration writers during the purge (196). Watts's observation is useful in locating the specific political engagements of Duras's writing, but I see Duras's subtle challenges to the left as noncollaborative, a legitimate critique of what she saw as inquisitional politics.

19. Tvetzan Todorov makes a similar observation about the cruelty of the French Communists during the Occupation: "The instructions sent out by the high command of the FTP Southern Zone on June 6 contain the following orders: 'Exterminate all the Kraut garrisons and all the militiamen of the Darnand Waffen SS; . . . kill without mercy the murderers and bastards of the militia, everywhere you find them.' " Todorov comments, "The term 'exterminate' is not chosen at random; these enemies are just barely human" (*A French Tragedy: Scenes of Civil War, Summer 1944*, trans. Mary Byrd Kelly [Hanover: University Press of New England, 1996], 23).

20. Sylvia Plath, quoted in Jacqueline Rose, *The Haunting of Sylvia Plath* (Cambridge: Harvard University Press, 1991), 195.

21. See Sandra M. Gilbert's comments on the father figures in "Daddy" and "The Colossus" ("Teaching Plath's 'Daddy' to Speak to Undergraduates," *ADE Bulletin* 76 [winter 1983]: 41).

22. In *Poetry of Mourning: The Modern Elegy from Hardy to Heaney* (Chicago: University of Chicago Press, 1994), Jahan Ramazani reads "Daddy" as a form of elegy: by "attacking him with the violence she once directed at herself, she inverts the restorative work typical of elegy" (279).

23. Sylvia Plath, quoted in James E. Young, "'I May Be a Bit of a Jew': The Holocaust Confessions of Sylvia Plath," *Philological Quarterly* 66, 1 (winter 1987): 134.

24. Sylvia Plath, *The Journals of Sylvia Plath*, ed. Ted Hughes and Frances McCullogh (New York: Dial, 1982), 60.

25. Richard Howard, quoted in *The Art of Sylvia Plath: A Symposium*, ed. Charles Newman (Bloomington: Indiana University Press, 1970), 11.

26. Horkheimer and Adorno, *Dialectic of Enlightenment*, trans. John Cumming (New York: Continuum, 1972), 193.

27. As Elizabeth Hardwick notes (and not favorably), "with Sylvia Plath the submission to, the pursuit of pain are active, violent, *serious*, not at all in a Swinburnian mood of spankings and teasing degradation. Always, behind every mood, there is rage" ("On Sylvia Plath," in *Ariel Ascending: Writings About Sylvia Plath*, ed. Paul Alexander [New York: Harper & Row, 1985], 105).

28. In "'This Holocaust I Walk In': Consuming Violence in Sylvia Plath's Poetry" (in *Having Our Way: Woman Rewriting Tradition in Twentieth-Century America*, ed. Harriet Pollack [Lewisburg: Bucknell University Press, 1995]), Jacqueline Shea Murphy suggests that Plath's fascist imagery is a commentary on the control and violation of women's and Jews' bodies, and is in this respect feminist. However, Murphy also recognizes that Plath "wanted authority," and thus poems such as "Daddy," the "bee poems," "Lady Lazarus," and "The Jailer" show Plath's "attempt to grapple with the doubleness of her desire" both for martyrdom and domination (115).

29. In her journals, Plath often wrote of her negotiations with her male partners, asking, "Why is he so afraid of my being strong and assertive? . . . Is that a sign that he must *compete* and *master* me?" (*Journals*, 40, 67).

30. Ibid., 33.

31. Sylvia Plath, quoted in Newman, *The Art of Sylvia Plath*, 65.

32. See Alan Bullock, *Hitler and Stalin: Parallel Lives* (London: HarperCollins, 1991), 7.

Conclusion: "This Cellar of the Present"

1. George Orwell, "Boys' Weeklies," in *Dickens, Dali and Others: Studies in Popular Culture* (New York: Reynal & Hitchcock, 1946), 103–4.

2. My reading of pornography has been influenced by recent feminist theorists who focus on pornography as a fantasy genre, as opposed to a genre of necessarily oppressive enactment. See, for example, Laura Kipnis, *Bound and Gagged: Pornography and the Politics of Fantasy in America* (New York: Grove, 1996); Snitow et al., *Powers of Desire*; Carol S. Vance, ed., *Pleasure and Danger: Exploring Female Sexuality* (New York: Pandora [HarperCollins], 1992); and Judith Butler, "The Force of Fantasy: Mapplethorpe, Feminism, and Discursive Excess," *differences* 2, 2 (1990): 105–25.

3. *Captured Virgins of Nazi Terror*, no author, year, or city of publication given, Kinsey Institute #WA 521; *Nazi Sadist* (New York: Star Distributors, 1982) was also published anonymously.

4. Both Holocaust histories and survivor testimonies describe cruel female Nazi guards. Margaret Higonnet mentions Dorothea Binz and Hermine Braunsteiner, and both Olga Lengyel and Dr. Gisela Perl identify Irma Griese. See Perl's *I Was a Doctor in*

Auschwitz (quoted in *Different Voices: Women and the Holocaust*, ed. Carol Rittner and John K. Roth [New York: Paragon House, 1993]) and Olga Lengyel's *Five Chimneys: The True Story of Auschwitz* (London: Granada, 1981), 155.

5. These cartoonish tropes have also made their way into mainstream Hollywood films, including Paul Verhoeven's *Starship Troopers* (1997) and *Barb Wire* (1996).

6. Liliana Cavani, quoted in Saul Friedländer, *Reflections of Nazism: An Essay on Kitsch and Death*, trans. Thomas Weyr (Bloomington: Indiana University Press, 1982), 129.

Works Cited

Adorno, T. W., Else Frenkel-Brunswik, Daniel J. Levinson, and R. Nevitt Sanford. *The Authoritarian Personality*. New York: Harper, 1950.

Aicard, Jean. Preface to *L'héroïsme français. Anecdotes de la guerre, suivies de réflexions et de questions pour les écoliers de France "par un Français."* Paris: Librairie Hatier, 1915.

Ajame, Pierre. *La double vie de Salvador Dalí*. Paris: Éditions Ramsay, 1984.

Alexander, Paul, ed. *Ariel Ascending: Writings about Sylvia Plath*. New York: Harper & Row, 1985.

Améry, Jean. *At the Mind's Limits*. New York: Schocken, 1986.

Anderson, Benedict. *Imagined Communities*. New York: Verso, 1983.

Arendt, Hannah. *Eichmann in Jerusalem: A Report on the Banality of Evil*. New York: Penguin, 1963.

Assouline, Pierre. *Gaston Gallimard: Un demi-siècle d'édition française*. Paris: Balland, 1984.

Atack, Margaret. *Literature and the French Resistance: Cultural Politics and Narrative Forms, 1940–1950*. Manchester: Manchester University Press, 1989.

Auden, W. H. "Romantic or Free?" *Smith Alumnae Quarterly* 31 (August 1940): 357.

Bailly, Jean-Christophe. "Le rêve et le désir: Au regard de la poupée." *XXè Siècle* 42 (1974): 101–8.

Balfour, Michael. *Propaganda in War, 1939–1945: Organizations, Policies and Publics in Britain and Germany*. London: Routledge and Kegan Paul, 1979.

Bartky, Sandra Lee. *Femininity and Domination: Studies in the Phenomenology of Oppression*. New York: Routledge, 1990.

Bataille, Georges. *Blue of Noon*. Trans. Harry Mathews. London: Marion Boyars, 1988.

———. *Erotism: Death and Sensuality*. Trans. Mary Dalwood. San Francisco: City Lights, 1986.

———. *Inner Experience*. Trans. Leslie Anne Boldt. Albany: SUNY Press, 1988.

———. *Literature and Evil*. Trans. Alastair Hamilton. London: Marion Boyars, 1993.

———. *The Tears of Eros*. Trans. Peter Connor. San Francisco: City Lights, 1989.

———. *Visions of Excess: Selected Writings, 1927–1939*. Trans. Allan Stoekl, Carl R. Lovitt, and Donald M. Leslie Jr. Minneapolis: University of Minnesota Press, 1985.

Baudelaire, Charles. *Les Fleurs du Mal*. Trans. Richard Howard. Boston: David R. Godine, 1982.

Beauvoir, Simone de. *The Second Sex*. Trans. H. M. Parshley. New York: Vintage, 1974.

Bellmer, Hans. *Hans Bellmer: Drawings and Sculpture*. Chicago: Museum of Contemporary Art, 1975.

———. *A Hans Bellmer Miscellany*. New York: Anders Malmberg, Malmö, and Timothy Baum, 1993.

———. *Petite anatomie de l'inconscient physique, ou L'anatomie de l'image*. Paris: Le Terrain Vague, 1957.

——. *Die Puppe.* Frankfurt: Ullstein, 1976.

Benjamin, Jessica. *Bonds of Love: Psychoanalysis, Feminism, and the Problem of Domination.* New York: Pantheon, 1988.

——. *Like Subjects, Love Objects: Essays on Recognition and Sexual Difference.* New Haven: Yale University Press, 1995.

——. "Master and Slave: The Fantasy of Erotic Domination." In *Powers of Desire: The Politics of Sexuality,* edited by Ann Snitow, Christine Stansell, and Sharon Thompson, 280–99. New York: Monthly Review Press, 1983.

Bernières, Louis de. *Corelli's Mandolin.* New York: Vintage International, 1995.

Bersani, Leo. *The Culture of Redemption.* Cambridge: Harvard University Press, 1990.

——. "Funeral Rites." *New York Times Book Review,* 15 June 1969, pp. 5–6.

——. *A Future for Astyanax: Character and Desire in Literature.* Boston: Little, Brown, 1969.

——. *Homos.* Cambridge: Harvard University Press, 1995.

Bettelheim, Bruno. *The Uses of Enchantment: The Meaning and Importance of Fairy Tales.* New York: Alfred A. Knopf, 1976.

Bland, Lucy. *Banishing the Beast: Sexuality and the Early Feminists.* New York: New Press, 1995.

Blum, Cinzia Sartini. *The Other Modernism: F. T. Marinetti's Futurist Fiction of Power.* Berkeley: University of California Press, 1996.

Boone, Joseph Allen. *Libidinal Currents: Sexuality and the Shaping of Modernism.* Chicago: University of Chicago Press, 1998.

Booth, Allyson. *Postcards from the Trenches: Negotiating the Space between Modernism and the First World War.* New York: Oxford University Press, 1996.

Breton, André. *Manifestoes of Surrealism.* Trans. Richard Seaver and Helen R. Lane. Ann Arbor: University of Michigan Press, 1969.

Bridenthal, Renate, Atina Grossman, and Marion Kaplan, eds. *When Biology Became Destiny: Women in Weimar and Nazi Germany.* New York: New Feminist Library, 1984.

Brittain, Vera. *Testament of Youth.* London: Fontana, 1978.

Brooks, Peter, and Joseph Halpern. *Genet: A Collection of Critical Essays.* Englewood Cliffs, N.J.: Prentice Hall, 1979.

Brossat, Alain. *Les Tondues: Un carnaval moche.* Paris: Editions Manya, 1992.

Brown, Norman O. *Life Against Death: The Psychoanalytical Meaning of History.* Middletown, Conn.: Wesleyan University Press, 1977.

Bruller, Jean. *The Silence of the Sea.* New York: Macmillan, 1944.

Bullock, Alan. *Hitler: A Study in Tyranny.* London: Harper, 1952.

——. *Hitler and Stalin: Parallel Lives.* London: HarperCollins, 1991.

Burdekin, Katherine. *The End of This Day's Business.* New York: Feminist Press, 1989.

——. *Swastika Night.* London: Lawrence and Wishart, 1985.

Burgin, Victor, James Donald, and Cora Kaplan, eds. *Formations of Fantasy.* New York: Routledge, 1986.

Buruma, Ian. "Depravity Was Contagious." *New York Times Book Review,* 10 December 2000, p. 13.

Butler, Judith. "The Force of Fantasy: Mapplethorpe, Feminism, and Discursive Excess." *differences* 2, 2 (1990): 105–25.

Canetti, Elias. *Crowds and Power.* Trans. Carol Stewart. Harmondworth: Penguin, 1973.

Captured Virgins of Nazi Terror. Kinsey Institute #WA 521, n.d.

Carlston, Erin G. *Thinking Fascism: Sapphic Modernism and Fascist Modernity.* Stanford: Stanford University Press, 1998.

Caruth, Cathy. *Unclaimed Experience: Trauma, Narrative and History.* Baltimore: Johns Hopkins University Press, 1996.

Catalogue général de la Librairie Française. Index to vol. 26 (1913–1915). Paris: D. Jordell, 1920.

Chancer, Lynn S. *Reconcilable Differences: Confronting Beauty, Pornography, and the Future of Feminism.* Berkeley: University of California Press, 1998.

Chasseguet-Smirgel, Janine. *Creativity and Perversion.* New York: Norton, 1984.

Clover, Carol J. *Men, Women, and Chain Saws: Gender in the Modern Horror Film.* Princeton: Princeton University Press, 1992.

Coe, Richard N. *The Vision of Jean Genet.* New York: Grove, 1964.

——, ed. *The Theater of Jean Genet: A Casebook.* New York: Grove, 1970.

Cole, Robert. *Britain and the War of Words in Neutral Europe, 1939–45: The Art of the Possible.* London: Macmillan, 1990.

Cowie, Elizabeth. "Fantasia." In *The Woman in Question,* edited by Parveen Adams and Elizabeth Cowie. Cambridge: MIT Press, 1990.

Cronin, Mike, ed. *The Failure of British Fascism: The Far Right and the Fight for Political Recognition.* London: Macmillan, 1996.

Daily Express. *Through German Spectacles: An Account of the Huns As They Are; Pictured by Themselves in Their Own Press.* London: Nisbet, 1917.

Daix, Pierre. "Entretien avec Pierre Daix." *Les Lettres françaises,* 6 April 1961.

Dalí, Salvador. *Diary of a Genius.* Trans. Richard Howard. New York: Doubleday, 1965.

——. *Hidden Faces.* Trans. Haakon Chevalier. New York: William Morrow, 1974.

——. *Oui.* Vol. 2: *L'Archangélisme scientifique.* Paris: Denoël/Gonthier, 1971.

——. *The Unspeakable Confessions of Salvador Dalí As Told to André Parinaud.* Trans. Harold J. Salemson. New York: William Morrow, 1976.

Deforges, Régine. *Confessions of O. Conversations with Pauline Réage.* Trans. Sabine d'Estrée. New York: Viking, 1979.

De Grazia, Victoria. *How Fascism Ruled Women: Italy, 1922–1945.* Berkeley: University of California Press, 1992.

Delany, Paul. *D. H. Lawrence's Nightmare: The Writer and His Circle in the Years of the Great War.* New York: Basic, 1978.

De Lauretis, Teresa. "Cavani's *Night Porter:* A Woman's Film?" *Film Quarterly* no. 30 (winter 1977): 35–38.

——. "On the Subject of Fantasy." In *Feminisms in the Cinema,* edited by Laura Pietropaolo and Ada Testaferri, 63–85. Bloomington: Indiana University Press, 1995.

——. *The Practice of Love: Lesbian Sexuality and Perverse Desire.* Bloomington: Indiana University Press, 1994.

——. "The Stubborn Drive." *Critical Inquiry* 24 (summer 1998): 851–77.

Deleuze, Gilles. *Coldness and Cruelty.* In *Masochism,* translated by Jean McNeil. New York: Zone, 1991.

Deleuze, Gilles, and Félix Guattari. *Anti-Oedipus: Capitalism and Schizophrenia.* Trans. Robert Hurley, Mark Seem, and Helen R. Lane. Minneapolis: University of Minnesota Press, 1983.

Derrida, Jacques. *Glas.* Trans. John P. Leavey Jr. and Richard Rand. Lincoln: University of Nebraska Press, 1990.

Dichy, Albert. "Paule Thévenin: La trahison comme ascèse." *Magazine littéraire* 313 (September 1993): 35–36.

Dijkstra, Bram. *Evil Sisters: The Threat of Female Sexuality and the Cult of Manhood.* New York: Alfred A. Knopf, 1996.

Dillon, E. J. *A Scrap of Paper: The Inner History of German Diplomacy and Her Scheme of World-Wide Conquest.* London: Hodder and Stoughton, 1914.

Duggan, Lisa, and Nan D. Hunter. *Sex Wars: Sexual Dissent and Political Culture.* New York: Routledge, 1995.

Duras, Marguerite. *Hiroshima mon amour.* Trans. Richard Seaver. New York: Grove, 1961.

——. *The Lover.* Trans. Barbara Bray. New York: Pantheon, 1985.

——. *The War.* New York: New Press, 1986.

Durham, Martin. *Women and Fascism*. London: Routledge, 1998.

Dworkin, Andrea. *Pornography: Men Possessing Women*. New York: Perigee, 1981.

Eatwell, Roger. *Fascism: A History*. New York: Allen Lane/Penguin, 1996.

Erickson, Steve. *Tours of the Black Clock*. New York: Poseidon, 1989.

Fernihough, Anne. *D. H. Lawrence: Aesthetics and Ideology*. Oxford: Clarendon, 1993.

Fest, Joachim E. *The Face of the Third Reich: Portraits of the Nazi Leadership*. Trans. Michael Bullock. New York: Da Capo Press, 1999.

Fichte, Hubert. "I Allow Myself to Revolt." In *Genet: A Collection of Critical Essays*, edited by Peter Brooks and Joseph Halpern, 179–90. Englewood Cliffs, N.J.: Prentice Hall, 1979.

———. *Jean Genet*. Frankfurt/Main: Edition Qumran, 1981.

Firchow, Peter E. "The Death of the German Cousin: The Great War and Changes in British Literary Views of Germany." *South Atlantic Quarterly* 83, 2 (1984): 193–206.

Ford, Ford Madox. *Parade's End*. New York: Alfred A. Knopf, 1950.

Foster, Hal. "Armor Fou." *October* 56 (spring 1991): 65–97.

———. *Compulsive Beauty*. Cambridge: MIT Press, 1995.

Foucault, Michel. *Foucault Live*. Trans. John Johnston. New York: Semiotext(e), 1989.

———. *Power/Knowledge: Selected Interviews and Other Writings 1972–1977*. Ed. Colin Gordon. New York: Pantheon, 1980.

———. "Sade sergent du sexe." Interview with Gérard Dupont. *Cinématographe* 16 (1975): 3–5.

Freud, Sigmund. *Beyond the Pleasure Principle*. Trans. and ed. James Strachey. New York: W.W. Norton, 1989.

———. *Character and Culture*. Ed. Philip Rieff. New York: Collier, 1963.

———. *Civilization and Its Discontents*. Trans. and ed. James Strachey. New York: W.W. Norton, 1989.

———. *General Psychological Theory*. Ed. Philip Rieff. New York: Collier, 1963.

———. *Group Psychology and the Analysis of the Ego*. Trans. James Strachey. New York: Bantam, 1960.

———. *Sexuality and the Psychology of Love*. Ed. Philip Rieff. New York: Collier, 1963.

———. "The 'Uncanny.'" In *The Standard Edition of the Complete Psychological Works*, trans. James Strachey, 17:219–56. London: Hogarth, 1953.

Friday, Nancy. *My Secret Garden*. New York: Pocket, 1974.

Friedan, Betty. *The Feminine Mystique*. New York: Dell, 1983.

Friedländer, Saul. *Reflections of Nazism: An Essay on Kitsch and Death*. Trans. Thomas Weyr. Bloomington: Indiana University Press, 1982.

Fromm, Erich. *Escape From Freedom*. New York: Avon, 1941.

Frost, Laura. "'Every woman adores a Fascist': Feminist Visions of Fascism from *Three Guineas* to *Fear of Flying*." *Women's Studies: An Interdisciplinary Journal* 29 (spring 2000): 37–69.

———. "'With This Ring I Thee Own': Masochism and Social Reform in *Ulysses*." In *Genders 25: Sex Positives? The Cultural Politics of Dissident Sexualities*, edited by Thomas Foster, Carol Siegel, and Ellen E. Berry, 225–64. New York: New York University Press, 1997.

Fussell, Paul. *The Great War and Modern Memory*. New York: Oxford University Press, 1975.

Gannon, Franklin Reid. *The British Press and Germany: 1936–1939*. Oxford: Clarendon, 1971.

Gättens, Marie-Louise. *Women Writers and Fascism: Reconstructing History*. Gainesville: University Press of Florida, 1995.

Gauthier, Xavière. *Surréalisme et sexualité*. Paris: Gallimard, 1971.

Genet, Jean. "L'enfant criminel." In *Oeuvres complètes de Jean Genet*, 5:381–93. Gallimard: Paris, 1979.

———. *Funeral Rites*. Trans. Bernard Frechtman. New York: Grove/Atlantic, 1988.

——. *Pompes funèbres*. In *Oeuvres complètes*, 3:7–192. Paris: Gallimard, 1953.

——. *The Selected Writings of Jean Genet*. Ed. Edmund White. Hopewell, N.J.: Ecco, 1993.

——. *The Thief's Journal*. Trans. Bernard Frechtman. New York: Grove, 1964.

Gibson, Ian. *The Shameful Life of Salvador Dalí*. London: Faber and Faber, 1997.

Gilbert, Sandra M. "Teaching Plath's 'Daddy' to Speak to Undergraduates." *ADE Bulletin* 76 (winter 1983): 38–42.

Gilbert, Sandra M., and Susan Gubar. *No Man's Land: The Place of the Woman Writer in the Twentieth Century*. Vol. 2: *Sexchanges*. New Haven: Yale University Press, 1991.

Glover, E. G. *War, Sadism and Pacificism: Three Essays*. London: Allen & Unwin, 1935.

Gordon, Bertram M. *Collaborationism in France during the Second World War*. Ithaca: Cornell University Press, 1980.

Graves, Robert. *Good-bye to All That*. New York: Doubleday, 1929.

Green, Eleanor H. "The *Wille zur Macht* and D. H. Lawrence." *Massachusetts Studies in English* 5, 2 (1975): 25–30.

Greene, Bette. *Summer of My German Soldier*. New York: Bantam, 1988.

Greer, Germaine. *The Female Eunuch*. New York: Bantam, 1971.

Griffin, Roger, ed. *Fascism*. Oxford and New York: Oxford University Press, 1995.

——. *International Fascism: Theories, Causes and the New Consensus*. London: Oxford University Press, 1998.

Griffiths, Richard. *Fellow Travellers of the Right: British Enthusiasts for Nazi Germany, 1933–1939*. London: Constable, 1980.

Gullace, Nicoletta F. "Sexual Violence and Family Honor: British Propaganda and International Law during the First World War." *American Historical Review* 102, 3 (June 1997): 714–47.

Hansen, Ron. *Hitler's Niece*. New York: HarperCollins, 1999.

Harris, Ruth. "The 'Child of the Barbarian': Rape, Race and Nationalism in France during the First World War." *Past & Present* 141 (1993): 170–206.

Harrison, John A. *The Reactionaries: A Study of the Anti-democratic Intelligentsia*. New York: Schocken, 1966.

Haste, Cate. *Keep the Home Fires Burning: Propaganda in the First World War*. London: Allen Lane, 1977.

Hayman, Ronald. *Hitler and Geli*. London: Bloomsbury, 1997.

Hawthorne, Melanie, and Richard J. Golsan. *Gender and Fascism in Modern France*. Hanover: University Press of New England, 1997.

Hearne, Betsy. *Beauty and the Beast: Visions and Revisions of an Old Tale*. Chicago: University of Chicago Press, 1989.

Herf, Jeffrey. *Reactionary Modernism: Technology, Culture, and Politics in Weimar and the Third Reich*. New York: Cambridge University Press, 1984.

Herzog, Dagmar. "'Pleasure, Sex, and Politics Belong Together': Post-Holocaust Memory and the Sexual Revolution in West Germany." *Critical Inquiry* 24 (winter 1998): 393–444.

Hewitt, Andrew. *Fascist Modernism: Aesthetics, Politics, and the Avant-Garde*. Stanford: Stanford University Press, 1993.

——. *Political Inversions: Homosexuality, Fascism, and the Modernist Imaginary*. Stanford: Stanford University Press, 1996.

Higgins, Lynn A. *New Novel, New Wave, New Politics: Fiction and the Representation of History in Postwar France*. Lincoln: University of Nebraska Press, 1996.

Higonnet, Margaret Randolph, Jane Jenson, Sonya Michel, and Margaret Collins Weitz, eds. *Behind the Lines: Gender and the Two World Wars*. New Haven: Yale University Press, 1987.

Hill, Leslie. *Marguerite Duras: Apocalyptic Desires*. London and New York: Routledge, 1993.

Hite, Shere. *The Hite Report*. New York: Dell, 1976.

Hobhouse, L. T. *Questions of War and Peace*. London: T. Fisher Unwin, 1916.

Hobsbawm, Eric. *Nations and Nationalism since 1780*. Cambridge: Cambridge University Press, 1990.

Hoffmann, E. T. A. "The Sand-Man." Trans. J. T. Bealby. In *The Best Tales of Hoffmann*, edited by E. F. Bleiler. New York: Dover, 1967.

Hooven, F. Valentine. *Tom of Finland: His Life and Times*. New York: St. Martin's, 1993.

Horkheimer, Max, and Theodor W. Adorno. *Dialectic of Enlightenment*. Trans. John Cumming. New York: Continuum, 1972.

Horne, John, and Alan Kramer. "German 'Atrocities' and Franco-German Opinion, 1914: The Evidence of German Soldiers' Diaries." *Journal of Modern History* 66 (March 1994): 1–33.

Horsley, Lee. *Fictions of Power in English Literature: 1900–1950*. London: Longman, 1995.

Howard, Lucy, and C. K. Binswanger. "Nuzzling with the no. 1 Nazi: Eva's Perspective." *Newsweek*, 8 December 1997, 10.

Hussey, Mark, ed. *Virginia Woolf and War: Fiction, Reality, and Myth*. Syracuse: Syracuse University Press, 1991.

Huxley, Aldous. *Point Counter Point*. New York: Random House, 1928.

"Images de la Libération" exhibition. Hôtel de Ville, Paris, France, July 1994.

Infield, Glenn B. *Hitler's Secret Life: The Mysteries of the Eagle's Nest*. New York: Stein & Day, 1979.

Insdorf, Annette. *Indelible Shadows: Film and the Holocaust*. 2d ed. Cambridge: Cambridge University Press, 1989.

Isherwood, Christopher. *The Berlin Stories*. New York: New Directions, 1935.

———. *Down There on a Visit*. New York: Avon, 1959.

"Jacques Chardonne et *Mein Kampf*." *Les Lettres françaises* (11 November 1943): 2.

Jameson, Fredric. *Fables of Aggression: Wyndham Lewis, the Modernist as Fascist*. Berkeley: University of California Press, 1979.

———. *The Political Unconscious: Narrative as a Socially Symbolic Act*. Ithaca: Cornell University Press, 1981.

Jay, Martin. *The Dialectical Imagination: A History of the Frankfurt School and the Institute of Social Research, 1923–1950*. Berkeley: University of California Press, 1973.

Jung, Carl. "The Fight with the Shadow." *The Listener* (1946). Reprint, *Essays on Contemporary Events*, London: Ark Paperbacks, 1988.

John, S. Beynon. "The Ambiguous Invader: Images of the German in some French Fiction about the Occupation of 1940–44." *Journal of European Studies* 16 (1986): 187–200.

Jong, Erica. *Fear of Flying*. New York: Signet, 1973.

Kaes, Anton. *From Hitler to Heimat: The Return of History as Film*. Cambridge: Harvard University Press, 1989.

Kaplan, Alice Yaeger. *Reproductions of Banality: Fascism, Literature, and French Intellectual Life*. Minneapolis: University of Minnesota Press, 1986.

Kaplan, Wendy, ed. *Designing Modernity: The Arts of Reform and Persuasion, 1885–1945*. New York: Thames and Hudson, 1995.

Kedward, H. R., and Nancy Wood, eds. *The Liberation of France: Image and Event*. Oxford: Berg, 1995.

Kershaw, Ian. *Hitler, 1889–1936: Hubris*. New York: W.W. Norton, 1998.

———. *Hitler, 1936–1945: Nemesis*. New York: W.W. Norton, 2000.

Kidd, William. *Vercors, "Le Silence de la Mer" et Autres Récits: A Critical Introduction to the Wartime Writing*. Glasgow: University of Glasgow, 1991.

Kinzer, Stephen. "Love Letters to Hitler." *New York Times*, 25 May 1995, sec. A6, p. 1.

Kipling, Rudyard. *Selected Stories*. Ed. Andrew Rutherford. London: Penguin, 1987.

Kipnis, Laura. *Bound and Gagged: Pornography and the Politics of Fantasy in America*. New York: Grove, 1996.

Klein, Melanie. "Love, Guilt and Reparation." In *The Writings of Melanie Klein*. Vol. 1. New York: Free Press, 1984.

Klotz, Marcia. "The Question of Fascist Erotics." *Faultline: Interdisciplinary Approaches to German Studies* 1 (1992): 69–81.

Knapp, Bettina. *Jean Genet*. Boston: Twayne, 1968.

Knightley, Phillip. *The First Casualty: From the Crimea to Vietnam: The War Correspondent as Hero, Propagandist, and Myth Maker*. London: Harcourt Brace Jovanovich, 1975.

Knop, W. G. *Beware of the English! German Propaganda Exposes England*. London: Hamish Hamilton, 1939.

Koestenbaum, Wayne. "The Aryan Boy Who Pissed on My Father's Head." In *Constructing Masculinity*, edited by Maurice Berger, Brian Wallis, and Simon Watson, 49–56. New York: Routledge, 1995.

Koestler, Arthur. *The Yogi and the Commissar*. New York: Macmillan, 1946.

Konstantinovic, Radivoje D. *Vercors écrivain et dessinateur*. Paris: Klincksieck, 1965.

Koonz, Claudia. *Mothers in the Fatherland: Women, the Family, and Nazi Politics*. New York: St. Martin's, 1987.

Krauss, Rosalind. *L'Amour Fou: Photography and Surrealism*. New York: Abbeville, 1985.

———. "Surrealism: A History?" Seminar delivered at Columbia University, New York, N.Y., fall 1992.

La Ferla, Ruth. "The Latest Look: Unforgiving." *New York Times*, 12 November 2000, sec. 9, p. 1.

Landis, Bill. *The Unauthorized Biography of Kenneth Anger*. New York: HarperCollins, 1995.

Langer, Lawrence L. *Admitting the Holocaust: Collected Essays*. New York: Oxford University Press, 1995.

———. *The Holocaust and the Literary Imagination*. New Haven: Yale University Press, 1975.

Langer, Walter. *The Mind of Adolf Hitler: The Secret Wartime Report*. New York: Meridian, 1985.

Laplanche, Jean. *Life and Death in Psycho-analysis*. Trans. Jeffrey Mehlman. Baltimore: Johns Hopkins University Press, 1976.

Laplanche, Jean, and Jean-Bertrand Pontalis. *The Language of Psycho-Analysis*. Trans. Donald Nicholson-Smith. London: Hogarth Press, 1973.

Laqueur, Walter. *Fascism: A Reader's Guide: Analyses, Interpretations, Bibliography*. Berkeley: University of California Press, 1976.

———. *Fascism: Past, Present, Future*. New York: Oxford University Press, 1996.

Laurens, Corran. "'La femme au turban': Les femmes tondues." In *The Liberation of France*, edited by H. R. Kedward and Nancy Woods, 155–179. Oxford: Berg, 1995.

Lawrence, D. H. *Aaron's Rod*. New York: Viking, 1961.

———. *Aaron's Rod*. Ed. Mara Kalnis. Cambridge: Cambridge University Press, 1988.

———. *The Complete Short Stories*. 3 vols. New York: Penguin, 1981.

———. *Fantasia of the Unconscious and Psychoanalysis and the Unconscious*. New York: Penguin, 1960.

———. *Kangaroo*. New York: Penguin, 1980.

———. *Lady Chatterley's Lover*. Ed. Ronald Friedland. New York: Bantam, 1983.

———. *The Letters of D. H. Lawrence*. Ed. Aldous Huxley. London: William Heinemann, 1956.

———. *Mornings in Mexico and Etruscan Places*. New York: Penguin, 1977.

———. *Movements in European History*. Cambridge: Cambridge University Press, 1989.

———. *Phoenix: The Posthumous Papers of D. H. Lawrence*. Ed. Edward D. McDonald. London: Penguin, 1978.

———. *Phoenix II: Uncollected, Unpublished, and Other Prose Works by D. H. Lawrence*. Ed. Warren Roberts and Harry T. Moore. New York: Viking, 1968.

———. *The Plumed Serpent*. New York: Penguin, 1961.

———. *The Rainbow*. New York: Penguin, 1981.

———. *Selected Literary Criticism*. Ed. Anthony Beal. London: Heinemann, 1973.

———. *Sons and Lovers*. New York: Penguin, 1983.

———. *St. Mawr and The Man Who Died*. New York: Vintage, 1953.

———. *Women in Love*. New York: Viking, 1975.

Le Bon, Gustave. *The Crowd: A Study of the Popular Mind*. New York: Penguin, 1960.

Lebovics, Herman. *True France: The Wars over Cultural Identity, 1900–1945*. Ithaca: Cornell University Press, 1992.

Leed, Eric J. *No Man's Land: Combat and Identity in World War I*. Cambridge: Cambridge University Press, 1979.

Leonard, John. "Portrait of the Artist as Narcissistic Hitler." *New York Times*, 19 June 19 1969, 43.

Linden, Robin Ruth, ed. *Against Sadomasochism*. San Francisco: Frog in the Well, 1992.

Lorentzen, Justin J. "Reich Dreams: Ritual Horror and Armoured bodies." In *Visual Culture*, edited by Chris Jenks, 161–69. New York: Routledge, 1995.

Lotringer, Sylvère. "A Conversation with Sylvère Lotringer." *Conference* 6, 1 (summer 1995):3–14.

Lottman, Herbert R. *The People's Anger: Justice and Revenge in Post-Liberation France*. London: Hutchinson, 1986.

"Love Notes to Hitler Are Basis for Play." *Boston Globe*, 27 October 27 1995, sec. 12, p. 5.

Mann, Thomas. *Mario and the Magician and Other Stories*. London: Penguin, 1975.

Marcus, Jane. "Laughing at Leviticus: Nightwood as a Woman's Circus Epic." In *Silence and Power: A Reevaluation of Djuna Barnes*, edited by Mary Lynn Broe, 221–50. Carbondale: Southern Illinois University Press, 1991.

———. " 'No More Horses': Virginia Woolf on Art and Propaganda." *Women's Studies* 4 (1977): 265–89.

Marcus, Greil. *Lipstick Traces: A Secret History of the Twentieth Century*. Cambridge: Harvard University Press, 1989.

Marcus, Steven. "The Upper Depths." *New York Review of Books*, 17 December 1964, 16–17.

Marcuse, Herbert. *Eros and Civilization: A Philosophical Inquiry into Freud*. New York: Vintage, 1962.

Marinetti, Filippo Tommaso. *Let's Murder the Moonshine: Selected Writings*. Trans. R. W. Flint and Arthur A. Coppotelli, ed. R. W. Flint. Los Angeles: Sun & Moon Classics, 1991.

Marks, Elaine, and Isabelle de Courtivron. *New French Feminisms*. Amherst: University of Massachusetts Press, 1980.

Marks, Peter. "Yes, Even Hitler Had His Groupies." *New York Times*, 11 January 11 1997, sec. A, p. 16.

Marriott, Michel. "The Eye of the Storm." *New York Times*, 13 November 1997, final edition, sec. F.

Marsh, Patrick. "*Jeanne d'Arc* during the German Occupation." *Theatre Research International* 2 (1977): 139–45.

Martin, Biddy. *Femininity Played Straight*. New York: Routledge, 1997.

Martin, Elaine, ed. *Gender, Patriarchy and Fascism in the Third Reich: The Response of Women Writers*. Detroit: Wayne State University Press, 1993.

McCarty, John. *Sleaze Merchants: Adventures in Exploitation Filmmaking*. New York: St. Martin's, 1995.

Mensch, Barbara. *D. H. Lawrence and the Authoritarian Personality*. New York: St. Martin's, 1991.

Merkin, Daphne. *Dreaming of Hitler: Passions and Provocations*. New York: Crown, 1997.

Meyers, Jeffrey. *D. H. Lawrence and the Experience of Italy*. Philadelphia: University of Pennsylvania Press, 1982.

Milfull, John, ed. *The Attractions of Fascism: Social Psychology and Aesthetics of the 'Triumph of the Right.'* New York: Berg, 1990.

Miller, D. A. *Bringing Out Roland Barthes*. Berkeley: University of California Press, 1992.

Miller, Francine Koslow. "John O'Reilly's Miniature Polaroid Collages." *Print Collector's Newsletter* 26, 4 (Sept.–Oct. 1995): 126–29.

Millett, Kate. *Sexual Politics*. New York: Simon and Schuster, 1990.

Mitchell, Juliet. *Psychoanalysis and Feminism*. New York: Vintage, 1974.

Mizejewski, Linda. *Divine Decadence: Fascism, Female Spectacle, and the Makings of Sally Bowles*. Princeton: Princeton University Press, 1992.

Morris, Alan. *Collaboration and Resistance Reviewed: Writers and the Mode Rétro in Post-Gaullist France*. New York: Berg, 1992.

Morrison, Paul. *The Poetics of Fascism: Ezra Pound, T. S. Eliot, Paul de Man*. New York: Oxford University Press, 1996.

Moselly, Émile. *Contes de guerre pour Jean-Pierre*. Paris: Berger-Levrault, 1918.

Mosse, George L. *The Image of Man: The Creation of Modern Masculinity*. New York: Oxford University Press, 1996.

——. *Nationalism and Sexuality: Respectability and Abnormal Sexuality in Modern Europe*. New York: Howard Fertig, 1985.

Mowrer, Edgar Ansel. *Germany Puts the Clock Back*. 1933. Reprint, London: Penguin, 1937.

Murphy, Jacqueline Shea. "'This Holocaust I Walk In': Consuming Violence in Sylvia Plath's Poetry." In *Having Our Way: Woman Rewriting Tradition in Twentieth-Century America*, edited by Harriet Pollack, 104–17. Lewisburg: Bucknell University Press.

Nazi Sadist. New York: Star Distributors, 1982.

Newman, Charles, ed. *The Art of Sylvia Plath: A Symposium*. Bloomington: Indiana University Press, 1970.

Nixon, Cornelia. *Lawrence's Leadership Politics and the Turn against Women*. Berkeley: University of California Press, 1986.

Ophuls, Marcel. *The Sorrow and the Pity*. New York: Berkley Windhover, 1975.

Opie, Peter, and Iona Opie, eds. *The Classic Fairy Tales*. New York: Oxford University Press, 1980.

Orwell, George. *The Collected Essays, Journalism and Letters of George Orwell*. Ed. Sonia Orwell and Ian Angus. New York: Harcourt Brace Jovanovich, 1968.

——. *A Collection of Essays*. New York: Harcourt Brace Jovanovich, 1981.

——. *Coming Up For Air*. New York: Harcourt Brace, 1939.

——. *Dickens, Dali and Others: Studies in Popular Culture*. New York: Reynal & Hitchcock, 1946.

Paxton, Robert O. *Vichy France: Old Guard and New Guard: 1940–44*. New York: Columbia University Press, 1982.

Payne, Robert. *The Life and Death of Adolf Hitler*. New York: Praeger, 1973.

Payne, Stanley G. *Fascism: Comparison and Definition*. Madison: University of Wisconsin Press, 1980.

——. *A History of Fascism, 1914–1945*. Madison: University of Wisconsin Press, 1995.

Person, Ethel S. *By Force of Fantasy: How We Make Our Lives*. New York: Harper Collins, 1995.

Peyre, Henri. Introduction to *Le silence de la mer*, by Vercors, 9–26. New York: Pantheon, 1951.

Phelps, H. C. "Plath's 'Daddy.'" *The Explicator* 52, 4 (summer 1994): 249–50.

Pierre, Jose, ed. *Investigating Sex: Surrealist Research 1928–1932*. Trans. Malcolm Imrie. New York: Verso, 1992.

Pick, Daniel. *War Machine: The Rationalisation of Slaughter in the Modern Age*. New Haven: Yale University Press, 1993.

Plant, Richard. *The Pink Triangle: The Nazi War against Homosexuals*. New York: Henry Holt, 1986.

Plath, Sylvia. *Ariel*. New York: Harper and Row, 1965.

——. *Collected Poems*. London: Faber and Faber, 1981.

——. *The Colossus*. New York: Vintage, 1968.

——. *Johnny Panic and the Bible of Dreams*. New York: Harper & Row, 1979.

——. *The Journals of Sylvia Plath*. Ed. Ted Hughes and Frances McCullogh. New York: Dial, 1982.

Ponsonby, Arthur. *Falsehood in War-Time: Containing an Assortment of Lies Circulated throughout the Nations during the Great War.* London: George Allen & Unwin, 1928.

Prager, Emily. *Eve's Tattoo.* New York: Vintage, 1992.

Preston, Peter, ed. *D. H. Lawrence in the Modern World.* Cambridge: Cambridge University Press, 1989.

Proud, Judith K. *Children and Propaganda. Il était une fois. . .: Fiction and Fairy Tale in Vichy France.* Oxford: Intellect Books, 1995.

Ramazani, Jahan. *Poetry of Mourning: The Modern Elegy From Hardy to Heaney.* Chicago: University of Chicago Press, 1994.

Read, James Morgan. *Atrocity Propaganda, 1914–1919.* New Haven: Yale University Press, 1941.

Réage, Pauline. *Story of O.* Trans. Sabine d'Estrée. New York: Ballantine, 1965.

Reich, Wilhelm. *The Mass Psychological Structure of Fascism.* Trans. Vincent R. Carfagno. New York: Noonday, 1970.

Reik, Theodor. *Masochism in Modern Man.* Trans. Margaret H. Beigel and Gertrud M. Kurth. New York: Grove, 1957.

Renonciat, Annie. *Livre mon ami: Lectures enfantines 1914–54. Catalogue établi et rédigé par Annie Renonciat.* Paris: Mairie de Paris, 1991.

Reshef, Ouriel. *Guerre, mythes et caricature.* Paris: Presses de la Fondation Nationale des Sciences Politiques, 1984.

Reti, Irene. *Remember the Fire: Lesbian Sadomasochism in a Post Nazi-Holocaust World.* Santa Cruz: HerBooks, 1986.

Rhodes, Anthony. *Propaganda, the Art of Persuasion, World War II.* Ed. Victor Margolin. New York: Chelsea House, 1983.

Rich, Adrienne. *Of Woman Born.* New York: Bantam, 1977.

Rich, B. Ruby. "From Repressive Tolerance to Erotic Liberation: Maedchen in Uniform." In *Re-vision: Essays in Feminist Film Criticism,* edited by Mary Ann Doane, Patricia Mellencamp, and Linda Williams, 100–129. Frederick, Md.: University Publications of America, 1984.

Ries, Lawrence R. *Wolf Masks: Violence in Contemporary Poetry.* Port Washington, N.Y.: Kennikat, 1977.

Rittner, Carol, and John K. Roth, eds. *Different Voices: Women and the Holocaust.* New York: Paragon House, 1993.

Roberts, Steven H. *The House That Hitler Built.* New York and London: Harper & Brothers, 1938.

Robinet, J., illus. *Carnet de route du soldat Fritz Bosch.* Paris: Berger-Levrault, 1915.

Roof, Judith. *Come As You Are.* New York: Columbia University Press, 1996.

Rose, Jacqueline. *The Haunting of Sylvia Plath.* Cambridge: Harvard University Press, 1991.

Rosenbaum, Ron. "Explaining Hitler." *New Yorker,* 1 May 1995.

———. "Hitler's Doomed Angel." *Vanity Fair,* April 1997.

Rossignol, Dominique. *Histoire de la propagande en France de 1940 à 1944: L'utopie Pétain.* Paris: Presses Universitaires de France, 1991.

Rousso, Henry. *The Vichy Syndrome: History and Meaning in France since 1944.* Trans. Arthur Goldhammer. Cambridge: Harvard University Press, 1991.

Rusch, Kris. *Hitler's Angel.* New York: St. Martin's, 1998.

Ruthven, K. K. "On the So-called Fascism of Some Modernist Writers." *Southern Review* 5, 3 (September 1972): 225–30.

Sacher-Masoch, Leopold von. *Venus in Furs.* In *Masochism,* translated by Jean McNeil. New York: Zone, 1991.

Sade, Marquis de. *Justine, Philosophy in the Bedroom and Other Writings.* Trans. Richard Seaver and Austryn Wainhouse. New York: Grove, 1965.

Sadler, William S. *Long Heads and Round Heads: or What's the Matter with Germany.* Chicago: A.C. McClurg, 1918.

Sanders, M. L., and Philip M. Taylor. *British Propaganda during the First World War, 1914–1918*. London: Macmillan, 1982.

Sanders, Scott. *D. H. Lawrence: The World of the Major Novels*. London: Vision, 1973.

Sartre, Jean-Paul. *Saint Genet: Actor and Martyr*. Trans. Bernard Frechtman. New York: Pantheon, 1963.

———. *Troubled Sleep* (*La mort dans l'âme*). Trans. Gerard Hopkins. New York: Knopf, 1950.

———. *What Is Literature?* Trans. Bernard Frechtman. Gloucester: Peter Smith, 1978.

Savage, Jon. *England's Dreaming: Sex Pistols and Punk Rock*. London: Faber and Faber, 1991.

Sayers, Dorothy L. *Begin Here: A Statement of Faith*. New York: Harcourt Brace, 1941.

Scheckner, Peter. *Class, Politics and the Individual*. Rutherford, N.J.: Fairleigh Dickinson University Press, 1985.

Schlink, Bernhard. *The Reader*. Trans. Carol Brown Janeway. New York: Vintage, 1998.

Sedgwick, Eve Kosofsky. *Tendencies*. Durham, N.C.: Duke University Press, 1993.

Serrié-Heim, M. *Petit-Bé et vilain Boche*. Paris: Delagrave, 1915.

Shaw, Bernard. *Bernard Shaw and Fascism*. N.p.: Favil, [1928?].

———. *Three Plays*. New York: Dodd, Mead, 1934.

Shirer, William L. *The Rise and Fall of the Third Reich*. Greenwich, Conn.: Crest, 1962.

Silverman, Kaja. *Male Subjectivity at the Margins*. New York: Routledge, 1992.

———. "Masochism and Subjectivity." *Framework*, no. 12 (1980): 2–9.

Simpson, Hilary. *D. H. Lawrence and Feminism*. London: Croom Helm, 1982.

Snell, Andrea Gisela. "'Die Franzosen' and 'Les Allemands': Cultural Clichés in the Making (1650–1850)." Ph.D. diss., Yale University, 1982.

Snitow, Ann, Christine Stansell, and Sharon Thompson, eds. *Powers of Desire: The Politics of Sexuality*. New York: Monthly Review Press, 1983.

Sontag, Susan. "Fascinating Fascism." In *Under the Sign of Saturn*, 73–105. New York: Anchor, 1991.

Spackman, Barbara. *Fascist Virilities: Rhetoric, Ideology, and Social Fantasy in Italy*. Minneapolis: University of Minnesota Press, 1996.

Sternhell, Zeev. *Neither Right Nor Left*. Trans. David Maisel. Berkeley: University of California Press, 1986.

Stevenson, Anne. *Bitter Fame: A Life of Sylvia Plath*. New York: Viking, 1989.

Stewart, Harry E., and Rob Roy McGregor. *Jean Genet: From Fascism to Nihilism*. New York: Peter Lang, 1993.

Stich, Sidra. *Anxious Visions*. New York: Abbeville, 1990.

Strube, S., and W. F. Blood. *The Kaiser's Kalendar for 1915, or The Dizzy Dream of Demented Willie*. London: Daily Express, 1915.

Suárez, Juan A. *Bike Boys, Drag Queens, and Superstars: Avant-Garde, Mass Culture, and Gay Identities in the 1960s Underground Cinema*. Bloomington: Indiana University Press, 1996.

Suleiman, Susan Rubin. *Subversive Intent: Gender, Politics, and the Avant-Garde*. Cambridge: Harvard University Press, 1990.

Szeman, Sherri. *The Kommandant's Mistress*. New York: HarperCollins, 1993.

Tashjian, Dickran. *A Boatload of Madmen: Surrealism and the American Avant-Garde, 1920–1950*. New York: Thames and Hudson, 1995.

Taylor, Sue. *Hans Bellmer: The Anatomy of Anxiety*. Cambridge: MIT Press, 2001.

Theweleit, Klaus. *Male Fantasies*. Vol. 1: *Women, Floods, Bodies, History*. Trans. Stephen Conway, Erica Carter, and Chris Turner. Minneapolis: University of Minnesota Press, 1987.

———. *Male Fantasies*. Vol. 2: *Male Bodies: Psychoanalyzing the White Terror*. Trans. Erica Carter, Chris Turner, and Stephen Conway. Minneapolis: University of Minnesota Press, 1989.

Tindall, William York. *D. H. Lawrence & Susan His Cow*. New York: Columbia University Press, 1939.

Todorov, Tzvetan. *A French Tragedy: Scenes of Civil War, Summer 1944*. Trans. Mary Byrd Kelly. Hanover: University Press of New England, 1996.

Traldi, Alberto. *Fascism and Fiction: A Survey of Italian Fiction on Fascism*. Metuchen, N.J.: Scarecrow, 1987.

Trial Balloon. *PartFantasy*. New York: Trial Balloon, 1992.

Trilling, Lionel. *Beyond Culture: Essays on Literature and Learning*. New York: Harcourt Brace Jovanovich, 1965.

——. *The Liberal Imagination*. Garden City, N.Y.: Doubleday, 1953.

Ungar, Steven. *Scandal and Aftereffect: Blanchot and France since 1930*. Minneapolis: University of Minnesota Press, 1995.

Vance, Carol S., ed. *Pleasure and Danger: Exploring Female Sexuality*. New York: Pandora, 1992.

Vendler, Helen. *The Music of What Happens: Poems, Poets, Critics*. Cambridge: Harvard University Press, 1988.

Vercors. *A dire vrai: Entretiens de Vercors avec Gilles Plazy*. Paris: Éditions François Bourin, 1991.

——. *L'apogée (1862–1932), "Moi Aristide Briand, Essai d'autoportrait."* Vol. 1 of *Cent ans d'histoire de France*. Paris: Plon, 1982.

——. *L'Après-Briand (1932–1942): "Les occasions perdues ou L'étrange déclin."* Vol. 2 of *Cent ans d'histoire de France*. Paris: Plon, 1982.

——. *Briand-l'oublié (1942–1962): "Les nouveaux jours. Esquisse d'une Europe."* Vol. 3 of *Cent ans d'histoire de France*. Paris: Plon, 1982.

——. *Le silence de la mer et autres récits*. Paris: Éditions Albin Michel, 1951.

——. *The Silence of the Sea*. Trans. Cyril Connolly. New York: Macmillan, 1944.

Viegener, Matias. "'The Only Haircut That Makes Sense Anymore': Queer Subculture and Gay Resistance." In *Queer Looks: Perspectives on Lesbian and Gay Film and Video*, edited by Martha Gever, John Greyson, and Pratibha Parmar, 116–33. New York: Routledge, 1993.

Vircondelet, Alain. *Duras: A Biography*. Trans. Thomas Buckley. Normal, Ill.: Dalkey Archive Press, 1994.

Wagner, Linda W., ed. *Critical Essays on Sylvia Plath*. Boston: G.K. Hall, 1984.

Waite, Robert G. L. *The Psychopathic God Adolf Hitler*. New York: Basic, 1977.

Watson, Peter. *The Nazi's Wife*. Garden City, N.Y.: Doubleday, 1985.

Watts, Philip. *Allegories of the Purge: How Literature Responded to the Postwar Trials of Writers and Intellectuals in France*. Stanford: Stanford University Press, 1998.

——. "Political Discourse and Poetic Register in Jean Genet's *Pompes funèbres*." *French Forum* 17, 2 (May 1992): 191–203.

Webb, Peter, and Robert Short. *Hans Bellmer*. London: Quartet, 1985.

Webb, Richard C. *File on Genet*. London: Methuen, 1992.

Weitz, Margaret Collins. *Sisters in the Resistance: How Women Fought to Free France, 1940–1945*. New York: John Wiley & Sons, 1995.

White, Edmund. *Genet: A Biography*. New York: Alfred A. Knopf, 1993.

Wieseltier, Leon. "In a Universe of Ghosts." *New York Review of Books*, 25 November 1976, 20–23.

Williams, Linda. "Film Bodies: Gender, Genre, and Excess." In *Film Genre Reader II*, edited by Barry Keith Grant. Austin: University of Texas Press, 1995.

——. *Hard Core: Power, Pleasure and the 'Frenzy of the Visible.'* Berkeley: University of California Press, 1989.

Willis, Sharon. *Marguerite Duras: Writing on the Body*. Urbana: University of Illinois Press, 1987.

Wilson, Trevor. *The Myriad Faces of War: Britain and the Great War, 1914–1918*. Cambridge: Polity Press, 1988.

Winnicott, D. W. "The Use of an Object." In *Psycho-Analytic Explorations*, edited by Clare Winnicott. London: Karnac, 1989.

Wood, Henry, and Ferdinand Hansen. *"Pictured Calumnies": Timely Comment on a Few Cartoons from The New York Tribune*. New York: New York Tribune, 1914.

Woolf, Leonard. *Quack, quack!* London: Hogarth Press, 1935.

Woolf, Virginia. *The Common Reader. First series*, annotated edition. Ed. Andrew McNeillie. New York: Harcourt Brace Jovanovich, 1984.

———. *Mrs. Dalloway*. New York: Harcourt Brace Jovanovich, 1981.

———. *Three Guineas*. New York: Harcourt Brace Jovanovich, 1938.

Wyatt, Jean. *Reconstructing Desire: The Role of the Unconscious in Women's Reading and Writing*. Chapel Hill: University of North Carolina Press, 1990.

Young, James E. "'I May Be a Bit of a Jew': The Holocaust Confessions of Sylvia Plath." *Philological Quarterly* 66, 1 (winter 1987): 127–47.

———. *Writing and Rewriting the Holocaust: Narrative and the Consequences of Interpretation*. Bloomington: Indiana University Press, 1990.

Index

Italicized page references indicate figures.

Clover, Carol J., 73–74
Communism, 39, 102, 105, 133, 141, 142
Corot, Jean-Baptiste-Camille, *Baccante with Tambourine*, 118

Dalí, Salvador: *L'Age d'or*, 63, 66; *Diary of a Genius*, 60; *The Enigma of William Tell*, 60; "Honneur à l'objet!," 63, 76; and politics, 60–61, 63–64, 152, 166–67nn. 2, 4, 167n. 4; *Unspeakable Confessions*, 60
D'Annunzio, Gabriele, 4
De Grazia, Victoria, 38
De Lauretis, Teresa, 10–11, 108, 125
Deleuze, Gilles, 29, 35–36, 73
Democracy, 3, 6, 18, 20, 24, 30; and fascism, 6, 15, 24, 151; and feminist theory, 131, 150; and German authoritarianism, 16, 20; and Lawrence, 14, 37, 38–42, 44, 46, 49, 52, 54, 56, 62, 142; and Plath, 142, 149, 150; and sexuality, 5, 6–7, 17, 29, 31, 33, 159–60
Derrida, Jacques, *Glas*, 101
Dijsktra, Bram, 158
Dillon, E. J., 18, 19
Doll/automaton, 66, 69, 70–78, 154
Drieu la Rochelle, Pierre, 4
Duras, Marguerite, 4, 5, 15, 28, 126, 131, 139, 144, 150; *Hiroshima mon amour*, 98, 126, 132, 133–37, 143; and Nazism, 7, 132, 133, 136, 137, 140, 141, 144, 157, 173n. 18; *The War*, 5, 126, 139–40, 141
Dworkin, Andrea, 124, 125

Eatwell, Roger, 1
Ehrenbourg, Ilya, 84
Eichmann, Adolf, 97
Eliot, T. S., 40
Eluard, Paul, 96, 114
Enlightenment, 13
Erickson, Steve, *Tours of the Black Clock*, 1
Eroticism, 3, 13, 15, 33–34, 129; and Bataille, 61, 62, 64, 66, 68; and cruelty, 34, 36, 108, 154; and fairy tales, 89, 90, 95; and feminist theory, 130–31, 149; and Genet, 100, 117–19; and Lawrence, 47–48, 50–51, 53, 55–56, 59; and Plath, 147–50; and power, 3, 34; and prohibition, 12, 13, 26, 28, 37, 117–19; and propaganda, 10, 26–28, 95–96; and surrealism, 59, 61; and Vercors, 81–83, 96

Fairy tales, 85–87, 89–90, 92, 93, 95, 97
Fantasy, 6, 9, 10, 11, 15, 32, 34, 36, 37, 62, 78, 99, 108, 124, 131, 150, 156–57, 159; and feminist theory, 10, 124–25, 127, 150; and Genet, 100, 102, 116–19; and Plath, 140, 141, 144, 149; and pornography, 153; and

propaganda, 11, 130, 154; and sadomasochism, 33, 35, 36, 73, 102, 111, 112; and violence, 73, 78, 158, 159
Fascism: and authoritarianism, 8, 9, 13–14, 16–17, 165n. 3; definition of, 8; and democracy, 6, 15, 24, 151; and fantasy, 6, 9, 10, 11, 15, 34, 36, 37, 124, 131, 159; fascist psyche, 74, 108–12; gendered theories of, 15, 114–16, 121–22, 150; and patriarchy, 15, 121, 122–27, 130, 131, 141, 144, 149, 150; and repression, 29–30, 32, 33, 37, 157; and sexual deviance, 1, 3, 5, 6–7, 12–13, 15, 29–35, 60, 67, 98, 119, 125, 151, 155, 159–60; and the unconscious, 23, 79, 156–57; and violence, 1, 4, 9, 12–13, 32, 33–34, 36, 64, 112, 131, 146, 164n. 24. *See also specific authors*
Fascist chic, 1, 161n. 1
Fascist modernists, 4, 5, 10
Female desire: and Duras, 131–32, 133, 138, 139, 141; and fascism and patriarchy, 124, 125, 126, 130; and feminist theory, 130–31; and Plath, 142, 143, 144, 146, 149
Feminist theory: and fantasy, 10, 124–25, 127, 130–31, 149–50; and fascism and patriarchy, 15, 121, 122–31, 141, 142, 144, 149, 150; and masochism, 119, 121, 127, 131; and Plath, 140, 144, 149, 174n. 28; and pornography, 124–25, 131, 174n. 2
Fetishism, 6, 12; and Bataille, 66, 67, 68, 69, 70, 79; and Bellmer, 78, 79; and Dalí, 63; and Genet, 100, 101, 105; and pornography, 153, 155
Films: and eroticized fascism, 2, 151–56; horror, 73–74
Firchow, Peter E., 19
Fletcher, E. F., 128
Foster, Hal, 60, 71, 74, 167n. 12
Foucault, Michel, 3, 8, 32–33, 151, 152
France, 2, 3, 5–9, 58, 62–63, 98. *See also* Militia/Milice; *Mode rétro*; Occupation; Propaganda; Resistance; *specific authors*
Franco, Francisco, 8, 58, 60, 129
Franco-Prussian War, 19, 58, 91, 93, 97
Freud, Sigmund: *Civilization and Its Discontents*, 18, 20, 51; "Fetishism," 67; "Psychoanalysis and War Neuroses," 18; "Reflections upon War and Death," 17, 18; "The Uncanny," 66
Friday, Nancy, 125
Friedan, Betty, 123, 125
Friedländer, Saul, 152, 157
Fromm, Erich, 30

Gauthier, Xavière, 72
Gautier, Jean-Jacques, 101

Gender issues: and eroticized fascism, 7, 144–50, 154; and Genet, 114–16; and Lawrence, 39, 56; and propaganda, 21, 26, 30, 87, 121; and sadomasochism, 73. *See also* Feminist theory; Homosexuality; Women

Genet, Jean: *Funeral Rites*, 4, 5, 14–15, 28, 100–119, 132, 135, 137, 153; "Members of the Assembly," 100; and Nazism, 69, 98, 100–102, 105–6, 114, 117, 119, 141. *See also* Sadomasochism; Treason

Germany: and Lawrence, 38, 41, 45; and national identity, 6; and Nazism, 9, 24, 64, 97; and propaganda, 18–19, 22–28, 84, 88–93, 95, 97, 98. *See also* Authoritarianism; National Socialism; Nazism; Occupation

Gilbert, Sandra M., 28

Graves, Robert, 23

Greene, Bette, *Summer of My German Soldier*, 98

Greer, Germaine, 123

Griffin, Roger, 8

Grossman, Atina, 122–23

Guattari, Félix, 29

Gubar, Susan, 28

Gullace, Nicoletta F., 21

Hansen, Ron, *Hitler's Niece*, 1

Harris, Ruth, 26

Haste, Cate, 88

Hayman, Ronald, *Hitler and Geli*, 1

Hearne, Betsy, 86

Herf, Jeffrey, 4, 111

Herzog, Dagmar, 31

Hewitt, Andrew, 4, 16, 100

Higgins, Lynn A., 104, 126, 134

Hill, Leslie, *Marguerite Duras: Apocalyptic Desires*, 132

Hindenburg, Paul von, 19, 23

Hite, Shere, 125

Hitler, Adolf, 1, 4, 5, 8, 11, 16, 23, 58, 62, 120–21, 127, 129, 158–59; and Dalí, 60, 166–67nn. 2, 4; and Genet, 101, 102, 104, 106–7, 109, 112–14; and Mussolini, 38, 55, 58; and sexual deviance, 1, 29–32, 106, 161n. 2

Hoffmann, E. T. A., "The Sand-man," 66, 71, 72

Holocaust, 121, 126, 140, 141, 143, 152, 175n. 4

Homophobia, 99, 100, 114

Homosexuality: and fascism, 4, 6, 7, 99, 100, 117, 119, 121, 164n. 23; and Genet, 100, 114–16; and Lawrence, 39, 46–47, 50, 51, 53, 56, 165n. 4; and prohibition, 12, 39, 117–19; and sadomasochism, 99, 101

Homosocial desire, 39, 46–47, 49–50, 51

hooks, bell, 172n. 6

Horkheimer, Max, 122, 126, 131

Horne, John, 14, 21–22

Horror (genre), 73–74, 152, 153, 154, 155

Howard, Richard, 145

Hughes, Ted, 146

Hutcheon, Linda, 126

Huxley, Aldous, 4, 5

Ilsa: She-Wolf of the SS, 69, 152, 154, 155

Insdorf, Annette, 155

Interwar period, 4–5, 7, 38; and Lawrence, 41, 42, 46, 49; and propaganda, 14, 21, 23

Isherwood, Christopher: *Berlin Stories*, 4; *Down There on a Visit*, 5

Italian Fascism, 8, 9, 24, 38, 41–42, 45, 46–48, 62

Jameson, Fredric, 10, 163n. 4

Jews: and Duras, 135; and Plath, 141–43, 147–48. *See also* Antisemitism

Joan of Arc, 112–14

John, S. Beynon, 83

Jones, G. B., 117

Jong, Erica, 125

Jung, Carl, 16, 164n. 14

Jünger, Ernst, 4, 111

Kaes, Anton, 152

Kaplan, Alice Yaeger, 4, 5, 87

Kaplan, Marion, 122–23

Kershaw, Ian, 31–32, 99

Kipling, Rudyard, 88; "Mary Postgate," 26–28, 95–96, 130

Kipnis, Laura, 125, 153

Klotz, Marcia, 164n. 24

Knapp, Bettina, 101

Koestenbaum, Wayne, 10

Koestler, Arthur, 83

Konstantinovic, Radivoje D., 87–88

Koonz, Claudia, 12, 154

Kramer, Alan, 14, 21–22

Krauss, Rosalind, 69, 71, 72

La Bruce, Bruce, *Skin Flick*, 152–53

Laplanche, Jean, 108

Laqueur, Walter, 8, 31

Laurens, Corran, 105, 115, 132

Laval, Pierre, 101

Lawrence, D. H.: *Aaron's Rod*, 38, 39, 42, 45–49, 50, 53, 54, 56, 57, 166n. 6; and authoritarian power, 34, 37, 38–40, 42–46, 48–57; "Blessed are the Powerful," 43; and democracy, 14, 37, 38–42, 44, 46, 49, 52, 54, 56, 62, 142; "Fantasia of the

Lawrence, D. H. (*continued*)
Unconscious," 42–43, 44, 47, 48–49, 52,
53, 57; *Kangaroo*, 34, 38–42, 45–47,
49–54, 56, 57, 64; *Lady Chattlerley's Lover*,
55, 56, 57; "A Letter From Germany," 38,
165 n. 2; and "libido/power" theory, 14, 39,
41–44, 49, 57, 63, 64, 70, 165–66 n. 6;
Movements in European History, 38, 40, 41,
42, 44, 48, 49, 51; *The Plumed Serpent*, 38,
39, 42, 47, 54–58; and propaganda, 40,
43, 51, 88; *The Rainbow*, 39, 45, 57; *St.
Mawr*, 57; *Sons and Lovers*, 44; "Tickets,
Please," 44; and the unconscious, 37,
42–43, 45, 59; *Women in Love*, 39, 44, 45,
46, 57. *See also* Homosexuality; Sado-
masochism; Women
Le Bon, Gustave, 43
Lenin, Vladimir, 60, 167
Leonard, John, 101, 171 n. 11
Lettres françaises, Les, 114–16
Lewis, Wyndham, 4, 40, 163 n. 4
Liberal politics: and fascism, 9, 100; and
feminism, 131, 150; and power, 157–58;
and sexual deviance, 125
Liberation: and eroticized fascism, 7, 14–15;
and Genet, 101, 102, 103, 104, 116; and
treason, 115, 126, 132, 136
Linz, Juan, 8
Literary modernism, 3–13, 153, 155, 162 n. 11.
See also specific authors
Livres roses, 88–95
Love Letters to Adolf Hitler, 120–22, 149
Ludendorff, Erich, 19, 23

Mann, Thomas, "Mario and the
Magician," 7
Marcus, Jane, 154
Marcuse, Herbert, 30, 32, 39, 57
Marinetti, F. T., *Let's Murder the
Moonshine*, 4
Marsh, Patrick, 113
Marxism, 61, 62, 157–58
Masochism, 15, 28, 35–37; and Bataille, 65;
and Bellmer, 74, 78; and Duras, 131, 138,
150; and Hitler, 31; and Lawrence, 55; and
Plath, 131, 143, 144–45, 146, 149; and
women's attraction to fascism, 15, 30, 54,
55, 65, 95, 115, 119, 121–22, 156
Mauriac, François, 101
Melville, Herman, *Moby Dick*, 53
Merkin, Daphne, "Dreaming of Hitler,"
158–59
Militarism: and Genet, 69, 108–12, 114; libid-
inal dynamics of, 3, 29, 30; and Plath, 142
Militia/Milice, 101–4, 109, 112, 139–40
Miller, D. A., 119

Millett, Kate, 123
Mitchell, Juliet, 125
Mode rétro, 116, 132, 138, 151, 156
Mon alphabet, 93, 94
Morgan, J. H., 19
Moselly, Émile, 89
Mosse, George L., 6, 22
Mowrer, Edgar, 24
Mussolini, Benito, 4, 8, 23, 25, 58, 62, 123,
129, 162 n. 9, 169–70 n. 25; and Lawrence,
38, 41, 54; Shaw on, 48

Narrative voice: and Duras, 133–36, 139, 143;
and Genet, 105–7, 108, 171 n. 11; and
Plath, 140–41, 142, 143–44; and Vercors,
80–82, 85
National Socialism: and Bellmer, 74, 76;
consolidation of, 62; and eroticized fascism, 8; and feminist theory, 123; and
Lawrence, 165 n. 2; and violence, 115. *See
also* Nazism
Nationalism, 3, 4, 6, 12, 22, 88, 98, 104, 105,
142, 151
Nazism, 8–9, 10, 14, 29, 34, 58, 62, 99, 111;
and Bataille, 65, 68–69, 70, 141; and
Bellmer, 71, 74, 75–78, 141; and Dalí, 60,
63; and Duras, 7, 132, 133, 136, 137, 140,
141, 144, 157, 173 n. 18; and feminist theory, 123, 124, 125; and Foucault, 32; and
Genet, 69, 98, 100–102, 105–6, 114, 117,
119, 141; and Plath, 7, 126, 140–41, 143,
144, 145; and pornography, 3, 151–56; and
sexual deviance, 6, 31, 33–35, 39, 99, 109,
114; and SS, 11, 99, 101, 102, 106, 109, 110,
112; and Vercors, 7, 78–79, 83–84, 86, 96,
97, 141
Nazi Sadist, 153, 154
New Wave, 134

Occupation: and Duras, 132, 139; and Genet,
101, 116; metaphorization as sexual encounter, 14, 85, 87, 96, 98; and perceptions of Germany, 80, 83–84, 93; and
treason, 115, 116; and Vercors, 78–79,
80–82, 84, 85
Ophuls, Marcel, *The Sorrow and the Pity*, 116,
132–33, 151
O'Reilly, John, 117; *Brinner*, 118, *118*; *Occupied Territory and the Dance of Death*, 118
Orwell, George: *Coming Up For Air*, 24; "Inside the Whale," 23; and Nazism, 24, 152,
154; *1984*, 28, 127; and propaganda, 19, 88,
153

Paulhan, Jean, 95
Paxton, Robert O., 31, 83, 116

World War II (*continued*)
erature, 4–5, 7, 8, 9, 79, 83–84; and
propaganda, 9, 13–14, 23, 24, 26, 93–94,
113; in relation to World War I, 6, 13–14,
16, 23–28, 58, 94–96; and sexual
metaphors for Occupation, 87, 96, 104–5,
115. *See also* Fascism; Nazism; Occupation;
specific authors and countries

Yeats, W. B., 40
Young, Ellsworth, 20
Young, James E., 141